D0387894

THE GOOD WANT POWER

Other books by Kathleen Nott

Novels
MILE END
THE DRY DELUGE
PRIVATE FIRES
AN ELDERLY RETIRED MAN

Poetry
LANDSCAPES AND DEPARTURES
POEMS FROM THE NORTH
CREATURES AND EMBLEMS

Criticism and Philosophy
THE EMPEROR'S CLOTHES
A SOUL IN THE QUAD
PHILOSOPHY AND HUMAN NATURE

General
A CLEAN WELL-LIGHTED PLACE
(a private view of Sweden)

Part-authorship
OBJECTIONS TO HUMANISM
WHAT I BELIEVE
THE HUMANIST OUTLOOK
ASTRIDE THE TWO CULTURES

THE GOOD WANT POWER

An essay in the psychological possibilities of liberalism

Kathleen Nott

BASIC BOOKS, INC., PUBLISHERS
NEW YORK

The author acknowledges assistance from the
Arts Council of Great Britain

Copyright © 1977 by Kathleen Nott
Library of Congress Catalog Card Number: 76-43391
ISBN: 0-465-02692-3
Printed in Great Britain
77 78 79 80 81   10 9 8 7 6 5 4 3 2 1

To
ARTHUR KOESTLER
with love and admiration

Contents

The good want power . . . the powerful goodness want.
                              Shelley: *Prometheus Unbound*

Preface

The subtitle I have given this book – 'An Essay in the Psychological Possibilities of Liberalism' – needs some explanation.

The Good Want Power is not directly concerned with practical or party politics although it offers some comments and opinions on historical and contemporary events, and occasionally uses them in illustration. On the other hand, it is not a work of political philosophy in the academic sense although its method is a kind of conceptual analysis. It is precisely as a would-be liberal, one of those who by temperament and upbringing want liberalism to have realistic meaning and to provide a working philosophy, that I have chosen this method; in the belief that liberal theorization, with its besetting weakness for emotive propaganda often based on false and woolly abstraction, has a particular need of examining its convictions and its language with scrupulous care.

Many of the chapters I have selected are analyses of particular texts, some more and some less familiar, some of them classics of the past, some of them works of contemporary political thought, and some not directly political at all. In the latter case, they have been chosen for their political and social implications. Some of these are liberalistic, some directly authoritarian: and some which may appear to be liberal, or anyway humanitarian, turn out on examination to be disguising an authoritarian temper under what appear to be benevolent social intentions. Examples are the schools of Behaviourism (Eysenck, Skinner) and some kinds of popular ethology (Lorenz, Ardrey), where the implications of specialist interference in social control may need to be unveiled.

The concepts I have selected and tried to analyse appear to me to be based on certain common assumptions which are often hidden or only partly revealed and also on certain historical ways of thinking which have become so engrained in cultural habit that they are used without criticism, reflection or even awareness. Because the habit has never been seriously challenged, the user may assume that he is referring to realities of agreed human experience when in fact the concepts on which he grounds his generalizations are conventions of classification, often indeed ancient and deeply rooted, from which he further abstracts his account of human existence and its potentialities, and on which he may even build his prescriptions for human behaviour and human social life. A list of these concepts includes, for example: 'Man' (his Human Nature or Humanity, his 'Brotherhood', and of course his 'Woman'); Individuality or The Individual; Freedom; Equality – notably in its modern version 'Equality of Opportunity'. (That last is rather different from most of the others and perhaps nowadays more dangerous because it stirs hopes of a practical programme.)

It is no less difficult than it has ever been for most of us to free ourselves from the assumptive automatism of these concepts: they belong to the historical structure of our European consciousness, our logic and our verbal usage.

The humanistic liberal characteristically believes in something he calls 'Free Thought'. Throughout the book I have been trying to show that he is usually as much as anyone else constrained in his thinking by inexplicit assumptions and conceptual prejudices which have arisen not only in his personal history, but in our common historical habits and customs.

That applies to the author too. My selection of concepts and texts to be examined is deliberately a personal one. More often than not the texts illustrate assumptions I have caught myself out in: their importance has been singled out for me by the mistakes and pitfalls of my own experience. That not only explains the subtitle; it is the reason why the opening section is largely autobiographical, in the directly personal sense, or as a description of the generation and the circumstances I grew up in.

For oneself, the main purpose in writing such a book must be to clear one's own mind of cant and of its historical lumber, to the best of one's ability. The method of course is fallible, but I do not know a better way of satisfying oneself that one's opinions are not only one's own, but that, after sufficiently thorough examination of one's own experiences and beliefs, one is at least entitled to hold them until they can be convincingly and rationally discredited:

without some such disciplined effort most opinion is little better than hearsay, often garbled.

Nor do I know of a better way of freeing one's thinking from automatic habit and thus at least of taking a step towards establishing an identity, a real place in a worthwhile society — what might be called a locus of genuine individuality. To become an independent, critical but still open, mind, still able to live in immediate and personal relations, is surely a better because more concrete ideal than the 'atomic' individualism whose conceptual validity the liberal may too facilely assume.

'Doing one's own thing' at all costs is not a new idea. On this, the second part of the autobiographical section uses the experiences of the last one to enlighten the present generation who think wrongly that it is their own invention (and have thought the same since the beginning of social records). The more mature discovery that nothing absolves people from the necessity of finding out how to live with other people is also not new.

Nevertheless criticism of current libertarian movements is aimed not so much at their youthful members and followers as at their ideological sponsors, who are often of an older generation and also often out of touch with this simple, recurrent and, as it were, familial situation. It is common for them to put all the blame on our technological society. If, with Marcuse, they advocate revolutionary change, they imply that 'Man's' Original Virtue and creative consciousness is only waiting for the release of social pressure. If on the other hand they demand a change of heart and consciousness, they may be suffering from Romantic nostalgia; they may not be actually saying that contemporary 'Man' is by nature much better than the society he has created: but they may, like Theodore Roszak, be insinuating that once upon a time he *was* much better and that we must find our way back to this moral prototype.

All that should have been an early warning that it is much easier to talk about changing one's habits, one's heart, or one's consciousness, than to do any of these things or to help others to do them. My concluding chapter was too optimistically projected as: *What is to be done?* As I approached the end of the book the problem of liberalism became much more clearly seen as chiefly moral and psychological: *How can we learn to think and feel both honestly and realistically?* (This realization was a good reason, among others, for lightening emphasis on practical concern and activity.) It still appears that we must first know what we are thinking and talking about. Contrary to Marx, we still — perhaps more than ever — have to learn to understand and to interpret our world before we try to change it. And our world consists in the first place of ourselves and of other people.

That brought me to a more detailed examination of the problem of identity, already referred to, and of its entailment of a reciprocal recognition of other identities. In turn, that implied an intersubjective understanding of justice between actual living human beings, to be opposed to the quantitative, egalitarian and legalistic definition which men of good will, but of insufficient self-analysis, have grown up with and continue to accept uncritically.

Here too the possibilities are not encouraging. The instrument of change would have to be educational: I believe that it is (just) more possible to change people's heads than their hearts. But the problem remains — even if the diagnosis is correct, what is the remedy and who is to apply it?

The book's title, quoted from Shelley, implies this unsolved dilemma. It means more than the descriptive fact that there is an upstairs world of the powerful and those interested in obtaining and perpetuating it for themselves — and a downstairs world of the powerless and unambitious. It certainly does not mean that all the sheep are 'good' in diametric contradistinction to the goatish Bad of Acton's 'All Great Men ... ' It means rather that if we confine ourselves only to the most fertile minds of every generation, they come in two distinct, even polar, types and in two not readily reconcilable attitudes towards human life. If we are to survive, as one humanity, they have to learn to make this planet habitable for one another. That perhaps puts more strain as well as responsibility on the active organizers who have the numerical power as well as the drive, than on those passive enjoyers (and even passive resisters) who have most of the 'negative capability'. (Liberals, like sexes and classes, are to be found on either side.)

KATHLEEN NOTT

I

Introduction
Liberal Background Noises

I A Liberal case-history

'Every boy and every girl' said Gilbert, 'That's born into the world alive / Is either a little Liberal / Or else a little Conservative.'

Gilbert died in 1911. When he wrote this quatrain, the chances for a viable infant may even have slightly favoured liberalism. It was the time of the great, probably justly famous, and last, Liberal governments of 1902–14. Those governments were undoubtedly responsible for some reforms which have helped to shape our subsequent history and contributed to some kinds of progress in education and social welfare whose benefit we may hope will prove irreversible; and included politicians who even in the light of epigonic research, so often inclined to concentrate on shady corners, may still appear both genuinely advanced and intelligent and not foolishly over-idealistic. But still they were the last Liberal governments, and it does not look very likely that we shall see another in Britain.*

We can see that the sense in which Gilbert uses the word 'liberal' was merely parochial. Over large areas of the world, most of what is now called the Third World, quite apart from the totalitarian states, liberalism is a term of contempt or abuse, and it provides no ideological cradle for the young of either sex.

Should we regard this change as irreversible? Should we even look upon it in a retrospective light? Did liberalism ever really mean what in its Victorian and Edwardian heyday it appeared to mean?

If we accept for the moment the Gilbertian dichotomy I should say that I was born 'a little Liberal girl'. That was not very long before the First World War. In those years, as I uncertainly

---

* The Liberal resurgence of 1973–4 looks like a flash in the pan.

recollect, news from the humming political world came to me, but it was as a noise rather than as articulation. Words here and there stick out. For example, I soon learned that my father was something *he* called a Liberal. Much later I pieced together what for him at least that implied: disapproval of war; disapproval of capitalism; disapproval of Labour; disapproval of God (and since he happened to be a first-class choir-bass, mild contempt of vicars); and a Utopian chiliasm based on a belief in Original Virtue, that looked forward to lotus-eating rather than general prosperity; because my father, though he worked daily, if unambitiously, thought that work was the curse of the working-classes.

But the personalized definition of a liberal came much later and would not have been accepted by my father and his contemporaries. I suppose he voted Liberal at the election of 1906 on behalf of his whole family, which was otherwise female.

What remains to me from this period is a thumping and banging background of 'argument' and war. (The 1914–18 war was often very noisy, even by general Second World War standards, because of the nightly barrage against zeppelins and later the taubes, and also the not insignificantly destructive bombs.) To a little girl, small for her age and by far the youngest and smallest of what appeared to be a large crowd of relations, older human beings also seemed to be very noisy and continually so. They and their 'arguments' have made a more lasting impression on me than the barrage and the bombs, although those were a necessary orchestration—partly I believe because they strained my attention; I was always on the brink of grasping what the elders were saying and always just missing it.

The strain was the greater because it belonged almost wholly to the detective work—I was too much occupied with trying to work out what they were saying to begin to think of it in my own terms of value and concern. I may have even sensed that it wouldn't interest me at my time of life. The noise they made kept me either up (if unnoticed), or awake (if driven to bed). They alarmed me too and left innervations of fear and evasiveness. I became and am still strongly tempted to browbeat, and I am also obliged rigidly, if often hypocritically, to observe the forms of debate. I detest losing an argument and if I have successfully made a case I suffer a compulsive and guilty reaction of self-paralysis while I decide whether or not I have been strictly fair and objective; I often decide that I have – and know very well that I haven't.

Even at the time, I believe, I was partly aware that my family and its callers were simply entertaining themselves. A 'political argument' was a game of Montagues and Capulets. (That is a better symbol than the Oxford and Cambridge boat-race – which is still, I suppose, more a sport than a battle.)

Even if they were a form of play, to me the 'arguments' always sounded near-lethal. 'Don't argue' was a frequent admonition from parents to children, particularly me. That speaks for itself. Certainly 'argument' was far removed from the Buberian ideal of a self-synthesizing dialogue – the aim was to do your opponent, and with a bludgeon not a foil.

It was also regarded as a masculine exercise. My mother, not noted for meekness, seemed to accept this departmental custom with a good grace, even pleasure, as she would have done if it had been, instead, the trooping of the colour or cockfighting. 'I love to listen to them argue,' she would say, and even talked of 'keen cut-and-thrust'. In other fields and among women and children she fancied herself at repartee and described her power – 'almost like a rapier'. I believe from what I have been able to observe in all classes that this situation has not significantly changed today. No doubt a far larger proportion of the people is better able than my parents' generation to carry on a specialist argument and come to some testable conclusions and, because of professional self-confidence and training, to avoid angry passions in the process. In politics there are many commentators on T.V., radio and in the 'quality' newspapers, with research departments behind them; therefore some facts to refer to and even a code or a lip-service of referring. But people still argue chiefly to win, and certainly not to expose either the structure of thinking or its relation to experienced reality. And though, in principle, many more facts are available, at least in democratic countries, than to my parents in their day, because of the spread of literacy and comparative ease of reference, the facts that are made use of in political or social discussion are often still taken from the not unprejudiced opinions and propaganda of the news-sheet that is brought into the house.

The electronic media today provide a dietary of facts, though a lean one, and perhaps the newspapers as one result of this are less influential than when I was a child. Even then you used to read the newspaper that reflected the opinions which you had first learned from it, and not its rival — as a wish to form an independent opinion would have prescribed. You were a committed man — to the Liberal Party or to the Conservative, and whichever paper you didn't read was 'that rag'. Thus indeed you could become — even if you were not born — a little liberal or a little conservative.

Moreover, not only the form but the subject-matter of 'argument' was in this way insidiously laid down for you. And often the more concrete it appeared the more abstract and ideal it really was and the less it had to do with the conditions in which you actually lived and worked.

The 'live' liberal issue, as far as I remember, was Free Trade versus Protectionism: but I think my father had no idea how one or the other, or the opposition between them, would affect him and his family or how either would make his living conditions better or worse. My mother had even less. She was not a fool — in the sense that she was shrewd in immediate concerns — and she would have made a good stump orator. All of that tends to confirm my belief that people are naturally more internationalist than parochial (and hence more contemptuous of the familiar: 'Labour can't rule' was said as often by the working classes as by the top classes). Abstract ideas come first and the capacity to apply them in experience (or to reject them when they are seen to be inapplicable to practice) is a development of maturity. All adolescents are ideological; and people who are uneducated or who have received no training in handling intellectual forms and ideas, remain so.

Probably in the days when the villages really radiated from the parish pump, informed interests went no further afield: but I expect that the arguments in tap-rooms were quite as abstract as at any later time. The Free Trade-Protectionism discussion is no longer live in its original form. But as far as the average family discussion goes it has simply been further diluted in another raging sea of international abstractions — Commonwealth versus European unity, for example. It's the Montagues and Capulets of today, and the wordy meaningless feud is without too much exaggeration typified by Alf Garnett.

The family structure in my early days was still very tight. It was part of an infrastructure or culture. A tight family structure may be a hive or bonnet of abstract bees. But 'Freedom' is not one of the bees. And to the individual members of such a family it seldom arises as a real need or a realistic goal. Individuals may have always wanted to break out—into delinquency, neurosis, on the one hand, or into higher social and economic achievement on the other —but people generally didn't, and probably don't even now, spend much time thinking about freedom, either in the abstract sense or for themselves as individuals.

Whatever flags they waved, my family in my generation were acceptant of the traditions, behaviour-patterns and conventions which had cradled their lives and which limited their possibilities. Much more so than the generation of my parents' parents. Really we were all born conservatives and it may be that most families still are.

Whatever it might have been, the appeal of liberalism, I think, at that time was not as a doctrine of individualism. Even my father who was in some ways idiosyncratic and rebellious against some of the more hypocritical conventions and interferences, and who certainly *read* for himself, took his political ideas out of the air where they flapped about with other bits of old newspaper. That might have instilled it into me, early enough to do me some good, that most people's 'ideas' and their conduct are so split as to force one to believe that they are quite unrelated. Putting it positively, to make any sense in education or in any field, we have to learn and teach how to unite theory and practice; or, rather, to reveal their natural unity. What most people call liberalism (which when examined is of many kinds, often quite disparate) suffers at least as much as any ideology from the shadow 'between the idea and the act'. In modern sociological jargon, one of many, it is a 'suprastructure'. My family's actual behaviour was part of the 'infrastructure' and as such was already receding into the cultural past. Whatever they said or whatever they thought they believed, my parents behaved as if they and their children were a distinct unit. Vertically the family had quite strong roots in the previous generation (naturally that was truer in my mother's case than in my father's) and struck out horizontally too, but much more feebly. My mother was both generous to the needs, and submissive to the plain selfish disagreeableness, of my maternal grandparents, quite beyond the call of duty (as I should conceive it anyway). My grandmother was an arrogant stupid old tyrant by whom my mother's childhood and youth had been ruthlessly exploited but whom she tenderly succoured in old age, poverty and sickness, and whom she never criticized to her face or behind her back. She could even describe my grandmother's most brutal and irresponsible behaviour towards herself with laughing admiration. All that is the more remarkable because she detested other women, apart from her own daughters and those whose material assets she revered (but did not envy — at least not consciously or in her behaviour).

My grandmother's early behaviour is not to be excused by poverty — my grandfather made quite a pile even by present standards because he was an unusually clever craftsman who was just in time to reap the benefit of a concealed and unpatented invention plus the sweated labour of his family; the pile of course was all kept under the bed and it dwindled as technology caught up.

The horizontal spread of the family unit was much more tenuous. My mother recognized (anyway in the diplomatic sense) her collaterals and in-laws. She genuinely liked one brother (the others had all disappeared); and because she was so trouser-minded — to a fantastically late age, all of course within the strictest sexual conventionality — she tolerated her brothers-in-law, with a certain contempt; they were mostly bachelors who all, in her view, resembled 'doctored Toms', a factual injustice, I early had no doubt. Her own and only extant sister and her sisters-in-law on either side she hated most self-righteously.

Whatever may be said of the others, and even if she acted in exactly the same way as everyone else, my mother was nothing if not an individualist. That may be because cultural or group-conventions are necessarily more stereotyped than the modes of behaviour they generalize. It may be that at least up to the time of her maturity and perhaps later still, kinship laws and customs were the real skeleton of society. Even if unreflectingly it might have been *de rigueur*, because of the unwritten and unspoken laws of exogamy, that one should hate, or at least that a married woman should hate, the tribe into which she had married. My mother, it is true, hated the wife of her admired and loved brother with adequate intensity. On the other hand she did not seek to impress her: it may be that she was rootedly confident of doing so anyway, being a native member of the family which the unfortunate woman (relatively intelligent but admittedly also Irish, Catholic, bossy, hysterical and fat) had joined comparatively late.

I should like to banish for ever the jargon word 'ambivalence'. People do not love-and-hate, anyway not at the same time. And in my opinion where they hate they do not, even in alternation, love. My mother, from time to time cordially inviting and lavishly entertaining, within (and far beyond) her means, my father's three sisters—'The Aunties'—was really pursuing a highly fantastic vendetta.

These activities had nothing even to do with pleasing my father —though he got on with his sisters he would much rather not have been bothered even by them. And ritual exchanges of family duties were not really demanded. To put it as my father put it in moments of candour and exasperation 'Your mother always wants to do their *dags*'.

My father, if he had been financially more fortunate, might have managed quite a high level of social and intellectual freedom. He was well-read, for his opportunities, musical, had sung at smoking concerts as part of a male voice quartet; and up to the time that I was about the scene he still had cronies. That is, he was allowed a drink on his way home from work; but family life had absolute priority. Family life meant my mother's matriarchal authority, which, whatever concessions she made to my father's masculine status—and they were clearly defined—was in practice unquestioned, naturally by herself, by her young, and even by my father however much he grumbled and from time to time laid down the law and made a scene. He had a terrifying empty ritual of putting on his boots after Sunday dinner and saying 'I'm off'.

It may be that our family culture had one or two unique elements —not only my mother's matriarchal assumptions but her own family history. After the industrial revolution until the time when my mother was adult, the family could still be the work-unit—and that was what her own had remained.

My maternal grandfather ran what might have been called a home- or cottage-industry. He was, I suppose, a 'master' jeweller: that is he must have served an apprenticeship—in Ireland (Cork) whence he and my grandmother emigrated to Liverpool in 1861. I am fairly sure of the date because it was in the first year of their marriage and his statement 'We were twenty-wan in sixty-wan' became a family slogan. He shortly moved to South London, somewhere round about the Old Kent Road, where he prospered both in money and seed. Fifteen children, and never less, for some number of years, than £50 a week (in those days real money). His children, boys and girls, mostly boys, became 'hands'; I have no doubt they were meanly paid and worked hours no Factory or Mines Act would have allowed, but they were very well fed and clothed. They had one maid of all work and even if it *was* all work, she was red-faced, bouncing and good-tempered. They had a 'Dame' school education – next thing to illiteracy, although my mother – an individual gift I am sure – had a staggering vocabulary which she used with remarkable accuracy. The only uncle I knew – they otherwise all disappeared except for one aunt – was a dab at all practical and technical things, picked up, or perhaps inherited. My grandfather, making compass-cups, invented a lathe 'which would do the work of sixteen men'. In addition his family provided a workforce of about ten (there were always some who were too young, for my grandparents though quite virtuously exploitative were not cruel, while my grandmother slept every afternoon in the periods between her pregnancies). Their output was considerable and he was invited by the American watch factory which commissioned him during this heyday to settle in the U.S.A. He didn't go in the end, for remarkable family reasons which hardly belong here; if he had gone, his and his family's economic and whole social future would have been revolutionized.

What we have here is no doubt an odd watershed in economic and cultural tradition. My grandfather, if you like, was a *proletarian* capitalist in a literal sense. The main source of his wealth, apart from his inventive ability, was his family. They worked at home in a family unit, in what, by the standards of the time, were comfortable conditions. They learned a useful craft. But they made no contribution to, and drew no benefit from, the rapid change going on in economic and social conditions. There are three striking and probably essential elements in their situation: (1) my grandfather did not patent his invention; (2) he kept the money in golden sovereigns in a big box under the marital bed; (3) all my grandparents' friends were Jewish – who alone equalled them in financial standing.

Thus for many years, while the technical and industrial revolution accelerating past him was splitting and scattering families, he remained a patriarch. My grandmother who always referred to him as the 'Master' – anyway always to those whom she regarded as her social inferiors, and sometimes to her sons and daughters in need of deflation – was in fact the 'Matriarch'. (And after all, although she hardly did a hand's turn herself, she did in fact produce the labour-force.)

Nevertheless, as honorary Patriarch and 'Master' – anyway in the craft- or guild-sense, the family being his unofficial apprentices – my grandfather, for this private Indian summer before the industrial capitalist winter closed in, was able to ignore the shop-floor, the boardroom and the bank.

That independence must in the shorter or longer run have shown itself to be illusory. No doubt the craft-unit, at least while they were growing up, provided advantages for his family which were considerably greater than those of most of their known coevals, while competing possibilities were few. They had a comfortable home, lots to eat and a fair amount to drink (strong ale and stout). They did not have to go out on bitter mornings or struggle home on crowded public vehicles. From dark hints my mother gave me – so dark in the obscure quality of her pride, that I don't know whether she cut out the acquaintanceship of most of her brothers in later life because they married 'skivvies', or because they *didn't* marry them – the sexual life of the sons was strikingly free, although exogamic and unrecognized.

And among their advantages (unless you regard it as a disadvantage) they had no T.V. or radio and sometimes went to a music-hall (in my mother's case, after she got to know my father, to a theatre, the opera or a smoking concert).

Theoretically it is just possible that my grandfather's 'cottage' craft industry would have lasted into the adult life of his 'hands'. If he had accepted the American offer the whole lot would have been drawn into the new economic and social machine much more rapidly than in England, churned about, minced up, moulded into new shapes, packaged, and centrifugally rail-roaded to different parts and aspects of the New World economy.

In England, as it was, the other opportunities were beginning to arise – and might easily have struck the second generation as more glamorous (even if they consisted only of the chance to go and work for a weekly pittance in someone else's modified treadmill, with the disadvantages of mobility and exposure I have mentioned, or, as it happened, of the call to the bloody muddy trenches in 1914–18).

My mother, always ringleader and much cleverer than my maternal grandmother at being the *éminence grise*, heard the call to emancipation (but of a totally non-feminist kind) much earlier than her friends or age-group.

Apart from exploitation in hours and wages which the family structure must have made to seem almost natural, the work must have been about as monotonous and boring as one can imagine. I am not certain, but I believe that the lathe (with possibly some hand labour) turned out tiny sapphire shafts which were used in watches and compasses. With the aid of the watchmaker's eye-glass and by hand, my mother and her siblings had to sort out the sound from the broken and imperfect. Fiddling work and very bad for the eyesight. My mother, a Rumpelstiltskin in reverse, told me that she sometimes relieved the strain and the monotony and had a bit of fun, by muddling up the more careful and competent work of the others after they had retired or vanished for the night. (I think I have not imagined that; if I have, it is logical imagination —it is the kind of thing she would have done.)

From a tender age she had been left in charge of the enormous younger brood (nearly all galumphing boys with huge appetites, leather lungs, rough sensibilities, and given to horse-play). I have no doubt that sooner or later she won and that in the process she also learned the will and the way to a domination which as naively as God she saw as her inalienable privilege for the rest of time. But she also revenged herself in day-to-day living while she grew to mastery, by odd devices of torment—e.g. weaving painful hillocks on to the inexhaustible basket-loads of huge masculine socks she had to darn; and other vindictive inventions.

And so at that time, about 1887 or 1888, my mother decided that she would be freer working for an ordinary individual boss than for her father. It was natural that she was bored with the work: but she would certainly never have thought that she was stepping forth into a life of ease or even anything easier. She never minded hard work. Moreover she had no notions at all about emancipation or even of the improvement of working conditions for herself, let alone for anybody else; she did not approve of the working class or conceive that they had any rights at all—'Labour can't rule' was as 'plain as the nose on your face'—and it would never have occurred to her that she belonged to them.

After her cramped and sight-marring day's work and therefore quite late on a winter evening and hence long after dark, my mother, aged eighteen, sneaked out of the family house and took a tram or a horse-bus to the City, wearing her usual mud-collecting long skirts, her bonnet and muff. She probably looked, for that time, very fashionable and smart.

(I have mentioned these details, sartorial, temporal, climatic or meteorological, and locomotive, not to add vividness to a bit of personalized history but to illustrate how great during this period of transition was the difference in attitude towards both work and leisure from the one that is most common today.)

Quite likely she fancied, or even expected, that she would go up socially in the world, but if so, by some automatic process — like a lift or perhaps a magic carpet. She had absolutely no intention of parting with tradition as she had lived it, and not the smallest wish to do so. The kind of 'living in' at close-quarters with the boss, which she would have to do in the work she went for, may have struck her as a natural extension of family life, not at all as exploited familial servitude. She wouldn't have thought of her goal in removing herself as 'Freedom'. Simply she wanted to get away from total family enclosure; not even that perhaps — rather see a bit more life: see for herself.

To exchange one autocracy for another wouldn't have struck her as a case of the frying pan and the fire. Rather, I imagine, she thought of autocracy as the natural state: and it wouldn't surprise me if she chose her work instinctively (although it must be admitted that the choice was limited), her own sense of natural domination being about ripe. But she meant to go on belonging to a family and to see that anybody she became responsible for should do the same.

My mother's new job was as manageress of a City restaurant quite well-known at the time though, I believe, fairly small. There were of course an owner and his wife, who lived on the premises and, in theory, his wishes had to be deferred to. My mother was very proud of this job, not only of the way she held it and organized it, but also of the way she had won it. She never again achieved that degree of external rule and her vivid imagination no doubt magnified its importance.

She had a remarkable memory for self-aggrandizing detail and I have heard the story so often that I feel I was a witness. But here I am only concerned with my mother in so far as she was representative or exceptional in a social structure that looked remarkably stable but was in boiling if not always visible ferment.

According to her account my mother obtained the job, abominably paid and cluttered with 'truck', with appalling hours and cramped conditions, over the heads of a number of eager and personable young women (less personable than herself naturally —something that is quite likely because she was exceptionally lively and good-looking: also with a flair for dress).

To her, the struggle and the victory added zest to the achievement. She had no notion at all of solidarity, either with her economic class or with her own sex. I don't remember any views of hers on the feminist movements but I am sure she thought suffragists were 'silly bitches'.

My mother used feminine wiles to get herself into the job and autocratic methods to maintain herself in it. If she had heard of Machiavelli, or anyway understood what he was getting at, she would have entirely approved of him.

My female parent was certainly exploited both by her family and by her employer. But it would never even have occurred to her that she was not 'free'. Or on the other hand that—because of the way the male members of her family voted (if they remembered)—she was not also as good a Liberal as they. And no doubt she was. In relation to her times perhaps even a better one: for whereas they merely *talked* a politics and an economics they could not possibly have understood even if it made sense, and which they could not even then have seen in relation to themselves, she felt individualism and free enterprise upon her pulses.

Free enterprise of the most buccaneering sort available *was* the 'rights of the individual', and the individual was herself. Quite unreflectingly—for what was there to reflect about?—she identified the rights of all others with her instinctive intentions: and these included the Lord's, so that an affront to her will was sacrilege. Though within her means she was capable of great generosity—*bounty*—it would never have occurred to her *not* to sneak or bully her way to the top of a queue, or *not* to talk everyone down in any purely female social gathering in which she was obliged to find herself.

She was able not merely to maintain but even to advance this individualism in her family role by a simple and consistent expedient: she identified with it all those budding individualities;

willy-nilly. It was only because it fortunately sometimes coincided with our interests that they were not totally nipped: for example, she believed in education and in my own case succeeded in propelling me into it, as the only way to get far enough out of the muddy rut and thus to 'do the dags' of *hoi polloi* (her expression): or to keep *ahead* of the Joneses as she might have put it today. Thus the family unit persisted: and it was not at all uncomfortable for her kind of individualism, which fitted very well into the tribal attitudes of her men-folk.

Politics at that time for the majority of the more vocal (but not necessarily articulate) working-classes was indeed an extension of tribal warfare; a matter of 'sides' and war-cries as well as of ritual entertainment. Gilbert for his time at least was right—there were only liberals and conservatives: that, for ours, extrapolates into libertarians and authoritarians; the structure further breaking down into those who know they have the right to rule and many more who would like to, but often let 'I dare not' wait upon 'I would'.

Of all this the family unit was the microcosm: and that is why the modern libertarians, particularly the Women's Liberationists, have attached so much importance to breaking it down.

From their own point of view they might be better occupied in trying to think of a viable alternative. The modern libertarian is often a bad interpreter of spontaneous behaviour and therefore of natural and inevitable reversions to type. A return to the family is at least as obvious in our time as any movement to supersede it: and seems to be something that many people really prefer, as well as being less ideological.

I believe that one's later political and social attitudes, either by acceptance or reaction, are learnt in early familial and cultural conditions, and are therefore more unconscious, primitive and persistent than anything one later comes to think: and hence that what one thinks are one's own thoughts are often unreflected habits. That is not to say that it is impossible to learn to criticize them and to free oneself from their automatic control. But it is to say that anyone who can call himself with genuine meaning a liberal must understand better than he commonly does this subworld in himself and others. And it is the reason why throughout the book that follows I have put most of the emphasis on our psychological and conceptual assumptions.

II   A pattern of generations

I feel fairly confident that the present student generation is not all that different from mine; as vague, if more – but not much more – vociferous than mine in its intentions and their practicability: and in its underlying motives no clearer. The differences, not all but many of them, if we consider them in themselves, strike me as superficial compared to the aboriginal similarities.

Our ideology was influenced – I cannot say consciously governed – by a more literary or 'humanistic' curriculum, which derived from Lawrence, Virginia Woolf and the Bloomsbury neo-Platonists, as well as from James Joyce, Freud, T. S. Eliot, or from their hearsay, or from the books and ideas they advocated.

That short (and quite inadequate) list gives some idea both of the opportunities of contradiction provided by our guides and prophets (who cannot necessarily be held responsible for our aberrations) and of their common want of social comprehension.

Why lump together that selection as 'literary'? Because the concepts these authors employed, whether consciously and critically or not (but generally not), were drawn not only from the literary work of art, but from what can be called the 'literature' of human thought and behaviour – the great perennial, even if alternating, generalizations, rather than from any open humble and tentative evaluation of their own experience as contingent beings who must trust their own perceptions but always be in process of correcting them.

Certainly these writers all used their own personal experience; more immediately perhaps than most previous generations: but their human acquaintance and its situations were restricted, while however much in practice they all contradicted each other they all retained the halcyon conviction that their experience was universal.

It may be objected that a similar limitation of range and vision is more common than not; novelists as different as Richardson and Austen have assiduously and to our ultimate profit cultivated their own patch. But that is the point. It is only when you get into the realm of ideas that you have to worry about credibility. (To poets or to writers about poetry it has been a recurrent problem because poets can't help making a universal claim – they have in their practice to show cause why their generalizations are more convincing than those either of science or of common experience.) Until about the 1920s—the time I have in mind—novelists put down as well as they could what they saw; they might be blinkered, their spectacles might be more or less accurate, but the question whether or not their characters were like real human beings— were, that is, convincing to the likely reader—usually arose only if the authors had undertaken some ideological or intellectual excursion.

At the time my generation was simultaneously being educated, rebelling against the false and authoritarian conventions of that education, and feeling round, whether it knew or not, for new authorities and conventions to take their place, heroes and villains were disappearing from imaginative writing. That soon became accepted as a commonplace and has continued to be so. There have been various explanations, for example that this is the century of the common or little man—meaning that only average-appearing people are real people and ignoring the question of how you define a real person. But that is only partial: the one thing certain about ordinary people is that they do not individually force themselves upon our attention; someone has to spot them and then see them as persons, even if as ordinary persons. I believe it is much more likely, and even that it was often the case, that writers began to feel uneasy about 'the individual'—his authenticity as well as the concept and its meaning. We ourselves were in no doubt that the 'individual' was the thing and that not only the human person but his 'personality' was sacred. But unless we were all really thinking of our particular selves or egos, as is probable, I doubt if we knew what could be meant by the individual, let alone what *we* meant. That was something we could expect from the literary generalizers, the novelists and sociologists and social theoreticians, or even of the historians and the biographers, but hardly of ourselves. I must say that now I find it hard to understand the concept of 'the' individual except as statistical. As such it has its uses for political and economic justice of an arithmetical utilitarian kind. But as a statistical or a political concept it is disheartening and bewildering to the liberal temperament which needs the quirky or gritty individual to animate its notion of community, and otherwise may find itself logically and irresistibly, if unwillingly, sucked in and drawn down by the powerful if vacuous abstractions of collectivistic generalizations and summaries.

On the other hand, 'personality', or the human person — which may in reality be just as abstract or just as difficult to discover and pin down — strikes me as one of the normative ideas we cannot do without, if we are to maintain the usefulness of any of our genuinely civilized achievements or continue to recognize and to prefer ourselves as specifically human beings.

But has the individual or even the human person ever been more than a working assumption of Westernized Christianity — a Christian moral 'fiction'?

Though I have always resisted the claim that the 'humanistic' (and anti-theological) liberal — who was sometimes a writer — E. M. Forster and Joyce Cary are examples — is a 'rentier' on specifically Christian moral values (T. S. Eliot's term) I hardly doubt that his psychological assumptions were originally derived from Christian concepts with the theology dried out of them.

To call the Christian account of the human person or personality a fiction is neither dismissive nor pejorative but merely literal. The Christian story or myth dramatizes 'Man' and, with many of its confessional and poetic writers, puts him, with as much circumstantiality of suffering and conflict as the greatest novelists and dramatists have been able to summon up, in an absorbing, exciting and convincing tragi-'Comedy'. But the concept convinces us, suspends our disbelief, only within this drama, so highly selective is it of our humanity and emotional, local and social concerns.

At this time when the idea of individualism or of 'sacred' personality for all, first became unquestionable to us, we were unlikely to be aware either of its historic sources — indeed we mostly assumed it as aboriginal — or that new and opposing theories and theologies were already eroding it and causing it to disintegrate; although we were often aware that these intellectual forces were in being. We might even have had some idea of the works that represented them; we had even read some of them or had read those who had read them. G. E. Moore, for instance, was mediated by the Bloomsbury Group, who helped thus to confirm us in what seemed to be our commonsense belief that personal relations of the kind the 'Apostles' and the Bloomsbury Group believed they had, were, if good, absolutely good. Malinowski, whether he meant to or not, helped to justify our rising suspicion that Western sexual and family arrangements were both stupid and corrupt and that what was needed was a combination of innocence and en-lightened commonsense—still unperverted among the Trobriand Islanders. The Noble Savage—in many disguises, sometimes no doubt even clothes—has always haunted and continues to haunt our societies as they recurrently settle into rigor mortis and their shrouds.

Freud of course was the great liberator: and we didn't have to read him, because Freudianism had a unique, almost magical capacity not only for infiltrating all conversation and discussion but for mastering the spoken word at source. It was thus the most dominating hearsay that has ever garbled understanding and undermined rational standards of criticism; and it provided us with a master-weapon against all rivals, particularly our parents. We could show that all our antagonists were always engaging in double talk, saying what they really and deplorably meant, but without meaning to, and thus demonstrating not only that honesty itself was a form of hypocrisy but convicting themselves out of their own mouth while putting their foot in it.

Often it was a certificated hearsay, since a majority of that student-generation was still middle or top class and could afford to be psychoanalysed. Unquestionably all this was undertaken, both by the sacrificial victims and by the priests of psychoanalysis, with a view to releasing the true and free individual.

In some cases at least the cult and ritual resulted in the eternal analysand, the twentieth-century counterpart of the nineteenth-century 'eternal student'. (This is more common now in Sweden and I believe in America.) Some of us in fact took ourselves apart and lost the screws; those who could, or whose parents could, afford it.

I shall pursue this topic in Part Two (Structures, Motives and Assumptions) instead of here because it has its place less as part of a historical sketch than as a generalization which is part of the structure of the book. It illustrates an essential problem or paradox of all philosophies of living—liberalism as much as any: that we have to assume, anyway in retrospect, that ideas and ideologies have been directly influential, even formative, on the behaviour of groups and individuals, whereas it has generally been the case and continues to be so up to the present, that the ideas as people actually receive and conceive them would hardly be recognized by their begetters. For one thing, not only literature but literacy has until the recent past been a minority accomplishment: not even full literacy – the necessary portal of literature – has been achieved and it may even now be diminishing from its maximum because of the multiple garblings by performers in many fields, as well as by the vast range of technical substitutes.

There may be an absolute hiatus between not only the idea and the act, but between the idea and the understanding. Nor can we console ourselves by believing that there is a natural upward pressure of common desires and instinctual feelings; that good (liberal) ideas somehow get into the air as if exhaled by the just, innocent and spontaneous but sleeping multitude, to be detected by systematic thinkers, formulated, and returned in better shape for use.

It may be that this split is the inevitable flaw of all ideologies and that liberalism cannot expect to be exempt. But liberalism is peculiar in having to rely on a belief that its philosophy is at least potentially 'natural'; the desire to be a free being in free relations is there to be elicited if we know or can find out how to do it; free personalities grow by gradual assent to the self-evident.

As we shall see, the human 'truths' of liberalism are far from self-evident: and as we have surely seen by now the continuing history of human behaviour could hardly have been much more illiberal.

I think my student-generation was born into a liberal assumptiveness which we had not yet learned to examine. There was no obvious immediately urgent reason why we should. It appeared that liberal strength was still in good supply (I am still talking of ideas, not politics). We had not long before won a war for freedom, and for freedom from war. There was a period – a very short one it now looks – when that was what we really assumed.

Hearsay assumptions especially if garbled are much better determinants than argued belief. We had been told by various ideologies that, if only as a by-product of our faith in them, we were liberated or in process of being liberated. Free personalities abounded; free relations flourished – no holds barred.

We failed to notice that most of the philosophies, rationalizations and ideologies to which we lent an ear were profoundly disintegrative both of the concept and the reality of personality.

Our relations with friends, lovers and those we even subsequently married often continued to be very high-minded. Everyone was free; everyone else must be left in freedom. Jealousy and possessiveness were out. They were an infantile disorder; and Freud had taught us to come to terms with the infantile, with the implied verdict that it was all the fault of our parents. However, as far as I remember we quarrelled just as much among our elected personal relations as anyone has ever done in the bosom of the family. And neither Freud nor Freudian hearsay taught us what to do about our parents; how to re-educate them or how to put in the balance the maltreatment they must obviously have received from their own parents. That may account for the fact that the doctrine of personal relations did not seem to apply to our progenitors; nor was freedom a retrospective award. And it never struck us as remarkable that we were the first generation to receive this gift or for that matter the first to have deserved it; because we were the first to have the properly certified *knowledge* of what it was, and how to use it – for ourselves.

If and when we had acquired some knowledge of history and could confirm that this liberation had never been achieved before, we continued *for ourselves* to 'blame God and our parents'* – or rather our parents. The rest of humanity throughout previous time we tended to excuse, or anyway the less successful part of it, for not having received our advantages of enlightenment. We certainly did not admit or even see that personality, like love or freedom, is an end-product of maturity, or indeed an unlikely synthesis of conflict, nor that self-realization could only be the fruit of travail in an environment of natural law.

That comparatively blissful stage dissolved with the disconcerting rapidity of all dawns. Most of us became aware that something was wrong very soon after we left our institutions of higher learning, if not before (I refer to the libertarians rather than to the practical or theoretical politicians among us). 'Gone wrong' is a better phrase, for we were always trying to prove, and thus to believe, that the distressingly recurrent bloodymindedness which historical human performance has so far illustrated was a kind of mistake.

* Dante, *Inferno*, Canto III 'Bestemmiavano Dio e lor parenti'.

All liberals (individualists, humanists) are Pelagians; they believe in Original Virtue. So the Fall of Man, however often it takes place, is not our fault. Because liberals are also (mainly) rationalists, they can no longer appeal to the Devil. So we had to believe in some *force majeure*; and Freudianism, blaming our parents and our early familial upbringing, was still the best available. It was also a way of putting the mistake right, not retrospectively, of course, but at least in our own generation.

The generation-gap though it may gape more or less widely and be more or less unbridgeable, is as old as the generations. And both the historical and the psychological judgments that it represents are false; for what is implied is not only that our parents could have retrospectively influenced the inexorable line of events by which they were unconsciously conditioned, but that we ourselves would be miraculously exempt from similar conditioning.

There was nevertheless an immediate practical snag for ourselves: the Freudian '*recherche du temps perdu*' couldn't produce results that were wide and lasting enough quickly enough (no doubt because of the obstinate 'resistance' movement of analysands).* Fascism was mounting, there was going to be another war; we needed another and more nearly instant explanation of the mistaken course; it had also to be both diagnosis and cure.** We might still believe that the psychological explanation (particularly of the causes of aggression) was correct; generally we did — it remained for many a matter of loyalty. But many of us chose Marxism. Marxism discounts the Individual's 'choice' and insists too that the significant part of his 'ideas' is a rationalization of his social and economic conditioning. But one of our 'ideas' was that we thought we chose it: and that had at least the advantage that we could attribute an equal 'choice' — the wrong one, of course, and therefore blame — to those we saw as deviants or intellectual

* How could it — taking years of time and bags of cash: while the number of those diagnosed (by the *fideli*) as in need, was astronomical.
** Freudian theory provided an odd Idealist mirror-distortion of the Marxian unity of theory and practice: total evacuation of one's past will eventually bring up the new man or woman; in learning — or thoroughly accepting — the truth of this generalization, you also learn how to perform the operation. At the time I am discussing it was a favourite intellectual game — quite as serious as chess, or even cricket — to try and reconcile Marx and Freud. (It still goes on, e.g. Norman Brown and Herbert Marcuse.)

drop-outs, *lumpen-Intelligentsia*: then as now, the young were not lacking in puritanical self-righteousness.

We can be fairly certain that not all are cradled into Marxism by direct economic and social pressures. The personal psychological pressures in my experience are much more important, and to avoid an infinite regress we need not go too far into the question of the way they in their turn arise. In the case of those who subsequently become liberals, negative or positive, the factor is probably guilt: and there is always our natural human assumptiveness — the complex of ideas and hearsays which at first we regarded as axiomatic and against which we rebelled.

The psychological factors were certainly more important in my own case, though I have no special reasons for thinking I was typical. Alone among my companions I had gone up in the world and was trying very hard to discard my family origins, on plainly snobbish grounds, as well as the Freudian ones which I shared. I am sure now that though my family was not totally A1 at Freud's — whose was, or is? — it was much livelier and more genuine than that of most of my friends and that I had never ceased to be at least vaguely aware of this superior merit (and its claim upon me). That accounts for my guilt, which was great, and for my projecting it on the poor and oppressed. I developed a myth that when my mother was left a widow, as I knew she would be, I not only must, but would, take her to live with me and be responsible for her keep. The notion (which turned out to be without an absolute practical warrant) horrified me into domestic insensibility: and I decided to dedicate my life to (all the other) poor and oppressed. That too has turned out not to be necessary — or anyway I have not found it so. During this time one of the set books in my degree course at Oxford was *Das Kapital*. Quite honestly the Labour Theory of Value impressed me — it still does — as simple moral, and common, sense. People who didn't, or who couldn't and who cannot, see that the exchange price of a product ought to reflect the amount of real work put into it, still strike me as morally obtuse. How it is to be divided up among the participants is a proper subject of discussion and agreement. But to deny that labour-power is the natural and prior basis of division is only possible in an immoral economy and an exploitative social system.

I was quite as much influenced by Marx's and Engels's description of the labouring classes: or so I thought. But in reality, or so

B

I have come to see, the main motivation was guilt and the need to compensate it—which caused great mental dissociation. In *What is Literature?* Sartre puts thus the paradox that Marxism involves:

> If I am absorbed in treating a few chosen persons as absolute ends ... if I am bent upon fulfilling my duties to them ... I shall pass over in silence the injustices of the age ... and finally take advantage of oppression in order to do good ... But *vice versa*, if I throw myself into the revolutionary enter-prise I risk having no more leisure for personal relations— worse still of ... treating most men, and even my friends, as means.

Although I have never known hunger or actual squalor, my background was near to the poverty-line and I had been brought up in a near-slum. I had also two or three years earlier spent a lot of time travelling, just before Hitler, through the shanty-town east of Berlin with its millions of unemployed. Here I could open my eyes to look at the descriptive evidence provided by Marx and Engels. But I was still obliged to shut them on my personal experience. My experience of poverty even in the days of com-munist 'slumming' has always remained wilfully vicarious. Intellectually, nevertheless, I have never been able to understand why early poverty causes shame. But I can well understand how easy it has been to let the Puritans and the Mr Gradgrinds con-vince the poor that their sinful idleness and ineptitude has incurred the wrath of the Almighty. That does not unify the poor.

A social theory which is convincing both in morals and logic is one of the best aids to passing by on the other side; thus liberal rebellion rapidly moves to some degree of Jellybism. I think this is as true of the great social philosophers as of the youthful ideologue. Though Marx proclaimed the unity of theory and practice, practice took no account of one's neighbour, and indeed was not supposed to do so. The victims were the evidence of the crimes of industrialism and capitalism; to attempt a piecemeal cure would constitute the worse crime of destroying the evidence. Moral adjournment was the truest morality.

I mention this here not just to advocate a philosophy of 'minute particulars' but rather as a fundamental and real dilemma; prone to it, the liberal—or the Christian—has no idea of resolving it.

It seems to me more and more obvious that all social political and religious creeds, individual and systematic, whatever their ambience or their complexion, are somehow alienated from their human subject-matter.

Thus in the kind of experience under consideration not only the theory but even the description never really fit the facts as they are lived or witnessed; and this applies both to the victims and to the examiners or theoreticians.

I must state emphatically that I disapprove of privation and, indeed, suffering, the more if it is unnecessary and unmerited, with all my heart and mind. All I am trying to say is that the experience of those who endure them and the experience of spectators, however imaginative, are different and even incompatible: anyway belong to different orders — to two different perceptual worlds. And it is injustice, or the sense of it, that makes people unhappy, much more than the poverty or pain in themselves; and that arises not from self-pity, still less from self-understanding, but in so far as they have the chance to see what befalls others.

I shall have to labour this further, because it bears on a fundamental thesis — that our sense of our own humanity and hence of our fellow-beings is insufficiently developed to provide us so far with a humane purpose that can be recognized and realized. We look at our fellows projectively, estimating their lot as better or worse than our own; but with calculation, seldom empathy.

The second alternative intellectual 'solution' was God. About that I have written too much elsewhere. It is relevant here for a reason which might seem paradoxical or even perverse: for what it shared, however much it might have been consciously opposed to any political diagnosis, with our Marxist alternative — that it was abstract, guilt-laden, equally lacking in the understanding of human beings, and even more obviously (and indeed often openly) in search of order and authority.

In England and France God was chiefly a literary movement, in the rather tight-lipped fashion of T. S. Eliot and his *Criterion* coterie: not at all evangelical or even enthusiastic and thus unlike its nearest counterpart today. The Marxist movement on the contrary was more attractive to the new young sociologists and students of economics and politics and to the new generation also of potential scientific boffins, those who almost at once, when they went down for jobs, were to be faced with the problem: *What do we do about armaments?*

At the beginning of the 1930s the Marxist moral line was fairly distinct, because so at the time were political alignments at least as seen by Marxist theory. Both soon became blurred and have since run into indistinguishability. In both cases that may be the result of our dramatic invasion and conquest by technology, which even then was not fully predicted or even perhaps predictable.

Those who look at this technological revolution from the other or recent end of the mere generation involved, who were born into the technological world, cannot, I believe, really imagine any other. That means that they also cannot imagine to what an extent that world was new and not quite credible to ourselves and how out of date were the categories in which we tried to conceive it: this in spite of our cars and our radios, and the war so short a time behind us which had been won by tanks and aeroplanes and bombs and the inner and outer mechanization of the fighting man (and woman). Nor how helpless we already were, although, with all the new techniques of mind and machine already available, we might have deemed ourselves less helpless than any previous generation.

For the young crypto-liberal then who happened also to be a natural boffin the Marxist moral line was at first simple (and, no doubt, a disguised, 'Godsend'). It confirmed his vaguely humanitarian upbringing which was unlikely to have roots in science; while it more than hinted at his key-role to come, and kept him on ice for the future: the epiphany of Science resurrected from its bourgeois corruption and restored to its natural and total innocence and beneficence. For the time being killing people was still wrong (killing of Fascist beasts or lackeys was also wrong for the time, in the sense of mistaken or inopportune) — just as he had always been told, and it was in any way that counted politically (that was morally too) only done by wicked profiteers in lethal machinery. So all you had to do was boycott and protest, or so you thought. Sabotaging and spying was probably going on already but we didn't know about it then. Killing members of the Soviet Union and their allies and adherents was peculiarly wrong because at that time and with the available means it was peculiarly likely.

Thus in that blissful time it was possible to belong to the

Communist Party and also be at the same time a member of the
Peace Pledge Union. I don't think that we grasped at the time
that by joining any of the permitted bodies (later to become known
as the Communist constellation) we were keeping the seat warm
for later infiltrations or were even unwittingly fledglings of this role
ourselves.

The Spanish Civil War and its United Front at first appeared to
stabilize the forces of freedom and the Left; but was later seen,
and fairly soon, as the 'dress-rehearsal' for totalitarian war and
was really the first unmistakable step towards the disintegration of
liberal morality in face of its political impotence and even loss of
meaning.

Most of the fighting on 'our' side of that war was done by party
socialists, the trade unionists (who had often been told off to act as
token martyrs), the communists and the anarchists, who also, to
be fair, did most of the talking and analysing. But we must remember that by us — liberals sometimes slipping in and out of Marxist
overalls — it was meant to be for and against liberalism, the freedom of the individual.

When the government Spaniards went down before Franco and
his Nazi and fascist supporters, we may still have remained aware
that there would soon be a much bigger battle; and that it would
be about the same sort of thing — totalitarianism versus the will to
freedom which, whatever our party alignments (if any) we still
hoped, even believed, would be revealed, in time and with luck,
as the real bond between human beings, cutting across parties,
prejudices, races and classes — the real definition of humanity.

In an important sense we can say that we were right, in our
diagnosis if not our prognosis. As a matter of moral and humane
definition, that *is* what the Nazi war was about — despotic force
and the will to absolute domination against the desire and the will
to learn to be free and just.

What was defeated was not the desire so much as the will. Or
we had better now say that liberalism revealed its own self-
defeat; and the illusion of having a will collapsed. A will seeks to
find a way; often by guerrilla — and makeshift, tactics and neglect-
ing no piecemeal and remote correspondence in all the fields and
works of human existence it tries both to stabilize and to advance
however infinitesimally.

In my observation the younger generations in the Western

world have not grasped their twentieth-century history — probably because they haven't been taught any in the memorable way that it demands.

They know, no doubt, many of the facts; those indeed which give an accurate if superficial picture of our contemporary world, both in its new structures and its new disorganization. They know that economically at least some of the defeated nations did not come off worst; they know that there was a new simplification in the political realignments, the superpowers arising in their blocs and with their satellites, like barely quiescent and new volcanic masses, with the new smaller nations emerging behind one or other of these barriers of finance and armament, to pursue, as best they could, the aims of their own internecine wars and devastations. They may even know — or rather they may have formed a more or less distinct idea — which of all the contenders, the big and the little, those who have and those who merely pursue decisive power, bear most of the genes of the moral future. For the most vocal young, disguised in the fashions of their generation, still believe in a moral future: that freedom, happiness, and the good life or better, for all, is not only desirable but attainable; even if they may often feel too that they have been forced, by our own foolish misconduct, on to devious routes and into unreliable and even disreputable alliances. That is to say that a number of them are still old-fashioned liberals at heart: with the implication that they are idealists, ideological, and unversed either in history or psychology.

What they haven't learned is that after the first totalitarian battle nothing of moral importance was ever the same again; nor will be.

And yet it may be true that the winning slogan of the whole campaign was not one of Churchill's; not the heroically archaic 'blood, toil, tears and sweat', nor the homely allusions to the beaches and the landing grounds, but something which can be expressed as *What you can do, that you may.*

We should all have learned that human beings could now do what had always previously appeared, at least to the typically innocent liberal, as the impossible. Now the impossible was to become, in the words of the old office joke, 'what takes a little longer'. In principle we 'knew how' — or would do next time: we 'knew how' to go to the moon; to feed the world's population or to control either its growth or divert its sources of supply; to save the environment, to ruin it or to discriminate against parts of it; to obliterate the ideological criminal (or his ideology, or both), as well as how to define him; to defoliate his vegetable nourishment (particularly in the places where he was a vegetarian); or to alter (for the better, according to our standards) his character and behaviour; to satisfy the material desires of all mankind or to modify and deflect them so that they ceased to be troublesome.

Here there is a somewhat cynical play on the use of 'impossible'. Some people and some acts are 'impossible'. That doesn't mean we are incapable respectively of being like the one and doing like the other; it means that we recognize that we had better not. And it was these 'impossibilities' we learned to accept and to do.

It is likely that the survivors of concentration camps, especially Jews, may have learnt some realistic lessons about human potentiality; in the case of the Jews more likely the confirmation of an old lesson—the limitations of human sensibility (including actual perception), imagination and even memory, the scotomization that afflicts the eye of the witness and blocks his ability to recall.

Liberal romanticism dies hard. Those who became either Marxist party members immediately before or immediately after the war still carried it concealed about their minds and were therefore open to an irrational disillusion: often turning not only against the communist values but the liberal ones which refused to fit with them, whereas the fault was in the shortsightedness which could ever have expected them to do so.

When it was seen, for instance at the time of the Russian march into Hungary, that totalitarian violence was not just an aberration or anyway a phase, but an increasingly common human habit, many fellow-travellers recanted: often still no doubt in the name of liberalism but not with much positive liberal hope. Some Marxists joined the Roman Catholic church, the rival firm, which reveals the abiding charm of authority, although, like the continuing protests, marches and demarches, it may have been chiefly a gesture and perhaps a gesture of despair. Meanwhile there was a quiet, unhurried, but uninterrupted procession along the corridors of the establishment. Many of our apparently like-minded contemporaries had been queuing since our blissful but delusive dawn and moved into the front seats which they had surely earned by a persistence comparable to Zeno's tortoise, and by their refusal in practice to be distracted either by abstract ideals or concrete injustices and woes.

That those of this type among us are content to be Establishment cogs or vehicles rather than wielders of immediate power does not mean that they are not interested in power, but perhaps only that they prefer operating a machinery whose efficiency they accept and respect rather than taking the responsibility of crucial decisions, even if that means being operated in turn and if the price they pay is generally anonymity except within a narrow circle. Few politicians become cabinet ministers; few priests move higher than canon; most of the legal profession will not become judges. Spies must by temperament prefer to remain expendable worker-bees. Some of the idealists were able to make the best of both worlds: the Via Media or the Groves of Academe, America and Redbrick. And they often found short-cuts or crawled through the old boy network at the back, emerging tangled with decorations but still able to sign a protest petition or a letter to *The Times* with an unshaken hand. There were also those puzzling few, the fellow-travellers, who had always kept quiet and travelled furthest, probably to Soviet liberation from critical adult responsibility; convinced Marxists and chiliastic revolutionaries, utterly loyal to their treacheries. Or perhaps they began by playing conspirators and found they didn't know how to stop: *The wind will blow* — as our mothers used to say when we pulled faces. Anyway, they may have found, for haunting, another kind of corridor and underground of power.

Those who remained above the surface while moving into the anonymity of power can often still be discerned through deliberate disguises — wigs or bowler hats — or waving order papers for emphasis or disapproval or umbrellas for cabs. Nowadays the deliberate disguises are admittedly different. Distinguished executives, publishers and publicity men are hairy, if balding, and wear (expensive and cunningly cut) casual clothing. It is all conventional unconventionality pretending it is not a livery.

Social clichés generally mean something but are often so loosely worded that they do not say what they mean; otherwise they wouldn't become clichés. One favourite, already referred to — 'generation-gap' — has an improbable air of precise reference; we use it as if we all knew what we were talking about and could point to and actually measure the distance.

The most important fact that characterizes the generation-gap is that the generations are compelled to look at one another across it. By no means always nor perhaps very often with love; sometimes with hate, though either may be unilateral. And, if so, the gap might be a trench on purpose dug to stop a flood or a conflagration and to give a start to a new definition of freedom where it is desperately needed for the benefit of both sides. But in fact, and as always up till now, the generations cannot escape from one another; they are inextricably involved.

The other favourite cliché is more often used with a deliberate vagueness in spite of its political and quasi-statistical sound – as if it were merely negating any public and vociferous content. Yet of the two expressions it may be the more meaningful.

It is among the 'silent majority' that real relations of the generations are silently carried on and destroyed or renovated, and where they may be the germ of a possible evolution. It is there that genuine change, including the change to freedom, may if anywhere be found. I believe that there is not a 'generation-gap' if that is to be taken to mean that there has been a sharp and irreversible change in the hopes, wishes, tastes, spontaneous emotions and primary reflexes of the generations (or even so much in their ideas, ideas being anyway more ephemeral and volatile).

No doubt the material technological revolution has altered that later generation rather more than our own. But chiefly in the sense that they live in a new public dimension. And, with those exceptions, we and they are not all that different. Take the case of so-called 'permissiveness' (where permission as usual is taken rather than given) – at one level so trivial and at another the representative symbol of 'liberty'. For us – the literate, vocal, aggressive, deliberately young, of our time (for youth is not and never will be a new invention) – everything, in so far as anything ever is, was permitted; with them it has to be seen to be permitted. True, we had to grasp the permission for ourselves, we had to make our own sexual and cultural morality or amorality: but then so do they, in so far as they do not jerrybuild on our so faintly blueprint and on our foundations dug with sweat and Freud. The difference is that nobody who can be taken seriously is seriously trying to stop them. The blaze of publicity in which they have to live is far more cordial, even enviously admiring, than adverse. The camera follows them into their bed and any of many remarkable conjunctions, with as much sycophancy as prurience.

Still there are some who see in all this something radically new
— Theodore Roszak for example or, in some aspects, Herbert
Marcuse (see pp. 221–32). Thus to believe that anything particularly reformative or reinvigorating, morally or socially, attaches to
youth in itself — one of the oldest conditions — is really only to hope
in hell's despite. It is a typical Either-Or, that binary ideological
construction with which we shall meet too often: because *we* have
made a shambles, there *must* be a resurrection; there is nothing
else that will reassemble the fragments and the *disjecta membra*;
entropy is unthinkable although, or because, we fear it.

I do not 'believe' in 'youth' any more than I 'believe' in any
other abstraction. The generations generate one another in the
process of succeeding one another. Most of their reciprocal criticisms are rationalizations of a partly natural, partly cultural,
antithesis which stands for both need and conflict. *Hungry generations* still means more than 'generation-gap': and the persistence
of types still stands for more than the artificial division of
generations.

As a member of the older of two generations then, one may
believe that the only certain and probably the most significant
difference between them is temporal — that they are in fact two:
and that our liberalism, and conception of liberation, was much
the same as theirs. That is not the same as saying that in both
cases the liberalism doesn't mean anything — although it may say
that the political and social expression of either often means nothing practical or in a variety of ways doesn't mean what it claims
to mean. It may be that we come back to a serious version of
Gilbert. We seem to be natural Manichaeans; in human thought
and speculation a duality of principle recurs: Yin and Yang,
Animus and Anima — there are plenty of them; and I shall suggest
that as an intellectual habit it can amount to a logical fallacy
which is typical of much Western thinking and leads and has led
to serious practical consequences.

I think nevertheless that it is a realistic observation and not
merely a hidden prejudice in favour of dichotomies that there are
two main types of human being with distinct attitudes and even
preferences about leadership and following, which do not result
merely from their opportunities or situation in their society; while
it seems to be true that rewards themselves will do nothing to turn
one type into the other: money in itself is no incentive to creative

endeavour but only to making more money. I am aware that this opinion cannot be quantified nor, therefore, given scientific backing. And it is based on an experience of human beings which, like everybody else's, is comparatively narrow. Its sampling, how-ever, unlike the statistical kind is not merely numerical – which is psychologically unidimensional – but arises in the web of ordin-ary human living and therefore at the convergence of multiple relations.

I am not suggesting that the two types, the leaders and the led, are totally distinct and immiscible. I am certainly not consenting unto the biological 'alpha'-* (and omega-) types of the ecological dramatist Robert Ardrey, whom we shall meet later, or to any similar doctrines. Rather I am saying that political and economic structures are too coarse and rigid to represent the oppositions in the living round; and that individuals are either more inclined to stay among the minute and immediate particulars of experience, or, on the other hand, are more projected and abstract in their outlook and ways of communication.

The majority, in all kinds of polity, are quite willing to let the first type run the show, or at least are very unwilling to think about the matter: and this can no longer be attributed solely to want of opportunity, if it ever could. Today, in the Western democracies anyway, it is more likely that there are a few mute inglorious Miltons than that there are village Hampdens unable to make their number in one form or another. In the dictatorships it may be different; there hiding among the frustrated democrats there must be many would-be autocrats who are genuinely deprived – by the other autocrats who have got there first.

Great men, either in politics or war (to single out the two main fields where the interests of the whole people are supposed to be vitally concerned), have often been great actors (or, if not 'great', impressive hams): and the majority of people prefer the habit of being an audience as they have always done.

We might compare two familiar adages, for the light they still cast both on the underlying dilemma of morality and power and on the kind of human misunderstanding in which the liberal has been educated or has educated himself.

* In political or economic politics, the cabinet minister (*a fortiori* the dictator) or the big business executive (or the 'pure' scientist, anyway in a technological world, if we are to believe James Watson the author of *The Double Helix*).

The first adage is Shelley's 'The good want power, the powerful goodness want'. The second, Acton's 'All power corrupts and absolute power corrupts absolutely'.

I think that both of these verbal formulations are to be preferred to the more fashionable introvert-extravert classification which the Behaviourists have adapted (but not adopted) from Jung because, unlike either of those two other usages, it at least allows that an individual may have had some insight into his fellows and even makes sense of some of his observable relationships, particularly within his family where his vital and universal quest for an identity is so obviously pursued.

It may be necessary to say that this dichotomy is rough, not rigid; the apparent preference either for passivity or for activity, for detachment or for involvement, may vary at different periods of existence or according to circumstances or pressures, though the latter case is often a matter of emergency (as in war or immediate danger) and reversion to type will follow.

There are other provisos that should be made: the classification has nothing essential to do with whether one is male or female; we are not talking of public roles as they are permitted or prescribed by contemporary Western societies but only of what we can glimpse, as far as is at present possible, of people being themselves when they are left alone (very difficult or unusual, admittedly, and requiring, as a form of psychological bird-watching, an imaginative telephoto-lens).

Moreover the classification, initially, has nothing to do with merit; it is not being claimed that it is absolutely better to be of one type rather than the other. Nevertheless both are subject to characteristic dangers, drawbacks and vices, with their compensations. Through inertia, the passive type may approach total insensibility in areas outside immediate and domestic gratifications; but it is also, among these people, if anywhere, that life is ever really *enjoyed*. The restlessly active are, we know, a nuisance, however useful, to the passive; and moreover, far more likely to be affected by 'Ideas'—ideologies—in an uncritical way; and also more likely to put those ideas that flatter or soothe their emotions, into practice—not always with strict intellectual relevance. It is a fairly safe and obvious generalization that if there is any exploiting to be done, as there is, it is they who exploit and the passive who are exploited. (None of this denies or diminishes the weight of class, and other handicaps and advantages; it does however suggest that some part of these material handicaps or advantages result from a kind of temperamental water-table to which individuals find their way by inertia.)

A further proviso is needed: that in the case of the restless, energetic, productive organizers and interfering few, we have the greatest difficulty in discerning how far they themselves are exploited by those—for instance among family, rivalrous allies and colleagues—who may well be rather more subtly manipulating them in turn or hanging upon their coat-tails.

All that may be obscured by their own unconsciousness, ignorance of the human situation or situations, and by the naivety they often hide, even from themselves; by bustle, as well as by connivance with the protective hypocrisy of their world of collaborators who may be more cynical and also shrewder in their own interest and, perhaps as a result, less willing to undertake the risks of active commitment.

It is possible then and also illuminating to look at the Nazi phenomenon, which we can distort but not ignore, and the events and intentions which fostered and led up to it (though these often seem disproportionate or even irrelevant to the result) as an extreme example of Prometheanism: how human beings have it in them to behave when they tap an unexpected source of unlimited power over others.

The source of Nazi power was impersonal technology and the development was logical in the sense that advancement in machines and organization could have been predicted in general outline and also in some detailed applications by engineers, even in specialized fields, and even by science fiction writers of scientific education; and often was so foreseen. But it would also in another sense have been unexpected. It may well be that some Nazis, like some classic examples of civil murderers, regarded other human beings, and perhaps themselves, with a totally insensitive objectivity and without awareness of a specific human identity, and would easily discern the advantages of the new impersonal techniques and lightly or automatically make use of them. But over the whole movement the transference from the material to the psychological must have been in a sense accidental. Obviously those who could make the plans, give the orders and switch on the power were remote from the actual dirty and literal spadework—the tortures, the gas-ovens, the mass and mingled graves. The unskilled operatives, the actual 'hands' were merely instruments of power, parts of the greed, themselves automatized as a result of the separation which had now become possible between the 'software' and the 'hardware' of technology.

None of that is to say that many of them, in more natural circumstances, would necessarily have had the light to refrain or to do differently. This is not a claim for Original Virtue.

On the other hand we must not deny, or refuse to make, a moral distinction between the varieties of non-resistance to evil, thus classifying all the passive as morally inert. Are all those who were cogs in the Nazi administration of death or those, for instance, often themselves prisoners or victims, who did not refuse to dig the graves, on the same moral plane as those minor functionaries who were capable of making lampshades out of murdered skins? And how do we apportion degrees of wickedness between all of them and the big executives of Nazi crime, who may never have soiled their fingers or even witnessed the intimate horrors of a concentration camp? Are those all one side of a moral divide, and the hands or instruments – willing or unwilling, conscious or ignorant – to be huddled together on the other? Neither the Nuremberg Trials nor the trial of Eichmann gave an explicit answer to these questions.

It might be better to try and reformulate the question. For however great the revulsion it seems natural to feel towards Nazi doctrine and treatment of humanity, and however fortunately common the feeling may be, the answer does not lie in trying to enumerate and classify particular acts and behaviour. The Nazi offence was against the sense of common humanity; that alone gives it enormity and moral meaning. Iniquity cannot be quantified and the merely social and legal attempts to do so – for instance in the Trials – were morally as irrelevant as our previous exactions of tribute have usually been; attempts to make the punishment exactly *fit* the crime are perfunctory performances in bad arithmetic. I am not saying that in this or any other case that we should let the criminals go, but that we should try to understand what we are doing and the nature of punishment. It is a mistake to believe that 1,000 cold-blooded murders are worse than one cold-blooded murder.

What we should instead be considering and what liberals in

particular should be mulling over is intrinsic attitudes to power. Here perhaps is the most urgent task of a dedicated psychology. ('Dedicated' is less objectionable than 'professional' because here as in many social employments which affect people directly, we need a far larger proportion of self-employed experienced and experiencing amateurs.)

To know how we ourselves and everybody else conceive and feel about power is not only the most far-reaching and urgent subject of human psychological investigation and the necessary substratum for political and economic realism, it is much more important than anything anyone thinks about 'sex' or the way to apportion one's income, or capital punishment or any of the other innumerable topics on which we are subjected to numerical surveys. Indeed it might well be found that all these themes, so often polled, acquired new — or perhaps some — meaning in the light of this more radical investigation.

It is a common and it was until recently a moderately justified complaint that the history books, certainly the school textbooks, were written as if history were an accumulating heap of hetero-geneous events. Even more serious, that on the contrary history was treated by historiographers according to some arbitrary and absurd principle of selection; as if, for one example, it were only the record of crowned heads, their births, marriages, begettings and deaths; or for another, of political and military 'heroes', aggressive men who 'seized power' and singlehanded diverted the course of events towards some direction of their own choosing. This was Tolstoy's complaint (in his reflections upon Napoleon in the Second Epilogue to *War and Peace* where he gives a comic parody of a section of a typical schoolbook). 'Seizing power' or 'being in power' here mean that the great man is totally responsible for everything contemporaneous; whatever happens during his ascendancy can and must be attributed to it.

If the standard of professional historiography nowadays is more impersonal and prosaic — more scientific no doubt we ought to call it — the myth persists in the journalism of current affairs. Obviously political commentary at the level of the gossip column can make one wonder about connections and influence; the Long Swim of Mao; the appearances, disappearances and reappearances of marshals on the May Day rostrum in the U.S.S.R.; the general haruspications that have been going on in living memory since the days of Mme Tabouis, famous clairvoyant (*literally*, if we take into account the bulletins on the bowels and other organs of Eisenhower and Johnson).

The recording of these and similar events doesn't of course need any deep political understanding. At most it is the study of form which might lead to a betting system that at least appeared to work; generally it is just on a par with astrology, simply unrelated to probability; or if there are any traceable effects they are a statistical accident, often the case when the assiduous reading of opinion polls accumulates a slant in opinion — which, it is true, can amount to a kind of feedback causation, or self-fulfilling prophecy.

Summit meetings on the other hand may not only make one wonder about the causal historical relation in general, but about the particular causal role of prominent political figures.

When Roosevelt or Eisenhower or Stalin met Churchill what did they actually decide across the table face-to-face which could not have been done over the telephone or by diplomatic bag? In wars (and otherwise) telephone conversations admittedly can be intercepted or diplomatic bags go to the bottom. But in war the risks of air travel or any kind of foreign travel are surely much greater than in normal times and they seem high enough anyway. Can it mean that we regard our deliberately elected indispensables as lightly expendable? More alarmingly, can it mean that our mortal (and often vital) affairs hang on private intestines, blood-pressures, whimsies, face-likings and degrees of alcoholic sociability?

It is more likely that the politician — or the 'powerful' in politics and other spheres — cannot afford to do without the tribute of drama and press sensationalism. But let us just suppose that the real social and psychological significance of political life, for the politician and for the political observer, either at the level of the informed critical analyst, not himself an active participant, or of the common passive newsreader, is chiefly or even considerably dramatic. If the statesmen themselves are protagonists, heroes, even in causes to which they are sincerely committed — cf. Lionel Trilling, *Sincerity and Authenticity* — should we not expect that the real and reasonable needs of most of their peoples must be crowded out or sidetracked? That life as it really has to be lived, including any moral progression in society or even the realistic and deliberate solutions of problems, is excluded? And that this is true even though the majority should prefer it that way? There are many parallels and analogies between political and business performances on the one hand, and the biological and practical needs of populations on the other, but few intrinsically logical connections. It is not that the majority of ordinary people even look upon the actual politicians as their instruments, for that would imply that there was a common and general political consciousness. People do not regard politicians as their representatives, but rather as their metaphors. Politics and life as we mostly have to live it from day to day are distinct spheres.

Whether the division into the 'Good' (or rather the Not-Bad) and the Powerful — even with the metaphoric provisos just made — is realistic or not, it is at least obvious that the 'powerful' do not represent the good, the disinterested or the passive and meek: in short, even in democracies — perhaps peculiarly in democracies — there is no such thing as truly representative government. Interested groups are what get represented: those who for whatever reason are uninterested — in the performances of the powerful — may occasionally include the genuinely disinterested (who may be genuinely *interested* too in something else which *appears* more interesting, and may genuinely and objectively even be so — and these are the most unrepresented).

That may be truer of the democracies even than of the totalitarian states or the better-established dictatorships where the masses may be forced to admit a real effect of politics on their daily lives because it is a dangerous enemy, while they learn not to deceive themselves that it has their welfare at heart. But even in those places the play persists, no doubt, and is found dull rather than intimately tragical or comical by an audience largely dragooned: they may have paid for their seats but reluctantly and even unintentionally. Politicians and the mass of their audiences do not inhabit the same cultural or psychological worlds.

Part One
The Current Scene

2
Talkers and Doers

Liberalism more often than not has had a bad press: from various sources, representing various definitions, often contradictory. Apart from the (literal) Supreme Pontification of the Encyclicals against it that have followed the French Revolution, it has been totally repudiated not only by Marxian socialism, but also in our time by the sometimes iniquitous but none the less self-righteous leaders of small emergent or re-emergent nations.

Those professed and articulate enemies flourish more in other parts of the globe than ours; and while the meaning that in any one of them attaches to the word liberalism may well be different from all the others, it is even more different from any of ours. Theirs have at least this much in common: that liberalism is a danger; either as a direct threat to the order they prefer, and wish to impose, or as undermining their propaganda and/or political doctrine.

For them at least liberalism still has political meaning and force. They do not yet have to distinguish an attitude or state of mind from deliberate action. In the West this separation has already taken place; and in that ideological confusion we label democracy, it is clear at least that there is no necessary connection between liberal attitudes and liberal politics whether of the Liberal Party or otherwise.

To the latter-day British liberal, the facts of this diverse enmity, heterogeneous though they may be, might be faintly consoling. Uncertain of his status and even of his definition, and in spite of any current symptoms of political resurgence, he can hardly help being surprised and a trifle flattered, to find that anybody should think he could hurt a fly.

It is true that not all the plentiful literature is unfavourable. It

includes histories, chiefly of political liberalism, accounts of
Liberal Parties, and studies and histories of Freedom-movements;
also histories of freedom of thought – which has generally meant
freedom of heretical opinion, particularly in the religious sense;
while in the background, the controversy over free will versus
determinism has kept moral (and much political) philosophy in
perennial business.

Recently there have been a number of analytical studies of
modern political Liberalism, in England and elsewhere, particularly and not unnaturally by German and ex-German authors.
These mostly adopt a diagnostic tone: and they are about the
failure or deviation of liberalism as a moral and cultural (as well
as political) force or direction and are usually written by troubled
well-wishers who seem to be seeking to rehabilitate a delinquent.
Some of these books assume a definite philosophical and moral
attitude for which liberalism is supposed to have stood: and therefore put the blame for Nazism on the German liberals on the ground
that they deserted certain 'eternal' or absolute values to which they
were implicitly committed. In this case the most important thing
about these 'values' is that they *are* 'eternal' or abstract: and thus
there is very little evidence on the ground, as to why the average
liberal ought to be committed to them or even as to how he is
connected with them. To be so perhaps registers a weakness or in-
capacity in analysing problems of human psychology: the wishes,
hopes and preferences of often conflicting individuals – which are
surely relevant to any philosophical as well as any historical view of
political existence.

To take into account the human psychological individual means
beginning with oneself; it also means trying to become clearer than
most of us are, including most liberals, about the concept of individuality; and includes seeing oneself and other individuals in sets
of relations, hence in a family and a culture.

I start from the position of wanting liberalism to mean something
both real and formative: that seems to imply as an initial conception
the belief that it needs to be self-critical and that it seldom, in its
contemporary manifestation, is sufficiently so.

If as a political and social movement liberalism has had more
enemies than true friends, as a psychological humanism it has been
rich in Trojan Horses – enemies from within; often high-minded
verbalists out of touch with real existence as it is lived either by

ordinary and unassuming people or by social and intellectual crooks at all levels of power and influence.

Thus, in spite of the subjective intention declared above, it seems best to begin with the contemporary scene because it projects in sharp and graphic form our schizoid conception of liberalism. One cannot think of any time in the world's history when so much talk about freedom — especially democratic freedom — was accompanied by so many assaults both violent and insidious upon it.

It is the talk which both makes and disguises the split. Much of it is double-talk, consciously hypocritical: but much more of it is double-think, genuine self-deception. The events and actualities may or may not be worse than in earlier times — only a divine omniscience could compare and estimate; while quantification, if it were possible, would be not merely misleading but irrelevant: a calculus of misery is just as meaningless as the utilitarian graph of happiness. It may be that more people — both absolutely, and relatively to the size of population — were abominably rejected from the human category by Nazism, and even by Stalinism, than by the Inquisition; but the suffering as always was individual and personal and we shall never know how representative the articulate samples have been.

That is not by any means to say that any of the contemporary events themselves are negligible: moreover, even when they appear heterogeneous, much of their relatedness is visible to a fairly simple inspection.

Old men and women are mugged in the public parks and thoroughfares; little girls and old women are raped and then strangled. Sectional groups, with or without physical violence, seek to impose not only their will, but their interpretation of fairness and justice; and not only on their fighting equals but on those who need and are entitled to communal protection, including their own; or on those whose moral and psychological authority, as implying agreed principles and as embodied in a rule, they have tacitly accepted by the act of joining an organization or institution. Hooligans and vandals destroy pleasures and wreck amenities and utilities which were designed for everybody and which, because of their age, were most likely earned and paid for by everybody else outside their group or gang; while the social worker's excuse of deprivation does not seem in our more generally permissive times much clearer or more valid than the social worker's programme of therapy.

Husbands beat wives with age-old assertion of virility and disregard of equality: and mothers and fathers batter their children even though the days of compulsory proliferation, at least in the Western world, are largely past.

Meanwhile obscenity and pornography flourish more than ever in a sexually 'liberated' society: and are still obscene for the same ancient reason, which alone has become less obscure than before. They are obscene in so far as they appeal to violence rather than to natural pleasure. Obscenity and pornography are predominantly masculine forms of behaviour which reify and thus violate female sexuality; and provide their own comment on the liberal's essential aspiration towards feminine equality.

Potentially women are in themselves a dirty joke as simple masculinity is not. Thus obscenity is one of the main prototypes of the dehumanization which is so alarmingly widespread in our present world; making nonsense of the ideals not only of liberalism but even of anarchism, which after all is put forward as a kind of social re-ordering based on an absolute morality of equal freedom for all individuals.

Those categories of description are quite enough for the British domestic scene. They are no doubt multiplied internationally; while it can be seen that in other countries, including the European, the climate of political violence is, so far, less temperate even than our own.

Political hijacking and other acts of political terrorism can be left aside for the moment. They are not new, although for technical reasons there may be more of them today: guerrilla fighting as well, although that too shares the category of extralegality. But to include them as concerning the state and direction of liberalism we should have to assume that such outlaws were against any kind of law, which is not necessarily the case. They may have opted out of our kind of law but they may be and often are genuinely persuaded that they want to substitute a different and better kind of law than the ones under which they believe they suffer. Generally the liberal (in the Western democratic sense) looks on law as intended to protect freedom and justice for the individual member of a society. It is the corruption of this concept and the filching, or insidious deterioration, of legal rights, achieved and guaran-

teed within our societies, which are more relevant here. And
from that point of view a liberal democrat may well think that our
present situation and prospects, at home and abroad, are discouraging enough. Beside the colonial 'liberations' we have plenty
of revolutions against obvious tyrannies where the contending
parties have had the chance of opting for democracy, for civil
rights and equality: in Greece, Chile and Portugal, for example,
but we have yet to see a genuinely liberal revolution.

Whatever the factions are fighting for and whatever names they
give to it, it does not seem to be for liberty, equality and fraternity,
as the liberal has historically expected: and it even casts a doubt
on the whole liberal version of history. Either before or after the
Peasant Revolts, either before or after the French Revolution
(not to mention the Russian) how far does it make sense to say
that *people* have been fighting for *freedom*. If they sometimes
have in conscious intention been fighting for freedom, *whose*
freedom?

The Third World of emergent or re-emergent nations presents
the liberal with a new element and perhaps with what could be
his most instructive problem – if he knew how to help to solve it.
Many of these nations, although by no means all, are our former
colonies and in a significant number of cases, and to a significant
extent, they have been able to emerge to their new status because
of our policies, however impure, of repentant liberalization. But
perhaps it does not matter too much to what extent this is true.
Obviously there is a vast number of other elements involved, including our own national interests and our need to shed responsi-
bilities we can no longer pay for.

'Freedom,' said Isaiah Berlin in *Essay on Liberty*, 'has never been
much of a rallying cry.' That is justified if, as I think we may, we
take him to mean *abstract freedom*. Up till now, people have been
rallied, if at all, to fight for particular and specialized 'freedoms'
which often turned out to be liberties taken by other people: and
they mostly rose in defence of their livelihoods, often their bare
subsistence, and against harsh regional and contemporary conditions. It was only this immediacy that made them aware of restriction and of frustration of need, and thus of freedom as something
they lacked. They rose against oppressions that they could actually
see and feel for themselves. And while, for instance, the Reformers
took advantage of this labour-force of social revolution, it was

done to further their own sectarian aims.

Here in the West where we retain, if we have not augmented, some if not most of the 'freedoms' for which our forebears had to fight and which they identified with 'Freedom', the one which is most notable for ourselves is the nearly absolute freedom to talk: and that is largely because, and while, we still retain those other 'freedoms'. And for the same reason most of our talk is about those who have lost them, or never attained them, or are in process – abroad or far from our homes – of fighting for them or believing that they are fighting for them, in their turn. (That doesn't mean, as I have already said, that in those still distant places the talk about liberalism and freedom doesn't still go on – however busy with death they may be: but the tone and the meaning are different.)

'Liberalism,' said De Ruggiero, in his *History of European Liberalism*, 'is a literary phenomenon.'

It began with talk – or anyway with words, written or spoken: with the Encyclopedists and in the pre-Revolutionary salons of France; and with the blissful and youthful Romantic proclamations that accompanied the French Revolution itself. As we know, it has continued to be 'literary' – in the sense that most of the 'Literary' are identified with it, in fact or in reputation; this is a fair generalization about the social and often the political opinions of the majority of the men and women writers in England and the U.S.A. The opinions and feelings are often fairly negative, more than anything a dislike of interference and authority and a preference, theoretical anyway, for uninhibited personal and sexual relations. A committed and intellectually elaborated attitude which may be called liberalism is not so easy to find in our century among professional literary men and women and its overt literary expression is rare. (Joyce Cary and E. M. Forster are the main exceptions.)

Nevertheless Ruggiero is right in the sense that the origins belong to intellectuals and verbal theorizers – people who talked or wrote or both – in a way which differs from the other important political and social movements.

Many other movements, perhaps most, have begun above the intellectual salt: and early modern liberalism often sprang from an aristocratic 'charity': and often meant that taking into account and wanting to be bountiful to, the poor and banausic, it hasn't really wanted to be mixed up with them. It has often been Platonic in the sense of looking for the Good, the True and the Beautiful: and that talk too has remained in the salon.

Today the talk is different, not only in those parts of the world that are hostile to liberalism. There is so much more of it of all sorts and sides that it is difficult for our ears to pick out what we need to hear or even what we need to know: and the difference is not wholly accounted for by the fact that intercommunication and chatter in the ether is now global. It is obvious that more people are using more words than ever before to conceal their thoughts and to distract from their deeds, which would otherwise be too painfully visible both to those who suffer them and those who, at a safe distance, deplore them. The events of history and technology —technology has made the most unavoidable parts of our recent history—have not so much altered our accepted notions of freedom as revealed that they have always been vague and generalized, even emotive. If generally grasped that could do no harm: and semantic optimists who abounded anyway in the 1920s and 1930s and at least up to the Second World War might even continue to believe that having at last understood and cleaned up our meanings we could proceed to change the world.

But it would also lay open the essential paradox of liberalism: that not only, as so often, those who talk don't do, but that in this case they can't; liberalism still remains a wish, and wishes have no horsepower.

The semantic optimists are much less common by now: linguistics of all sorts has gone over to structure and given up content.* Nevertheless even if knowing the exact meaning and use of all the discrete words we might employ won't help, it is just possible that an honest conceptual analysis might at least put the liberal in an appropriate moral attitude to begin with: although there he might well stay.

One of the first concepts his definition has to subsume is the freedom of the individual. Freedom has shown itself to be a vast vague notion or set of notions; but the nature of individuality, if we can detect it at all, is surely to be quite concrete and immediate,

---

* This is not true of 'Structuralists' in the special sense: e.g. Lévi-Strauss, Barthes and others; but they have given up the comparative evaluation of content.

presenting itself to our minds and eyes in any discussions of current situations.

Individuality is the essential and inalienable behaviour of individuals: and the vocal (and talkative) leaders of eighteenth- and nineteenth-century liberalism, whether or not they felt able to spot 'the individual', were quite certain that he was potentially as real as Jack-in-the-Box. When certain undesirable social pressures were relieved he would spring into existence: and moreover he wouldn't bob down again.

Whether the pressures are yet relieved or not, it is beginning to look unhappily as if he doesn't after all count for much: that the well-being of *anybody in particular* is not a goal and can never be more than a by-product of any of our societies, whatever their political and economic type and whatever their stage of development; although it can be and often is the concern of private charities. Indeed it may begin to appear that this individual person was never more than a figment in the liberal mind; the ideological attacks on the very concept of a self-determining person come powerfully from many disciplines outside the political and economic: for example from branches of psychology which otherwise often appear in reciprocal contradiction. Both Freudianism and Behaviourism are varieties of determinism based on the assumption that an individual, if he thinks he knows his own mind and can make it up or (with extreme Behaviourism) if he thinks he has one, is deluded. On the other hand there are new studies and developments such as evolutionary ethology which lay much more stress on hierarchic social groups than on the human units which compose them: most of the existing social and economic studies and disciplines which speak with statistics rather than with human tongues.

Moreover in the present context, 'self-determining' person is even a modest concept. It does not extend to a claim for influence or even social significance, but only to the pursuit of a self-knowledge or self-realization which, outside even more than inside the orthodox religions, still provides many human beings with the hope of growth and the belief that they can count at least to themselves and to their neighbouring fellows. No society that we have ever known has characteristically liked this literal eccentric. In tribal and totalitarian societies this is obvious; but even our democracies have never really done more than tolerate him; while those we can still recognize as carrying out a working definition of the democratic are getting worse. It is not only forceful protests, vocal or physical that are found objectionable or even intolerable; original individual opinions, the more so if clearly thought out and formulated and ready to their own defence, are painfully embarrassing if not exasperating. They are dangerous bad form.

This generalization is not significantly affected either by the increase in violent behaviour, particularly among the younger generation, or by the contemporary disregard of convention, for example, of dress or sex. We are not yet breeding a generation of *desirably* eccentric individuals: but mainly of new groupings of conventionalities. There is here a parallel with nationalistic 'freedoms': it is the conventional group that is 'free' in relation to the opposing and antagonistic 'freedoms' of other conventions.

There is no special evidence that the younger generation has done anything new for 'the individual'; or that, on the average, they have any more recognition or respect than their elders for 'individuality' as a universal right or quality. Certainly the more vocal and active among them favour the freedom of counter-talk, (or 'answering back') to their opinions, often dogmatically held, as little as any parental generation: and stand it from their parents as little as that and any preceding generation stood it from theirs. The young, without much concrete experience, are often absurdly as well as highly ideological—something which can easily be confused with liberalism. Unless they construct formally revolutionary groups, they either tend or drift towards anarchy (a failure to grasp the value of institutions); or towards middle-aged established apathy (a tendency to use institutions as crutches—which can also be used as offensive weapons); or to exaggerated and often doctrinaire permissiveness which is in part a clamour for the right to self-destruction (taking others with you) in various forms. Whichever their extreme of development, they seem to do no better than we did to solve the liberal problem of power with responsibility.

To say that liberalism began—and begins—in talk is not meant to be contemptuous: at the moment it merely draws attention to a fundamental essential element of liberalism—freedom of thought and discussion, meaning the right to hold and air our eccentric views in public and social life (but, too, the prior *duty* to make sure that they are *really* our own).

I believe that the dislike of this verbal and vocal form of individual eccentricity is more marked, as it always has been, in Britain and other predominantly Anglo-Saxon countries than it is elsewhere. This may be in part because the Continent (where liberalism may still have a dangerous and often anti-clerical meaning) grew up in a tradition of disputation; that does not of necessity imply a genuine concern with freedom of thought and expression: it may mean not much more than that in some of these countries philosophy and dialectics are school subjects.

In Britain anyway you still (after a certain age even in the case of professional intellectuals) don't, on purely social occasions, engage in political or religious argument: if, rarely, you do, it may literally break up the party.*

In Continental countries where discussion, even mildly warm, is a respectable form of entertainment, its content and its relation to action are not, in my experience, more substantial than our burbling and gossip. It may be that, imbibing abstract dialectics with their school milk, the French, the Germans and others also absorb a certain sceptical immunization against hot air – and even learn that verbal battle may be a healthful exercise, like static bicycling.

The only common element which emerges without much doubt from talk and counter-talk of present and past is that 'Freedom' is something you are forced to fight for (or less equivocally something or some idea for which your present political bosses, after their own definition, will involve you in fighting for).

Superficially that marks no great change in human history or tradition. Most wars so far among the civilized have been wars of liberation from someone's, or some group's, point of view (often enough, at least to the spectator or victim, in the sense of 'liberating' used by the troops in the First World War). That the wars of times earlier than ours – the pre-Reformation struggles and

* The High Table conversations in C. P. Snow's novels strike me as authentically dull and empty of content.

In his *Autobiography* J. S. Mill, one of the more insistent advocates of absolutely free discussion—infinite too, with all the old and long-buried conversational bones repeatedly dug up for re-examination in case some truth has been preserved in suspended animation—gave almost equal emphasis to the appallingly low standard of 'educated' English conversation, of which he took what might be called a hygienic or prophylactic view: a good intellect should simply keep clear of this high level of lead, for fear of debilitation, even loss of capacity.

religious wars of the sixteenth century used a concrete and limited definition of freedom—freedom of conscience and the claim to private judgment in some matters at least—is some merit. Nevertheless it has always been true that the majority of those who either directed or performed the actual fighting were in it for some other reason; not the ideal of their own liberation or anyone else's: they were professional; mercenary; pressed in one way or another; or just drawn into it willy-nilly.

Most of that still applies today; the categories are much the same—although their distribution, the scene being global, may be different. But it is still a question whether, following on the Second World War and the events that led up to it, humanity has suffered some deep psychological change which may prove irreversible.

Before our time, it was comparatively easy, if one was of average intelligence and had thought about the matter at all, to have a decided and arguable opinion on the question: *Who is oppressing whom?* And therefore, Who is trying for whatever end to be 'free'? That is to say, whatever the participants, winning or losing, may have claimed or actually believed, it was easier for outsiders, even at the time, to decide which party was actually the aggressor; and in historical retrospect much more easy—an advantage which obviously may be expected to apply to future historians of our own struggle (if we fail to prevent them from being born).

To some extent already it applies to the contemporary historians of our own World Wars, but though their researches and the release of documents still leave them—rather obviously, like many lay others—pointing at Germany as the prime mover, it seems fairly clear that at least in the case of the First World War, her significant role was that of initiator of a struggle that would have proved inevitable. Her unforgivable crime was getting her blow in first (and included failing to bring the thing off—moral disapproval, as in other matters, is always divided between the two). She too moreover was fighting for 'freedom' (from encirclement or whatever else fitted her own definition). That the Second World War, the culmination of the struggle against German Nazism, the spearhead, or rather (not to risk anachronistic euphemism) warhead, of the fascist movements of preceding decades, was the first that had been fought for freedom as a universal, necessary, realistic and realizable human goal, is a point of view still widely held, and one which I myself hate to relinquish. That Nazism was a mutation which represented or possibly engendered a major and irreversible change in human outlook seems more likely: and hardly gives ground for hope.

Thinking again of Isaiah Berlin's 'freedom has never been much of a rallying cry' one would find it encouraging to be able to prove him wrong. In retrospect which may blur or romanticize, one might still believe that the democratic response to Nazism – whether or not we now admit that we were fighting for mere survival and at first looked like going under – meant that millions of people had been liberals all their lives without knowing it. Nevertheless this subsided and it could be seen that if there was a mutation it was in the kind of challenge rather than in the response. The Nazis had injected a new virus or a new variant into the body of humane humanity; and the antibodies adapted and proliferated to contain the attack for as long as they were needed. One may still be left asking if this 'body of humanity', after convalescence of a sort, had done more than master a particular vicious strain; and, on the other hand, whether the Nazi virus was as exceptionally vicious as it seemed. After all, we have had torture and mass extermination of unassimilable or scapegoat groups before: the Inquisition and the Albigensian Crusade, as well as recurrent pogroms at any time or place where they served a tyranny in need of blood sacrifice.

Looking both backwards and also around the contemporary scene, one may not – perhaps one had better not – believe that those were fascist or Nazi beasts of a wholly new species; but rather that the scale and the kind of the horror that the Nazis developed was an outrageous illustration of the adage – *What you can do, that you may.*

But in respectably abstract philosophical language it had been foreshadowed by Plato, Hegel, Fichte – and some rather less academic *Untergang* publicists.* What was new was that you *could* do it backed by the enthusiastic and active support of many (and

---

* It is not really agreeable for a liberal to have to accept that ideas have no important direct influence; still less, we hope, that the function of philosophers in armchairs and with intellectual binoculars, is to watch the bloody battles they stir up (if they do) from a safe and uninfluential distance. Nevertheless – and this will recur because it is a basic theme of the analysis of liberalism – he may have to face the likelihood that it is only disagreeably authoritarian philosophers who directly affect action.

certainly the tacit compliance of multitudes). You could do this new thing in history because of the proliferation of technologies; in the automatization of the machines of destruction; in the logistic calculations; and in the manipulations of men and women — practical psychology. Dehumanization certainly: but as an effect rather than a cause? Or so we hope: so that the question, lugubrious especially for the liberal Humanist, *Did the new opportunities only reveal and facilitate a predominantly evil slant in human will and feeling* — still remains open (though perhaps unanswerable).

Yet if we adopt the Marxian dialectical principle that 'quantity changes into quality' we may indeed have ground for believing or fearing that the totalitarian evil of our century marked a radical departure in human psychological behaviour: that the accumulation, scope and direction of material power permitted an irreversible change in the way people thought and felt, both about themselves and about their relations with their fellows; and in the working definition of humanity.

But that is still statistical: it refers to the behaviour of masses; and it does not entail that all human individuals, in their several wills and temperaments, either suffer or accept the change. And it is hard to doubt that in those black decades a considerable number of individuals, in and outside of the roughly democratic framework, were prepared to fight and risk death and torture for something they called and really believed to be freedom, whatever the rest of their amalgam of motives; that is why they too often finished up inside a Spanish prison or a concentration camp; they were not necessarily typical of the majority of the inmates and there were not enough of them to stop the camps from being constructed. It still remains another open question whether or not any idea, including those of universal freedom and justice, can be successfully *fought for*. Certainly many of the foreign idealists who volunteered in national liberation movements, from Byron to the International Brigade, quite apart from the fact that they liked a fight, have been motivated by passion rather than by rational integrity, or by a reasonable and humane *judgment*. On the whole they have advertised the liberal paradox that reason does not teach freedom and justice; and that nothing less will do.

It appears unlikely, and more unlikely as we look back from another generation or two (the new generations are less and less interested in looking back), that those heroes and martyrs of the

C

Resistance and guerrilla movements had a very significant effect on the victory over totalitarianism – which proved to be temporary. Naturally they helped, and they were for a time an inspiration to others fighting for their stakes in life and home, or even doing merely what they were told in the Allied war efforts.

Their type persists, at very different levels of integrity and wisdom. No one can help admiring and, at his degree of pusillanimity, envying, those who will put their convictions to the final risk. But that is not evidence that they serve emancipation from human bondage more or less than the genuinely convinced or deeply indoctrinated terrorist or political hijacker of today: or more or less than that rugged individualist Winston Churchill whose rhetoric did so much to encourage us against the Nazi menace but whose real powers had been called out only by an enormous emergency, and who made a far less notable contribution to the rebuilding of a world that looked as though it might have a greater potential of freedom. Peace bores what Robert Ardrey calls 'alpha-types'* – leaders whose climate is war and domination. Individual and personal freedom needs peace. Surely we must admit that the world's experience in this century, if we look back no further, has shown that the wars, revolutions and counter-revolutions tend to diminish it or stifle it except by accident or privilege here and there.

It is true that a large number of people have been partially let out of the absolute straitjacket of poverty; at the same time on the average they have been given less, not more, encouragement to think for themselves, for even where their governments are not totalitarian, their education is illiberal rather than humanistic.

Meanwhile the existing totalitarianisms go on; and the newly emergent nations look like providing more: often with help from the older 'liberal' democracies or from not too repentant former colonial imperialists, not too discouraged from moving back in a new financial disguise.

Even if we allow that, apart from other more material motives and pressures, the American intervention in Vietnam and Indo-China and elsewhere along the Cold War frontiers was also impelled by a Jeffersonian resistance to totalitarian communism, hardly anyone could honestly say that it increased the liberties of

---

* See Robert Ardrey, *The Territorial Imperative* and *The Social Contract*.

individual Vietnamese (or facilitated their pursuit of happiness); least of all of those men, women, children, babies and foetuses who have died, with or without consent, for an American idea: or that it offers any comprehensible hope of freedom to the majority of the survivors, either side of the 20th parallel, or in the remaining world, including America. Yet some American leaders and many American citizens, whether or not the most influential, almost certainly believed that they were *defending* the freedom of the ordinary person everywhere; those people believed that they were carrying the anti-Nazi Resistance movement into its next logical phase against what may well appear to be its hardly distinguishable communist isomorph. Later some of those American believers, including politicians and generals, were shaken by their experiences of the Vietnam war. Even some of their non-American supporters, far removed from the razed and sheltered ground of the conflict (which was, however, available on T.V.), but perhaps with their noses brought up against the fantastic revelation of the Pentagon Papers, thought that they could avert their eyes.

The interest of the remarkable Pentagon Papers (see Hannah Arendt, *Crisis of the Republic*) lies on the intellectual and moral side, even more than on the political, but is none the less frightening for that: indeed more so, for they show the delicate precision with which the intellectual methods and techniques (software and hardware alike) that have been developed in our computer age can corrupt moral sense by their unnaturally abstract detachment; and they do this by corrupting not only ordinary common sense as well, but *sense* itself.

What war revealed in the calculus of nuclear megadeaths was a neo-scholasticism quite as distant from reality as the angels dancing on the needlepoint were removed from the possibility of normal perception.

From those reluctant revelations we know that the computer-commanders in Washington ignored the pessimistic reports of their own spies on the ground at what would have been, before napalm, the grassroots. The wood was blindingly etched on their vision so that they could not have seen the trees even if any had been there. It is hardly surprising then that the cultural undergrowth has also been trampled on and torn up; if we are to believe the more impartial and less macroscopic and aerial survey of Miss Frances Fitzgerald in *The Fire in the Lake*, the American idea of liberation has cost their South Vietnam allies, for many years, if not for ever, most of what made their traditional way of life and perhaps – for how can we tell? – what made it worth living.

Yet all is still done in the name of democratic freedom. And always in the rest of the world, even in the places which reject liberalism either as disruptive or as bourgeois-idealist humbug, it is unusual if not unknown to find that dictatorial governments or military juntas are ever doing anything worse than *defending* freedom: they never seem to be attacking it. And they seldom proclaim an open and unequivocally authoritarian regime or one that is totally pollutive because undisposable: but much more often an emergency that demands 'national' consolidation and national 'freedom'.

Here Marcos of the Philippines and Park of Southern Korea are types of those who have seen that the defence of 'national' freedom requires the abrogation of all democratic and constitutional rights (that is, the suppression of *individual* freedom) and apparently entails their own sempiternal incumbency. They are notable and long-established examples but there are more every year.

In those undeveloped, poor, or recently ravaged parts of the world 'liberalism' must be fought because it might lead to communism – or even mean business. And perhaps this is even a correct judgment: anyway more honest than the kind of liberalistic assumption that often flourishes in Western democracies – that we *are* free, or at least that we are well on the way to greater real freedom for everybody.

It is often forgotten or remains totally unrealized that liberalism begins as a moral doctrine (as does socialism in so far as it is liberal). But because any political or moral philosophy is obliged to come down to compromise with economic and social institutions the most characteristic moral behaviour of democratic societies is adjournment. Even when states have achieved social affluence the moral goal, while still beckoning, seems to recede. There are Swedish functionaries, for instance, who still say '*When* we have finally solved our economic and social problems *then* we will deal with our moral and psychological ones'. Anyway they said so quite lately (see my *A Clean Well Lighted Place*); and so did the Russians.

Is this hypocrisy and sharp practice based on the hope of fooling at least enough of the people enough of the time (while you think what to do next)? Or is it what might be called a genuine lip-service? — a genuine belief that the desire for freedom, whatever one may mean by it, is a deeply human as well as cultural preju-dice which demands, like religions, at least a conventional and outward respect, and which conceivably could turn dangerously nasty to the point of heroism if deprived of it. I incline to the belief that hypocrisy often has a solid foundation of self-deception: the alternative here is what Popper in *The Open Society* calls 'the con-spiracy theory of society'. This is without prejudice to the convic-tion that the arts of manipulation and hoodwinking are advancing rapidly; nor that kinds of brainwashing which can obliterate the illusion or even the notion of freedom are not only credible but are probably already in operation, not only in totalitarian coun-tries but in our democracies. Nevertheless I believe that the *knowledge* of what constitutes genuine liberty is still too little advanced and too confused for ease of detection and therefore of eradication; and hence that for the sake of those who hold to a humane ideal, who care at all about real human beings, it is better that those who do not should feel compelled to serve it with their lips.

The Nazis were exceptionally impudent and honest in openly proclaiming their evil intentions to the world which, as Dr Goebbels guessed, would not listen (— the cynical principle con-tained in Poe's *The Purloined Letter* may not have been rightly appreciated by democratic politicians): but even they ruled by essential fraud as well as by force. They might *announce* that they were working for eternal domination, but hardly for total or even selective assassination. Deceit may at least be a sign of recognizing that you had better not challenge head-on a widespread prejudice in favour of information and assent: and the convention of hum-bug is preferable to brute and immediate force in so far as it allows the undeceived some little breathing-space and opportun-ity to infiltrate among the less-informed, and even to the more timid some hearsay of juster and truer ideas. (Liberals cannot help faintly trusting that larger hope.)

It must also be said on the other hand that deceitfulness and self-deception and the deliberate manipulating of illusions, be-cause we have the opportunity and the means, is more character-istic of our present scene than any authentic attempt to spread enlightenment: and it is more likely to be the prelude to overt violence than to any kind of humane conversion. And since fraud is only the slower version of force, to countenance deceit or illusion is to connive, however unwillingly, with violence. The liberal's first — and endless — task, it appears, is 'to clear his *mind* of cant'. He may come to believe that, anyway in our present condition, that is the most he can achieve and even that to arrive at such a mature psychological realism is far beyond most existing capacities.

To clear one's mind of cant, moreover, is a permanent exercise for the liberal: not merely a therapy to cure or halt degeneration, nor a way of keeping mentally in trim for more propitious times.

For the liberal the two most important, because most dangerous kinds of cant are themselves separately at war: and they employ forms of jargon which are even more dangerously confusing because they are apparently distinct and even opposed. The two commonest jargon words of religion are probably 'love' and 'God'. T. S. Eliot said that liberals — liberal humanists, that is — were *rentiers* on the morality of Christianity. I have argued this elsewhere (see *The Emperor's Clothes*) and believe that now it is not much more than a not very relevant debating point and that it was always a red herring. It may nevertheless be more than ever important that liberals should not be *rentiers* on the *jargon* of religion. I shall have more to say about 'love' — often an abstract and emotive word like 'freedom'. Leading theologians of our time have done their best to lighten 'God' of all concrete content, which doubtless makes for manoeuvrability in handling the term; or even for sleight of usage.

But it is even more important nowadays that the liberal should remain critical towards the jargon of science. Since he finds another essential of freedom, political or personal, in *consent* to government or direction, his morality is bound up with seeking what, in all situations, is the case and what is not. But to find the relevant truth in moral or social life needs practice and skill, as well as information and faith, especially when, whatever the form of one's faith, it relies heavily on those who appear to be the appropriate experts.

Increasingly over the last two or three centuries liberal humanists have been inclined to look on 'Science' as the impartial guardian of their own particular humanistic morality. It is true that the sciences have made enormous advances in knowledge: and that what continues to appear as knowledge must, morally as well as reasonably, be accepted and respected, and acted on where we believe it to fit; in short, that in particular fields it is wise to follow the prescriptions of experts, provided that they are in perfect or very substantial agreement. Nevertheless everyone, not least the liberal, tends more and more to seek advice from the scientific expert, or the 'expert' who claims to be scientific, on problems of being human: and experts are increasingly inclined to boost their guardian-status with quantitative credentials which should lend genuine, if limited, authority only to the non-human sciences.

It is largely through inevitable ignorance which, because of the real complexity, departmentalism and obscurity of present scientific and technical knowledge, may also remain incurable, that we find ourselves taking the experts that come our way on absolute trust. But anyone who has the capacity to maintain any kind of criticism should do so. One can hardly call oneself a liberal if one does not believe in criticism, in the sense of keeping one's mind open as long as possible and taking all authority, even the most scientific, with a grain of salt: salt of course in sufficient quantities is an emetic.

Scientific experts are groups with closed communication. That can sometimes provide an excellent technical excuse for the short cut in expression and a high risk of a short cut in thinking: particularly dangerous if what is cut short too is the real subject-matter — a fellow human individual living in a society of his fellows.

A moderate scepticism is part of mental health: and it is safer than not to assume that the claim to impartial objectivity in any matter that bears on the independent well-being of human individuals is suspect or has something to sell. Scientists claim not only impartial objectivity in general but moral neutralism (while some philosophers, too, look on value-judgments and what they call 'psychologism'* as unsavoury habits). I advance the dogma or hunch that even in the exact sciences this may disguise a preference for one's own product: hence the rhetoric, jargon and cant — all sales talk which is incompatible not only with impartial

---

* The assumption in any form that philosophical, logical or mathematical truth depends on the individual or subjective act of thinking. It is used with different shades of meaning: for instance, Popper (see *The Open Society*) uses 'psychologism' to refer to the mass effect of individual variations in thought and behaviour. The term's philosophic usage is usually pejorative.

objectivity, but with the whims, wishes, and preferences of ordinary human beings if those could be made informed, articulate and respected.

Living in this world of cant and jargon the liberal had better remind himself penitentially that he makes and has always made his peculiar contribution of moral hot air; in particular that he is prone to Jellybism as well as to moral adjournment; a way among other things of hiding from himself the fact that people in society are still more often than not indifferent or actively selfish about the needs of those near to them: and that, in contradiction of the socialist morality he has often uncritically adopted, better material conditions have not achieved the promised cure and can even sometimes be seen as hardly relevant.

Clearing his mind of cant, his own and everyone else's, the liberal may come to admit that we live in a Darwinian world: and then he can ask himself whether by taking thought and action he can help to modify and civilize it. While seeking the most realistic and informed answer to that question he will at least learn a lot about human beings: their behaviour, regular or unpredictable, their attitudes to freedom, and the meaning, if any, that they give to it. And the conditions which favour or thwart it—particularly no doubt the latter. It may well be that he will come to believe that liberalism is not of this world, anyway not of this present world or any he can foresee; even that it never has been of this world: that whatever the human struggle, economic, political and psychological, is about, it is not yet, or visibly, about release from automatism or about emancipation into full and as yet unrealized humanity.

3

A Darwinian World?
Individuality and Individualism

In the fierce mid-century argument about evolution, the nine-teenth-century liberal would naturally incline to the side of Darwin and Huxley, but he would not necessarily or probably have foreseen our Darwinian world where 'fitness' to survive has little to do with his values and often seems opposed to them. Even before that time it is probable that temperamentally and intellectually he would have preferred to discard supernatural origins and explanations and to believe that mankind had not Fallen but Risen; a continuing process which the doctrine of progress based on industrial and economic, if not imperial, expansion would help him to interpret optimistically. Moreover, articulate and reasoned liberalism was represented by the class which had solid grounds for optimism. It would take some time for the implications of the Malthusian and Darwinian doctrines of the struggle for existence to sink in. Even today the liberal may believe or anyway hope that the conflict between individuals and between warring groups and social conceptions cannot reflect an ineluctable scientific law of evolution but is somehow caused by a mistaken human development through which it has adopted the wrong political and economic forms. At least up to the period between the two World Wars the twentieth-century liberal, both in private and public relations, in many cases succeeded in maintaining this optimism: and he was even reasonably justified in believing that the Second World War, by the time it came, certainly had to be fought to defend our existing democratic liberties, which were really endangered by the Nazis.

For some time even after that war was over, in supporting Roosevelt's programme for the Four Freedoms, he showed conviction that the increase and spread of real freedom entailed a fairer distribution of the world's wealth as among both individuals and nations: hence in turn both individual and class co-operation which would establish peace. His ideals were still those of Liberty, Equality, Fraternity. He could very likely even foresee that this would cost money and other material sacrifices, even of status. Redistribution of wealth meant that he who hath much shall have less than before. These aims were not too different from those of the milder social democrats, although he differed and was probably vaguer and sociologically less informed in his ideas about how to achieve them.

It is only in our post-war world that it may seem more likely than not, even to the liberal, that co-operation is only a millenarian ideal, not even in the order of nature, and that the competitive struggle, even as among the majority of individuals, quite apart from warring groups, is eternal.

It is interesting, and points again to another typical liberal dilemma, that J. S. Mill, the most representative of liberal intellectuals and individualists, not only believed that co-operation – a warm concern for our fellow-beings – would reveal itself as our second nature, but, with some apparent inconsistency, saw the chief danger to the future health of individuality in a preference for group-mindedness (after all a form of co-operation). He foresaw the sameness which would afflict us and put it down to the spread of communications (as did Tocqueville).

In many ways this has been borne out, as any air-traveller to once exotic and romantic parts can see for himself as he views the façades of airport buildings and shoots up his Hilton hotel. But verbal communication is not in the same case. The spread of tele-communications (which Mill could hardly have foreseen) may have revealed a sameness among us, but did not create it: and it does not generally arise from an under-individualized and over-socialized propensity for co-operation. It is rather an overt atomic competitiveness which makes most of us alike. These communications, being technological and artificial, have no natural limits; and allowing instant participation they allow also instant showmanship: all business is in part or whole show-business – which is easier than interest or empathy as well as more internecine. At all levels above an extremely depressed destitution many, perhaps most, people seek prestige and status as a way of life or at least accept it as the social ideal – not merely because they are having a natural fling after generations of being deprived of creative personal expression.

Neither Tocqueville nor Mill looked on democracy as much better than an inevitable *faute de mieux*. Mill comforted his resignation by trusting in the prestige of intellectual leadership. His 'clerisy' was not only a self-justifying logical development; people were going to welcome it and even like it: once, we must suppose, they were in an educational condition to recognize it and that it was for their good.

The hope is not only incompatible with equality—that would not have troubled Mill unduly—but it also appears inconsistent with Mill's ideals of a proper individual eccentricity and of permanent criticism. But in any case, and in the event, he would have been disappointed. The most powerful form of technological communication, television, has shown that even authentic, social and moral criticism is practically forced to don the motley before people are able to observe and listen to it long enough even to misunderstand it. Most T.V. discussions are a staged performance which rejects the natural co-operation the theatre itself finds necessary; the audiences, which are supposed to participate, are invited, and in some way selected, and their performances to some extent stage-managed. More seriously the Box daily confirms and visually advertises what we now know, although Mill did not, that however much people rely on experts of all kinds (as they once were obliged to rely on witch-doctors) they tend to dislike and distrust intellectual ability or even an unusual intelligence that makes its own observations and judgments: something that not only suggests that they get the wrong sort of 'clerisy'—an elite elected by a fishy electoral procedure—but that they themselves distrust or envy authentic individuality.

It is not that people are either worse or more stupid than they used to be; or that people in another country or time are, or were, better; or in another class or category are worse—although all of us seek those consoling and magical projections now and then. People have generally been different from what we mostly assume, not least the liberal: often living at great moral density under the pressures of autonomous groups from which the individual hardly distinguishes himself and is therefore not likely to be much troubled by ideas of freedom and choice.

The liberal particularly is likely to forget that the individual—

'self-choosing' as Sartre calls him — whose 'freedom' provides him both with his goal and his pattern, is not easy to spot or even to recognize: it asks for at least the patience and the skill of the bird-watcher. Individuality is recognized, often tacitly, and only in real encounters, perhaps reciprocally: and it is, even so, hard to discern, while what is harder still is to estimate its influence beyond these limits of neighbourhood. It is only in close-up and possibly under the psycho-moral microscope, that you can see what people want and in what *they* feel their freedom to consist: and that you can recognize yourself in them. And this cannot really be generalized.

If the 'individual' or 'individuality', in the sense the liberal accepts, is hard to find psychologically, historical detection is even more difficult: history and historical events have a large say in all matters of individual development. It is a liberal axiom that society exists, or anyway ought to exist, for the full flowering of this individual: or that society ought not to hamper it. In this doctrine of a unique individuality the Christian axiom of human personality has no doubt influenced him but it does not help him to discover how this flowering could be brought about in any society we can at present conceive, nor where indeed to look for the seed; he would certainly feel safer if he could find in history the support of a tradition, preferably both of thought and behaviour.

So would we all: but the need is greatest if one's ideas demand a change in general human behaviour and are in any way proposals for bringing that about: or if they appear too novel; or if one regards them, maybe secretly, as too weak. The liberal will be hard put to it to trace this supportive tradition. Or he may discover two traditions and try to make them into one when they are really distinct and even at times in conflict.

One is that of the thinkers who have made it their business to define the individual's right to freedom. This is significantly an 'ought' — or normative — definition and thus, although it claims to describe a natural law, is inherently suasive or propagandist. In its pure form, moreover, it is not much more than two centuries old. As Herbert Butterfield (*The Whig Interpretation of History*) implied, it turns into a kind of philosophy of history, with the common characteristic of those philosophies — that it prophesies the effects it would like to bring about — and with the essential (and sometimes complacent) optimism that goes with it. Just as one such philosophy of history inevitably and logically moved towards Christ, and another to the ideas of the Spirit, so liberalism (whiggery, for Butterfield, includes liberalism) moves not only towards the perfected individual, but also to the apotheosis and theophany of liberalism (or whiggery). The free creative individual whom the ideological liberal sees as the type to which the whole creation moves is not in fact a historical phenomenon. And if the liberal looks back beyond the small cluster of his nineteenth-century intellectual forebears, it is only rarely that he will find this significant, and 'self-choosing', atom who among other things, and to fulfil the liberal specification, has also to be representative of universal 'Man' – born to freedom and desirous to establish or re-establish it for himself and his fellows. It is true that he will find plenty of forceful individualists: indeed those will largely create his impression of history for him.

It is this other 'tradition' and its intellectual Romanticism in which he is quite likely to find himself: the romance of Renaissance humanism whose emotive attraction, we might note in passing, may result from unconscious personal vanity. It may be true that liberals are less prone than conservatives and crypto-authoritarians to praise times past as compared with the present but that is mainly because they have an equally ideological, if not mystical, fixation upon the Future. And certainly, just like everybody else, they can identify themselves, if unconsciously, with the more splendid figures of past history – the condottieri, the alpha-types. (Actuarially, most of them would have been serfs, beggars or, of course, for one reason or another, *premature corpses*.) Those splendid 'individuals' as they certainly were – condottieri, Leonardos, secularizing scholars breaking out of medieval superstition and intellectual inhibition – have really nothing in common with the liberal's 'individual' and his 'individuality', or, therefore, with liberalism: or anything that we nowadays call humanism.

In so far then as he pays any attention to the history of events and behaviours, the liberal may become eclectic and thus perhaps self-deceiving; selecting his ancestry from doctrines and faiths that may indeed proclaim a humane ideal and which may even have inspired him during his formation, but which on closer examination seldom seem to be on the side of the individual trying to realize his own freedom, to become a free person in free relations. Liberals it seems are capable of detecting in ideologies as varied as those of the Platonic idealist, the Renaissance humanist or the Lutheran reformer, what we might call the *premature liberal*; and to credit freedom movements with a historical continuity and development they have never possessed.

It is even possible for the secular liberal to maintain this illusion about the battle for religious freedom and to see the whole of protestant post-Reformation history as in the line of genuine individual liberation.

Nevertheless, we may agree with Berlin that 'freedom has never been much of a rallying-cry' if by 'freedom' or 'liberty' we mean what the liberal would like us to mean or would like to think he means himself: — the willingness of individuals to fight for liberty of conscious and consciousness — for the right to truth and knowledge, and for freedom of expression; and if necessary to sacrifice themselves for all this as a universal disinterested aim: thus for the beliefs and opinions of others, on the assumption that they are sincerely held. In this sense freedom indeed has been a cry with a shortage of wool: and it is significantly ironic that, as we saw, the shorter the genuinely liberal content, the more the cry has become useful to tyrants and factions.

It is true that the most powerful and influential battles have been fought under the banner of *religious* 'freedom' and have made a great contribution to revolution either as a base or as a parallel. These have certainly been of major interest to the liberal, while at the nineteenth-century peak of individualistic liberalism religious emancipation was a central issue and liberal humanism was essentially secularist.

But it has been rare to care about liberty of conscience in an absolute sense: that is, to care about other men's liberty of conscience except in the sense of trying to check it in favour of one's own. It has been other 'liberties' which have preoccupied the rebel: and the attack — as in the pre-Reformation struggles — has been not so much in support of anybody's religious freedom as against outmoded or unjust economic and social structures with which the Church was identified or which it supported. Luther himself cared no more for 'liberty' than for the other 'freedoms', which were used rather as a bait to lure peasant and working-class support while he established upon them his own preferred dogmatic discipline. Rebellious peasants and other workers, during pre-Reformation and Reformation times, attached themselves to the movement for religious reform and its leaders, but chiefly because they were being ousted from their land or their craft status. It is true that some recent researches, particularly in England, make a case for believing that the workers of the twelfth to the fourteenth centuries both in agriculture and industry were also inspired by values which the modern liberal (as well as the primitive Christian) might recognize as like his own (in their more generous and disinterested form or as he would like them to be).

Rodney Hilton, for example, says in *Bond Men Made Free*:

In our consideration of these simple and basic issues in the earliest period of peasant demands the desire for freedom emerges clearly and ... is continuously present in peasant movements sometimes more and sometimes less strongly.

Admittedly he adds that

Freedom, then as now was a concept that acquired significance only in specific contexts, in terms of concrete gains and losses ... Freedom, it has been put at its crudest, was an aspect of the development of real estate.

(which means that free status and tenure were the best for the colonization and clearing of virgin lands). Nevertheless, by the fourteenth century there entered 'an ideological element which instead of being confined to the clerical intelligentsia was spreading to other social groups'.

But all this concerns only political and economic liberty: indeed freedom as a physical notion – although Hilton suggests that something more disinterested, more 'liberal', was present in germ. It is true that the Peasant (and other revolutionary) movements allied themselves with 'heretical' religious leadership, but that can hardly be regarded as a forerunner of the liberal notion of liberty of the individual conscience. Indeed the quotations suggest that the religious leaders were often converted to political means rather than the other way about.

The pre-Reformation Conciliar Movement was in one sense a step towards democracy and equality in Church governance. Nicolas of Cusa argued for power in the Church as in the State, based on the consent of the people. But according to Mackinnon, in *Origins of the Reformation*, neither Nicolas nor the other Conciliar leaders were prepared to go the whole length of their theory of popular sovereignty. The Conciliar Movement did have its martyrs and it appears that John Hus (whose ideas were based on Wyclif's) died for the freedom to believe and promulgate whatever one believes to be the truth. We may find so obstinate an integrity admirable and even sympathetic. Indeed we must do so: no more and no less than in the case of the secular martyrs of resistance movements or of scientific freedom of thought. Willingness to die is likely to impress many of us at some time as a strong argument for the truth of a proposition. But of course it is nothing of the kind; it is at best an argument for the strength of a belief that one's proposition is true: but no sign of willingness to listen to the possible case of the other side: rather the contrary — it may be choosing the best exit from the discomforts of an argument you fear to lose.

No movement of religious reform, then — still less the religious wars and conflicts — has primarily been about freedom of conscience and thought, nor therefore about what the liberal must regard as an inalienable right of individuality. Like all wars and conflicts they have been about one set of alpha-types against another: about who is going to win.

That the liberal is often a humanist in practice means, not necessarily that he is in favour of Man, but that he is against God, and that may provide him only with a rather thin and negative notion of his free and creative individual.

Liberty of conscience too — even on the most disinterested definition — is markedly distinct from liberty of consciousness.

Up to the time of the battle around Darwin's *On the Origin of Species*, and until the reverberations had died away, there was good reason or excuse for identifying liberty of conscience with what was called 'Free Thought'. But it has never followed that being able to choose and proclaim what one feels obliged to believe, and to reject interference in this respect, means that one is able to think freely. Freedom of thought is inextricably bound up with open awareness and inquiry: and with open-mindedness, the willingness to be proved wrong or misled. It is not clear that liberals think more freely and impartially and without exclusion of subject-matter, than anyone else.

In the case of religion especially, the humanistic liberal does not always want others to have the freedom to think freely. *He* also possesses the Truth and finds it a duty to impose this 'freedom' on others. And whether he is willing to die for it or not, he is certainly willing to prohibit religious education in schools. He has his own orthodoxy: he wants to be *right* – to win: he is battling for his side. Otherwise he might see a case at least for letting religion die a natural death.

On the other hand I have no doubt that if the Church or any of the 'Churches', religious or secular, which have been strong could regain their strength they would likewise show that they have learned next to nothing about liberty of conscience or of consciousness – freedom of thought. But that they are down is not because any form of genuine liberalism is sitting on their heads. We need not go here into the causes of the decline. What matters as far as the liberal humanist is concerned, is that he himself has helped to turn religious orthodoxy into a decoy duck. Shooting at it will do nothing to free either thought or feeling: and it may very well waste the fire which badly needs to be aimed in other directions.

In the Twelve Articles, asking for Luther's endorsement, it is clear that the Swabian peasants, anyway, saw social reform and economic improvement as inseparable from the Reformist demand for greater religious freedom. Luther's reply (*Enjoinment to Peace on the Twelve Articles of the Peasantry in Swabia*) showed that to him the distinction between political and religious liberation on the one hand, and a free conscience on the other, was unmistakably clear, and his understanding of the new spirit as old as Papal sin; or of the Princes and overlords whom he indeed blames for the disturbances and for the conditions of the poor and dispossessed while in the same breath he enjoins them to slay and if necessary exterminate the peasantry 'as one would slaughter a mad dog'. He categorically denies the right of rebellion against established authority, even in self-defence: the purpose of government is to preserve property and, as he put it, 'keep men above the level of the beasts'.*

Luther preached woe to the overlords by whom, no doubt, the offence cometh. But God could be relied upon to punish them,

---

* A contemporary Luther would have caught up with ethology and the territorial principle which shows that the beast which is an evolutionary success has developed a strong property sense. Luther was here, though no liberal, a forerunner of Locke – a founding father of our civil liberties as liberals have mostly conceived them – who rooted them firmly in property.

while they in turn would punish the peasants, who appeared to have a choice only between two bad ends – starvation or slaughter. The liberal may have to admit that even those who look like possible 'freedom heroes' are often governed not by any disinterested search for truth (an impartiality which would be necessary even to wish for liberty of conscience for others), but by an aggressive drive towards the establishment of one's own partisan definition, including the definition of 'freedom' itself. Here again leaders of religious reform can be and generally have been honestly if disagreeably self-deceived. They believed that they possessed the truth and believed it firmly enough to be willing to die for it. It is no doubt possible to believe that the truth shall make one free: and if one then believes that one possesses the Truth, it is perhaps no less than one's duty to force it on others and thus compel them to be free. This sense of duty has often continued into the secular and political movements of our time: thus they are not easily identified with a liberal spirit if that entails the priority of the individual and freedom of thought and conscience (or *your* right to hold views which *I* detest).

The liberal association during the rise of industrialization with Puritanism, and its gospel of Gradgrindery, is not accidental. Politically and economically boosting individualism (of the alpha-type) Puritanism probably did more harm than Rome to genuine individuality. Clearly it favoured hard work and the success of materialistic projects whether in politics, economics or intellectual, scientific and technological inquiries and skills. But the liberal ought perhaps to agree with Christopher Hill* that it turned up-

---

* After the defeat of the radicals in 1666 ... the protestant ethic dominated at least those thoughts and feelings which could be expressed in print. The society produced great scientists, great poets ... Newton and Locke dictated laws to the intellectual world. It was a powerful civilization, a great improvement for most people on what had gone before. But how absolutely certain can we be that this world was the right way up, the world in which poets went mad, in which Locke was afraid of music and poetry? This society which on the surface appeared so rational, so relaxed, might perhaps have been healthier if it had not been so tidy, if it had not pushed all its contradictions underground: out of sight, out of conscious mind. The protestant ethic so dominated the moral attitudes of the middle classes ... that the Licensing Act could be allowed to lapse in 1695, not on the radicals' libertarian principles, but because censorship was no longer necessary. The opinion formers of this society censored themselves [Hill, *The World turned Upside-Down*].

side down the world of genuinely humane possibilities which depends so much on the poetic and imaginative power and insight of literature and art: at least that is the vision the liberal himself has mostly hankered after.

Thus if the authentic individual has always existed he has failed to generate the power to rejuvenate and take over the world. Individuals of genius, like all desirable nonconformists and eccentrics, are also like lunatics — 'they don't organize'. And theoretical liberals may well ask if they themselves historically have done much to help.

The temptation may be to escape into other chains: to find new orthodoxies which may look rational or critical, and therefore liberalizing; but which are sometimes straitwaistcoats of a more modern or fashionable pattern. They may be scientific as well as ideological. When faith (or hope) exceeds understanding one can turn any science into an acceptable ideology — and a new orthodoxy. To this the liberal humanistic mind is specially susceptible: and finding that the 'creative and disinterested' individual is elusive, both in the past and in the present, it is apt to solace itself with hopes of 'Man', of whom it also tends to trust that 'Science' will give us one day not only a perfectly correct, but also a much more acceptable picture. That is particularly and essentially the case in so far as the liberal rejects the realistic psychological and moral insights of which the religious as well as the artistic spirit has from time to time been capable.

It is true that the liberal, like many others, is likely to be dissatisfied with the Darwinian and neo-Darwinian account of evolution — the war of survival among species, carried on at the human level as the struggle for the individualistic upper hand. But he is all the more likely to substitute a new faith in moral evolution (and thus even in a 'developmental' individual) — to which some biologists as well as some ethologists give support. (As we shall see, it is more often, and perhaps ironically, the so-called 'human' sciences, with their popularizers, that subscribe, on animal evidence, to the static notion of intra-specific 'aggression' and its social containment.)

But with or without 'scientific' support, the hope for moral evolution is slanted to the future. We cannot assert that it is a Utopian fantasy, only that the badness of the past is no evidence that the future must improve.

It may well be that the hope is only a particular (and liberal) illustration of a habit that specially characterizes European thinking – the habit of thinking in sharply discrete opposites or alternatives: the 'Either-Or', which is also the habit of thinking in 'sides' or contrary generalizations (generalizations are often in part emotive or suasive). Or perhaps we should say it is the habit of taking sides instead of thinking. To adopt a generalization, however plausible and however strongly vouched for by professional experts of human and social sciences, is a partisan commitment and not an aid to authentic thinking. One thing we ought to be able to say about the genuine individual – if he is to exist – is that he must be trying to think – or 'see' – for himself. That means he has the right (sometimes the duty) to be wrong – something which may make for freedom though not necessarily for order.

Part Two
Structures, Assumptions, Motives

4

Either-Or?

In the authoritarian regimes the split between the powerful and those who 'want power' has at least the (perhaps dubious) merit of being sharply defined. In the democracies there is a great variety of splits, hiatuses and dichotomies: and the confusion is greatest in the world of ideas where the liberal is not much less likely than anyone else to seek the comfort of those over-simplifications which generally lead to illiberalism.

One of the splits is longitudinal: the traditional opposition in European thinking between Idealism and Materialism; or, preferably in this context, between Monism and Dualism, since Idealism and Materialism are both monistic. The argument here is epistemological, about what we can *know* to be real; and this has certainly had wide-ranging intellectual effects, particularly theological and economic. But for the present discussion it is more important that the purely philosophical ideas, one side or the other, have had so little direct influence: not only ordinary people but most scientists — and they more than most deal with and intervene in 'reality' — do not think about its nature; as an epistemological description they are mostly naive monists; they take their perceptions of the world for granted.

The splits are also horizontal: between the ideas or theories of ideologues, thinkers or theoreticians and their own practice or application or even their own potential material of observation; and also — more important here — between the conceptions or theories of these professional thinkers and the behaviour of other people, including those who listen to them and whom they no doubt hope to guide or influence.

I have elsewhere referred to this progression of ideas in the world as either 'The Church' or 'The Game of Scandal'.*

* The progression of influence is either circular or wildly tangential. In the case of the 'Church', the founder has a good idea (a realistic generalization of

Of this hiatus where 'the shadow falls', traditional (and academic) detachment is an essential perhaps, but not the sole cause. That the hiatus exists is true of all formal thinking, as I have said, but it is particularly the case with political ideas or those which have a necessary political entailment. Certainly political thinkers though they may be working within a tradition of study, and even an unreflected one, often draw their evidence from what they can see in the conditions of the world around them; as we can readily accept when we look at almost any of them from Plato or Aristotle to Hobbes. But this does not make them impartial. A political idea (and probably most other Ideas) is part of a *side*: which means that it is sooner or later up against an opposing side. However unversed in political practice, political thinkers are unlikely not to wish that someone in the executive field would see their conclusions as sound advice or at least consonant with his own wisdom, yet on the whole they do not seem to establish much in the way of prescriptions* – with the notable exception of the Utopians, particular Plato – and these, even where political doers or would-be doers are sympathetic, have never been found workable for long. Part of the explanation may be that a 'side' cannot be put across by a completely rational (i.e., among other things, a disinterested) argument. This is of peculiar importance to the liberal who has to put his faith in *rational* persuasion even if it means flying in the face of 'reason'.

Nevertheless the long-term ineffectuality of Ideas comes from still other causes: not only from the thinker's detachment or, on the other hand, from his over-persuasiveness: nor even from literal incomprehension which leads to misinterpretation and garbling.

---

visible circumstances). But promptly he attracts disciples who proceed at once to garble the Message. On that garbling is founded the Church (or other permanent institution). In course of time there appear splits and splinters and on these new sub-garblings are erected new sects (churches or institutions). Comes the revolution, the new light, and the retrospective research for the *original* or authentic Message: followed by a new accretion of disciples; the garbling; the Church; and so on. We have all played the game of 'Scandal' and registered the disparity between the message originally whispered and the final version.
* I do not suggest that economic and social ideas have no direct influence, at least in the short-term sense, or do not offer prescriptions: but practice— varieties of application, inevitable in their case—tends to cancel out: so that their prescriptions fail and their influence is nullified.

It is at least plausible that there is something wrong or inadequate with the way that human beings use their minds: and that this infects all of us including the professional thinkers; which would imply that our common assumption that thinkers naturally or by training know how to think realistically is an illusion. One psychological characteristic which is common to both professional and amateur (and to those who hardly ratiocinate at all) is our preference for certainty; we must have answers even if they disappoint our wishes, often powerful, even if vague; and we are not trained to patient expectation of what, disappointing or not, is necessarily difficult to arrive at.

In fact we are not trained in thinking at all: and the logical training of the specialist thinker is highly theoretical and abstract; whereas natural and unavoidable thinking has inseparable psychological and emotional innervations and ganglia – and is often a highly rebarbative process. This will hardly yield early or commonly to an improved education even if we could conceive or work one out. A disinterested open mind which will make itself up only when it accumulates evidence to satisfy its critical interest and which also has the insistent energy of curiosity to sustain it, is rare – even among scientists, otherwise they would not so easily become specialized, nor so soon and so often reveal that their interests both within and between their specialities are competitive.

For this intellectual hiatus and for the uninfluentiality and frequent irrelevance of Ideas the professional thinkers are not entirely to blame: nor indeed is the situation one only for regret – particularly in the case of political thought. Among ordinary people, on whose behalf thinkers often claim to be thinking, there may be a real resistance to Ideas as such. Shelley's rather negative 'good', who are not interested in power or organizing other people, may not necessarily have Ideas or even formal thoughts, but often have perceptions and feelings of their own. They may, for instance, not care about 'Freedom', while still having a sense of their own freedoms. But these kinds of awareness are also not 'represented' by ideologies or by the subtler speculations of highly trained philosophers.

There is a case for believing that this ineffectuality is worse for liberal ideas than for those of the authoritarian: for those are more easily sold by action than by reason and, because they are more likely to be conventional, traditional and unoriginal, can afford to do without the uncomfortable and generally resented means of explanation and argument.

There is also a case for believing that those who do not take kindly to formal thinking are easily sold the bad habits of those who do. There are a number of these habits — I do not say that they are all bad and certainly many of them appear to be natural (in the sense of 'spontaneous'). Some of them are intellectual structures and others are psychological mechanisms (there is nothing to prevent these, in either case, particularly the bad ones, from cohabiting with ease).

Of course, too, I am not saying that we are not *affected* by ideas. That would be patently false and absurd: nothing could have affected us all more strongly and inescapably, whatever we made of them, than the conceptions and beliefs associated, say, with either Jesus or Machiavelli. I say only that we mostly get them wrong and that nobody is really in a position to certify what would be right: reciprocal hearsay is our portion and sooner of later there is an inevitable failure of communication between the original pioneer and ourselves — *it is not what* he *meant, at all** — until another thinker arises to promulgate what he claims to be the original true version. If this one attracts sufficient support he will be able to silence doubt and 'settle' our questions until he can safely institutionalize his new error, as it will have become: for the original 'good' and formative idea was an intelligent but immediate reaction to the universal elements in an immediate and real human situation; the rest of us cannot for long see with the eyes of another: even where we caught a glimpse of his vision, we lose it; at the best we are always coming back to find him in the fog and in the hope that he will tell us again.

General ideas affect people as assertions, as instructions, as slogans or cries (college- or war-cries quite often). They are credited, when they are, more often for their energy or self-confidence than for their logic or realism. This is an important component in the *Either-Or* which is one of the most fundamental structures in European ratiocination.

I have adopted the expression Either-Or to avoid limiting a useful classification of our habits of thought and perception to the purely philosophic varieties of dualism. Intellectually we may

* Eliot, *Prufrock*.

subscribe to none of these even if we understand or are interested in them. Admittedly it would be a mistake to think that the post-Cartesian mind-body dualism, probably garbled, has not provided a matrix for some of the unreflected assumptions out of which we construct a world: a world not only of perception but of values. Most of us for instance have a slight, or even a great, penchant for the mental and spiritual, often just in so far as it is incomprehensible and therefore mysterious; and this is in itself a help towards making us blind to the laws and necessities of natural or human existence and behaviour which otherwise we might more easily learn to trace and accept.

In fact the Either-Or classification primarily refers to our natural difficulty, as ordinary human beings and perhaps as philosophers too, just in maintaining an intellectual dualism or pluralism; it represents rather our natural invincible monism and the way we adhere either to *Either* or to *Or*: how we like to make up our minds or have them made up for us; how we adopt one side of a question, become identified with it, and having expelled its contrary from our minds, take up a permanently defensive position and haul up the drawbridge after us. It may be said in passing that there are no obvious signs that if we could be freed from emotional and economic pressures we would behave with open rationality. This will be referred to again in the later parts of the book because it is an important premiss of liberal hopes of melioration.

It must be emphasized that the Either-Or is a subjective not an objective description. It describes the way human beings especially in the West habitually feel, think and even perceive, unless they are able to criticize themselves into greater disinterestedness. But since to criticize one's ingrained mental habits is as difficult as trying to see the back of one's own neck it can often be found embedded or fossilized in the products even of high intellectual training which may be intended to prescribe actual standards of objective 'reality'.

Early logical positivism with its rule of referential verification attempted to do just that: and itself committed one of the most notable Either-Ors of our time, encouraging the rest of us to follow. According to logical positivism, assertions and judgments were either logical or emotive; that is, they either referred to the 'real' (meaning the positive or factual or empirical world), or else they were in some sense suasive. Being based on purely subjective premisses they could not claim any universal (logical) or factual warrant; referring only to our feelings they had an internal axe to grind and our statements in this case were attempts not to describe but to influence. It is much easier to see nowadays that the logical positivists *favoured* a certain (allegedly scientific) description of the real world and demoted spontaneous apperception which may indeed be 'emotive' or suasive, but may also at the same time be strictly factual. To cry 'murder' is undoubtedly, as Ayer said in *Language, Truth and Logic*, a shriek or exclamation, and therefore 'emotive' (trying to persuade the police to come?); but suppose that you *are* committing a murder under my eyes, this language is both realistic and logical as well, although it is not primarily intended even to be referential. I am not interested just in accurately describing this bit of the perceived world, I chiefly want something to be done about it. When it comes to the necessities of action human beings, if sane, think with limited but real accuracy. As witnesses and describers – that is, in our average and common intellectual passivity – we are inclined to be partial: to what we believe are our own observations and to our own arguments, when we have them. Those seem not only true and sufficient but, if *seen*, bound to prevail. The clearer our own ideas to ourselves, the more we are inclined to believe that they are also simple and ought to be obvious to the honest and pure in heart. Hence we often attribute obduracy to what we regard as error; we forget that perfect clarity may be shallow. It is true, especially if we have read some contemporary philosophy, that we are inclined to attribute rhetoric to other people's arguments: people are *either* logical or emotional – which can hardly help meaning that it is not ourselves but *other* people who have emotive motives.

I refer here to logical positivism, which in its cruder form has been philosophically criticized out of significance, just to illustrate that up to its period philosophers were strangely and perhaps peculiarly unaware that we needed a psychology of thinking: and perhaps still are, since philosophers seem if anything to have retreated still further from analysing the processes of thought and, possibly in the wake of the Behaviourists, have confined themselves to its products – our logical constructs and the meaning of our usages.

The Either-Or is put forward as one of our commonest and most retarding intellectual *structures*. There are others which one can sometimes discern as auxiliary or subsidiary formations, but perhaps it is better to keep the term 'structures' for those which like Either-Or are most obviously intellectual, or, rather, logical. The basic Either-Or is simply a classic case of the logical fallacy of Undistributed Middle Term.* As such it might strike one as technical and therefore corrigible. But it is also an example of the gradual merger between the intellectual or philosophical and the psychological; we must always remember that psychologically we can at present function only with a minimum of self-criticism.

Thus structures tend to merge with formations perhaps better described as mechanisms. There are a number of these too; and again we come across these only when we happen to do so, not theoretically, but in practice and when, rarely, we have become aware and critical of our own thinking processes. The distinction lies in the fact that what can be called mechanisms are even less accessible to consciousness than 'structures'. And the value of the distinction, if any, may lie only in the possibility already suggested that our logical or technical errors are more open to purely intellectual—that is, educational—means of correction: with the usual chicken-and-egg proviso: someone or some people have to make a start and pull up their psychological roots: catch themselves out in their buried and sub-logical assumptions.

Projection is no doubt one of the commonest of unreflected mechanisms: and rooted too in what appears to be a psychological necessity. Human identity, mere identity as such, has been treated by twentieth-century novelists and dramatists not only with a curious or subjective interest, but with a widely appealing imaginative power. Identity seems to be hardly won and to be felt at least as highly precarious: and in ourselves and in our feelings we equate it not only with being socially recognizable and viable, but with being human. It appears that it is not possible for most people to think far beyond this or to think themselves into other skins; and we are quickly led to the projective belief that other people who appear to us (naturally) to be in the same general

---

* For those not familiar with the phrase, the following syllogism provides an example of undistributed middle terms:

All cats are quadrupeds; some quadrupeds are cows; therefore all cows are cats.

Here 'quadrupeds' is the middle term.

situation as ourselves and who yet behave unexpectedly, are 'really' behaving out of character (as we define human character), are eccentric, mad or bad.

For it is bare identity that is our working psychological assumption: we have no axiomatic knowledge or sympathy in relation to the content of other identities, perhaps rather a resistance: hence the importance of projection and the obscurity which it imposes on human motivation.

It was suggested earlier that the structural Either-Or seldom remains on the purely intellectual or ideological level because if it did so it would have to maintain the strain of a protracted internal dialogue with oneself. The struggle becomes objectified and its commonest resolution is a habitual identification with one or other of two main classes of mentality. This gives us two more complementary mechanisms: and we should be at least as aware of those who cannot see the trees for the wood as of those who cannot see the wood for the trees. People can suffer from one or the other at different times: sometimes, in varying proportions, at the same time. Immature intellectuals and ideologues, including trainee sociologists and psychologists, as well as those with theological intentions, often suffer from *silvagigantism*. People in professions which train them to believe that they have to compete by producing quick yet lasting results (technological science, maternity and charring) may be afflicted by *dendropygmaeism*. But even potential silvagigantists may as working curates or therapists turn to a stunted dendropygmaeism: troubled like Martha about many things which refuse conformity to the patterns of belief they have absorbed. Thus the intellectual attempt to understand and genuinely humanize our experienced world may too often founder between mega-abstraction and obsession with detail.

If that is another illustration of the split between theory and practice – and the discrepancy between general ideas and their application – it is also on the other hand an argument for examining a number of concepts and assumptions whose real existence we assume because they are part of our habitual daily speech. Some of them we feel we are born with – for instance 'human nature' (or even 'nature'). Others, like *The Social Contract* (Rousseau's at the moment, not Harold Wilson's) are clearly inventions but may seem necessary ones, like God: and are commonly revived in what seems to our contemporary eyes a more realistic setting. To the liberal, prone to intellectualize and abstract, there should be some value in trying to identify some of the psychological mechanisms and assumptions that, even if they do not invalidate these conceptions, may support and slant them and often disguise their character as fictions.

A fiction is often a useful working tool; it is often an adequate convention for representing social reality, as we see in the cases both of the novel and of theoretical law. But the thoughtful contemporary liberal must see that many of those which used to be his working concepts have already become slogans or counters: 'equality' or 'fraternity', for example; while even 'liberty', which he can hardly do without, is in a shopworn condition. This may not be only or even predominantly because the world has changed or even because these concepts have changed their meaning and applicability. It may be because, in the sense I have been using the word, they were always 'structures' which had embedded themselves in European thought, often below the level of conscious ratiocination; and have become habits not only of conceptual logic, but of perception: the way we look at, see and hence unreflectingly assume, our world, and receive it as reality. What has changed, sometimes painfully, is not these ideas, or rather their definition, but our consciousness of them. In becoming conscious of their inapplicability, it is true, we have made some sort of advance, and even in a liberal direction. For in so far as we grasp that these 'structural' assumptions have shaped not only our thinking and perceiving, but have even decided and selected for us the topics we shall be capable of thinking about, we prepare the terrain for our psychological freedom even though we may never occupy it. It also practises us in the acuteness with which we shall detect the rising class of false structures and strengthens the moral vantage-point from which we can criticize and attack them, especially if they belong to the other (or authoritarian) side: as I shall hope to show that they often do.

Conceptual analysis, where we are capable of it, may help us to reach this point of criticism. But in the case of conceptual analysis as it is practised by some contemporary philosophers, the usual hiatus is to be found. They do not in general teach us how to do it; for one reason because their choice of concepts to be analysed is seldom directed to the more prevalent misusages of abstraction: ideas like 'individuality', 'individual', 'human nature', 'nature' (as found in 'state of nature' and 'natural law'), perhaps 'free will' and 'free thought'; 'freedom', particularly as it exists in 'freedom-and-order'; and even some apparently more practical notions such as 'equality of opportunity': as well as a number of psychological ideas: domination and subjection; love; sex.

With these notional topics we think we are referring to a common and accepted reality which we can all assume as a basis of discussion; we assume that we all know what we are referring to and that therefore we not only know what we are talking about but that what we are talking about exists in some substantive sense. The structural concepts embedded in our mostly unconscious processes of thought and feeling are what encourage us, even oblige us, to make these working assumptions, so often distorted and even erroneous, which however, enable us to survive in a society or culture as right-thinking (or left-thinking) human beings. Or rather as 'Man', for that is of all the all-purpose structural concept.

And since we all share these structural concepts, unanalysed and assumptive, the uncultivated or the unintellectuals with the more critical, it may turn out that the oppositions and divisions of political and social thinking are less profound than they are often taken to be: and the extreme libertarian and the extreme authoritarian, both claiming commonsense experience to back their judgments, may both be haunted and automatized by the same figment. Political philosophers of all complexions have often based their generalizations upon them, disregarding or unaware that they are abstractions of a partial or selective kind, masquerading as empirical laws or descriptions.

'Man' is one of the most fundamental of these pseudo-inductions.* While the underlying structural assumption was theological (it often still is), it has been easier and perhaps in the past more pardonable to use this concept: because of a common understanding and even agreement not seriously challenged, it appeared to have a clear reference. Nowadays when we commonly use it with more ignorance and vagueness while claiming to refer to an agreed and established biological and evolutionary background, the meaning is probably more fluid, less profound and even less realistic as far as the users are concerned.

---

* A perfect induction is a generalization based on total enumeration of particulars without exception.

Theologians may have been psychologically mistaken but they often went deeper into a common if limited sense of our human being: into something ordinary people could recognize as at least part, and an operative and influential part, of themselves and of life as they lived it. But professional scientists, including some geneticists, ethologists and behaviourists, sometimes seem to be palming off their own generalizations—their structural concept of Man—in place of the field evidence which would enable us to recognize a specimen.

Mill, shortly to be discussed as our classical libertarian, speaks mostly, and probably by preference, of 'mankind'. We might believe that in his peripheral imagination a crowd of distinct phantoms pressed their pallid faces against this conceptual window. But also there seems little doubt that the barrier remained— between the concrete and the experiential on the one hand, and the abstract and statistical on the other. Abstraction, whatever the subject-matter, tends to side-taking and case-making.

In practice, the structural habit works out to the advantage of the authoritarians, as compared with the libertarians. They usually do not feel any need to concern themselves with individual psychology: and as their generalizations about ambiguous human nature must always be half-correct, they can be more confidently dogmatic.

Hobbes, for instance, can speak unflatteringly of 'Man' (and his nature) as 'solitary, poor, nasty, brutish and short' because individuality and freedom in the liberal's sense have been expressly ruled out as nonsense according to the definitions and the task he has set himself: he is only concerned with ordering the average life-span of the miserable creature so that he may be saved from destroying himself and his fellows. The self-organization and development of an individual life-style is no problem to Hobbes because it has no meaning.

It *is* a problem to the liberal, and not only because it is part of his creed that social organization ought to be for the ultimate benefit of individuals (real living people), but because, like all of us, he does not know how to think that far; as a rule he does not know enough about any individual, including and even primarily himself, to know what kind of society would fit him best, would provide the best compromise between fulfilment and restraint. It is no wonder that he hypostatizes his limited and selective experi-

D

ence of being human into one of the abstract names – Man, Humanity. Because he is partly aware that this is a vital failure he does it with less clarity and honesty and probably with much more of a bad conscience than his authoritarian opponents; and much more than they do he tends to support his definition with whatever looks like professional evidence and guidance. The social and human sciences study cases, don't they? Freud kept him going for a long time: and even Marx, anyway in the 1930s before we had experienced the totality of totalitarianism, could be interpreted in terms of moral adjournment: *when* you got the material chains off him, then the individual, that free creative spirit, would come for the first time into his own. Today the social and 'human' sciences instead of helping the liberal rather tend to leave him in his quandary or to intensify it; partly because they model themselves on the non-human sciences, physical or biological; the ones which I shall shortly discuss are certainly of more use to the authoritarians, in so far as they may feel the need for confirmation. Even Freud (who certainly intended to be an authority and resented any suggestion that he might not always be one) was really dealing with a projected abstraction of his own: his case-studies produced only wider and wilder generalizations which, moreover, because they could not account for present and existing human beings, had to seek support in an extension of abstraction, for example in an imaginary history and anthropology. See, for instance, *Moses and Monotheism*.

Contemporary psychologists and sociologists may well appear to be more willing than Freud to submit to the case and learn from it. But where they do not content themselves with being purely descriptive of human individual behaviour, abandoning explanation and prognosis, their cases tend to dissolve in mass-statistics which are always on a more advanced level of abstraction from needs and fears as they are actually felt by individuals. Obviously there is a great and increasing need in societies, compelled by the ideal of organized welfare, to establish some agreed laws of human being. Thus we have to believe that our generalized picture of human reality whatever it may be is truly representative – and that it has not neglected any particular which would be contradictory and which might suggest that our world of others is ever more alien and unmanageable than we have present reason to believe. This leads us to think in exhaustive opposites: our opponents when we are at all aware of their arguments must be shown to be totally wrong, to have misconceived the very structure of human existence; as in a sense they have, for their abstraction of human existence is polar to our own: they have abstracted the very elements we have rejected in ours. Hence not only the fruitless arguments about other groups and classes, and other individual human beings, but hence also the psychological and sociological 'schools'. And even perhaps the futility of trying (or pretending to try) to see the 'other point of view'. If you lean over to peer too eagerly into the enemy's camp you may fall into it. We have seen this happen; the Western communist, traumatically disillusioned with the Soviet Union, has been known to jump straight into the Roman Catholic Church.

These political and other splits seem to be subject to a law of opposites that affects (and afflicts) human ratiocination; and one might think that to detect their fallaciousness it often needs hardly more than textbook logic. They might for instance take the form: It is human to be irrational, or All human beings are irrational: all women are human beings: therefore all women are irrational (substitute appropriately 'over-sexed' or 'violent' and 'Blacks').

This is the concise pattern of what in its larger and therefore less easily detectable form I have called the principle of Either-Or; and we shall meet it lamentably often. Either-Or is not only a fallacy: it represents our ingrained habit of opposing two abstractions, each of which necessarily becomes a side, with all the polemic entailment of distortion, and sometimes falsehood. We do not naturally see, and do not easily become versed in, the practical details of our own experience which could be relevant to our case and make good our arguments: we see far more clearly and willingly that those which our opponents may produce are indeed irrelevant to our own generalized commitment.

This partisan abstraction is both more noticeable and more serious in theorizing liberals than in the more heterogeneous group of their authoritarian opponents; and has helped to make it more difficult to develop a realistic liberal philosophy. Moreover it has earned them much of the obloquy which their opponents, often authoritarian themselves, who do not have to pretend to be philosophical but only 'realistic', visit upon them.

5

Mill and his Individualism

Whatever we think about the direct influence of ideas it is useful to examine the intellectual structures and psychological mechanisms of those who have produced our most striking (and most influential) misinterpretations; and to look for examples among both libertarians and authoritarians. It will be at least illuminating if opposing 'sides' sometimes share some of their assumptions, not readily visible to us, and possibly hidden even from themselves; the more so if the assumptions are of a kind which one side or the other would consciously repudiate.

Liberalism in its modern sense and with most of its modern elements was fully present at least in England by the end of the seventeenth century. It was characteristic that, with increasingly powerful hints, political and mercantile, to state government to mind its own business as far as possible, there should have been instant disagreement as to exactly what that business is, which Liberalism certainly has never succeeded in settling. The result has been a compromise which the consciously idealistic liberal, especially among the young, cannot help seeing as of a specially immoral kind: since it must appeal to him as not just pardonably between alternative means of working towards the ideal, but as between idealistic principle and worldly practice.

The laissez-faire economic origins of Liberalism no doubt hang round him like a caul: in so far as the contemporary Liberal Party shares the Mandevillian version of free enterprise with the Tories, he must regard it as unethical; and quite apart from that he can hardly join it because even in attempting to put that dubious principle into practice it has shown itself much less successful than the conservative opposition. He cannot trust the collectivist methods of the Socialists to make a moral society work; he can hardly trust the individualistic methods of the Tories much more – their image of the individual is one he has in principle forsworn, although he may be uneasily aware that it has essentially helped to make him what he is.

In short he feels morally obliged, as they do not, to distinguish between individualism and individuality, however much in practice 'liberals', younger and senior, often confuse the two.

There are, it is generally agreed, two main and contrasting divisions of liberal thinking which, among other things, reflect this distinction between the 'individual' and his 'individuality' – and do little to sort out the confusion. There are those who believe in what is called 'positive freedom': that we are truly free, not just in so far as no one interferes with us, or we are left alone to do what we please or to do nothing if that pleases us better, or if we do not please to be pleased by any particular goal or purpose; but that on the contrary we have to be helped to be free, in order to realize our full potentiality; and in some cases this is regarded as an educational role of government.

Among the chief proponents of this concept of intervention are Hegel and neo-Hegelians, like Bradley and Green. But to believe that 'positive freedom' is a notion entirely confined to state interventionists is perhaps somewhat specious. Those who sincerely believe that freedom is developmental – something a human being comes into in his maturity, when he has been offered and has taken the fullest opportunities of developing what individual powers he has, by being, doing and creating to the best of his abilities and chances – may be unreflectingly maintaining it in another form, even though they claim that the moral and social business of others, including families and governments, is merely to clear obstacles as far as possible out of the way of this development and purpose, or goal-directed activity. There is certainly something both prescriptive and assumptive about 'developmental individuality': it prescribes the fullest development as an absolute value or ideal: and it assumes that all individuals at least potentially share this ideal.

These advocates of a 'positive freedom' in the individual-developmental form are faced with an immediate difficulty from which the Hegelian school is more or less immune, and for which they have to make provision: all developing personalities have to respect the development of other personalities. It might appear that we are all, all of us, free only within rather narrow limits of one among many Tom Tiddler's grounds, as in many respects we must all of us, in honesty, feel that we merely are. In similar honesty, and indeed with realism, we have to admit that if any other personality flowers so fully that it overhangs our particular plot, we shall feel fully justified in pleading Ancient Rights.

This second school of thought, with its predilection for 'freedom from', has some roots in a prelapsarian notion of an original freedom which men are supposed to have bargained away for domesticated security: it believes that all restraints are artificial, at best a necessary evil, often with a half-suggestion that we have merely lost the way out of the Golden Age when the lion lay down with the lamb; and that we have only to find the way back.

The freedom these theorists hanker after is negative; freedom from all external restraint is their basic definition and their only fulfilling goal. This is the idea of Original Virtue in its extreme form: and perhaps that psychological assumption is one without which the liberal would lose all faith and hope. Yet it is held only vaguely, not only, no doubt, because of its theological flavour, but because it tallies so poorly with observation: and because it entails so many dilemmas and contradictions in the definition of freedom. For example, if the free man is one who reveals and realizes his freedom by successfully resisting external restraint, he can come into his kingdom of virtue only by also revealing his capacity for self-regulation. Moreover any apparent maieutic means to this rebirth must be an intervention and therefore wrong or less than ideal. All education, for example, is an inhibition of other potential interests, at least at any given time. And though it is true that since Freud some liberals have thought that they clearly recognized the undesirability even of internal restraints, if they are repressive, it is not true that all of them recognize that all 'therapies' interfere before they deliver.

Those who hold the other, the 'positive' view of freedom, whether in its neo-Hegelian form or not, haven't the same trouble. To them the state, or government, is the great agency of fulfilment. Moreover it gives the only possible meaning to the notion of freedom, and perhaps even to that of the individual person. That is the Hegelian view: freedom belongs to nations or states: and individual 'freedom' is in no sense atomic but is an end-product of belonging to the whole. We have seen already that in the new nations today that is often the acceptable definition.

On the other hand the pro-authoritarian political thinker may not find it at all necessary to justify or rationalize state supremacy by any appeal to freedom, positive or negative. With Hobbes, he may see the advantages of the authoritarian or paternalistic state as so pre-eminent that they make nonsense of any ideal of a natural or 'original' individual freedom.

For Hobbes, the hypothetical 'state of nature'—for which the liberal still half hankers and which he often still unconsciously assumes, at least in a psychological sense—is 'nasty, brutish and short' and therefore as far from freedom as is the life of the hunted animal, always pursuing its subsistence: and incomparably inferior to the peace and order of the sovereign state whose benefits require in exchange only the surrender of eleutheromanic illusions. On this view, the 'individual', anyway an empty conception, can at best be described as 'free' at the moment when he thus surrenders his 'freedom'. And even those who, like Rousseau,* have claimed to believe in an original state of natural freedom, have never been able to detect its practical manifestation except as the freedom to contract out of it into the state—and that is an a historical fiction.

It will be seen that it is perfectly easy to talk about a 'state of nature'—an original and culture-free condition of individuals— and equate it either with freedom or servitude. But if we identify it with servitude, we may or may not think that the political state, inaugurated by contract or consent or else imposed, gives us freedom and one of a better kind. We may simply think that freedom is a myth, probably an undesirable one.

There is a third possibility, and this is perhaps not only most natural and common, but most logical for a liberal: that we really are 'born free' at least in the sense that we all potentially want to be self-dependent and also want to make the most of ourselves; but that this freedom is precarious and needs organized protection. Thus the state of government is a necessary evil, a *faute de mieux*, out of which we ought to, and must, one of these days, develop and educate ourselves. This hope was the Holy Grail of classical

* Rousseau himself rises to an inconsistent panegyric on the developmental freedom of life in society.

communism: and continues in neo-Marxism. It is also one of the hallmarks of natural or temperamental liberalism. In emotional intention it cannot help leading diametrically away from 'positive freedom' and thus of course from anything except the most formal acquiescence in state intervention or authoritarianism. And it lands itself in an inevitable dilemma for which its leading theoreticians have never found any acceptable working solution, while indeed, under one aspect or another, they may even find themselves in the opposite camp. In practice not all liberals, not many perhaps, are genuine egalitarians or even democrats.

J. S. Mill was neither. Moreover if he could be reincarnated today we could hardly forecast where he would stand either politically or socially: or how far he would recognize libertarian developments as inheriting his own liberalism. We may think that at least there have been and still are many movements of liberation and some local successes. It is more than doubtful that Mill would sympathize even with these in the form they have taken as much as one ought to expect from his theories and basic tenets. That we might expect anyway from the general rule of 'Churches' (see pp. 75–6) of the Founders and their epigones: and also from the certainty that Mill like everyone else was more deeply embedded in the culture of his time – dominated by the moral, earnest but self-deceptive Victorians – than he could realize.

Nevertheless it is natural to begin this short study of contrasts and parallels with Mill; in some ways he is more our near-contemporary than any other well-known liberal thinker, and is likely to be found fairly sympathetic by modern liberalizing and humanistic movements, whatever he might have thought of them. His better-known works are still perhaps surprisingly readable: for example, the *Autobiography*, *On Liberty* and *The Subjection of Women*. He not only appeals to the necessary anarch in all lively minds and characters, he has a way of sounding indefeasibly and obviously right, at least to the general emotions and also the special interests of the rather heterogenous class of liberal reader. He is characteristic, too, in the way that no doubt gives liberalism the attraction of perennial youth, not being unduly troubled with historical sense or by informed criticism of the cultural past or by realistic foresight; he was rather abstract, too, about the human potentialities of the time.

All this could be at least instructive for our present generations. Whatever one thinks about the real influence of ideas there is every reason to study and to learn from the mistakes of our intellectual forebears, especially the most prominent.

Apart from the misinterpretation which affects all general ideas when we try to apply them, political and social ideas, as we said, are partial to fictions: no doubt because, more than most, their creators are aware of the urgency of concrete action: or of giving the appearance of it. This self-deception and the need for it may help to account for the general failure of political ideas noticeably to improve our lot in human societies. Both 'society' and 'the state of nature' as conceived in varied versions by political thinkers of opposing schools, were fairly obvious fictions. But 'the individual' as expressing an opposition to 'society' is yet another: it is the one most favoured by liberal theoreticians: a fiction inhabiting a 'state of nature' — for there is nowhere else for the 'individual' to live.

One can suspect something wrong (unrealistic) in all political thinkers who make a sharp opposition between the state and the individual (whether we conceive him statistically or as a natural state) — whichever side of the division they prefer to take their stand. We may suspect in the first place that they don't sufficiently distinguish 'state' from 'society'; or recognize that states and governments come and go but 'individuals' are born into societies (families, clans, tribes), and that to some limited but essential extent the two reciprocally define one another. In political thought, the concepts 'state' or 'government' are not being used clearly and accurately, or probably even honestly, unless as referring primarily and no doubt even predominantly, to power, not to morality or psychology; otherwise they are likely to entail an insidious question-begging: to depart from description into evaluation almost certainly reveals partiality in a political thinker.

In so far as the liberal recognizes this characteristic of political and much sociological thought he is justified in conceiving his individual as a necessary focus of resistance. Nevertheless that does not entitle him to give his opposing idea any other particular or practical human content; or even to try to do so. For even if he could do so, he would be unable to think up a form of society which would fit or even be relevant to him. Liberal thinkers have shown that they do not know how to invent a truly social individual (or thus to solve Shelley's dilemma).

For Mill, being the best judge of his own interest is the only or chief qualification for individuality and what — at least by contemporary standards — makes the individual recognizable. But this is already a considerable assumption and a considerable claim. It assumes that he knows what his interests are and what he wants, apart from what his social connections tell him they are or what he wants and ought to want: moreover that he knows naturally where to look for them and for their satisfaction and development and that he can either communicate this self-knowledge to us or that we can have some natural insight into it. In short what is assumed by Mill's 'individual' is a real 'state of (developed) nature'.

The fact that this natural self-interest cannot always stand up for itself is the only excuse that Mill allows for state — or external government — whose job is essentially to provide the necessary protection. Outside this protected area in which conflicting interests are to be balanced and settled, government has no justifiable role. Mill follows in the Benthamite utilitarian tradition that all restraints on individual freedom are inherently evil, and government hence only a necessary evil. The sphere of its encroachment must be demarcated with the sharpest vigilance.

Mill is reasonably well aware that the boundary is difficult to draw, but in one example solves the problem to his own satisfaction by acknowledging that an habitual drunkard may well damage the interests, not least the economic interests, of his family and associates and on that ground alone be reprehensible and possibly punishable; but what he does to himself remains his own inalienable business.

Apart from the difficulty of deciding what *is* his own business and how far that indissolubly merges with the business of others, this sharp separation opens up an even larger and a more definitely moral question. It includes among other things the reciprocal relation of rights and duties, as between individual persons. Logically the individual drunkard would seem to have the right to proceed to total and unrestricted self-destruction. Mill appears to have thought that that was covered by the prohibitory clause: everything stops short of damage to the legitimate self-interests of the others concerned. But in theoretical morality have we the right to let another individual person kill himself? Whatever the means he chooses and whatever the motives, including the acceptance of an unselfish euthanasia, have we not a duty to try and prevent him or at least hold him up till it is quite certain that he knows what he is doing with all the supporting reasons for making it a sound judgment? The self-destruction of alcoholics can hardly come in this category. The short moral question for everyone concerned (all of us) is: Are there any individual rights which do *not* dovetail into corresponding duties of and towards other individuals?

It cannot really be held that Mill has settled for all time the problems nor the area of individual moral privacy. Our contemporary problem of widespread drug addiction is by many who believe that they are liberals, anyway in spirit, not to be so lightly dismissed, nor indeed the problem of alcoholism, from which it is not either logically nor realistically to be distinguished. And certainly Mill did not uncover any moral rule which was to show itself as transferable to problems of individualism that had not yet in his time arisen. Moreover there is at least one example which shows that his feminism, a cause with which concrete human individuality was surely, more than most others, most intimately and inextricably involved, had areas of abstraction if not total blind spots; an example, too, which suggests that Mill had not outgrown the immature liberal's characteristic confusion between a strictly laissez-faire individualism and a moral individuality or personality. Believing that in principle all restrictions on trade are undesirable, he was prepared, it seems, to extend this franchise to the trade in prostitutes: pimps too were to be emancipated (see *On Liberty*).

This curious blind spot might be considered as evidence that no one can think himself wholly free of the situation combining class and culture in which he happens to be born; and there is all the more credit to Mill for his more usual sensitivity towards women and the immoral anomalies of their conditions. In general one would like to know what Mill would have had to say on our present social morality. It is true that he is trying to confine his definition of limitation of liberty as far as possible to actual intervention by governmental authority; and he relies heavily on public opinion and its structures (while disapproving of them) to maintain an acceptable social unity: a 'secular-arm' attitude, like condoning prostitution in the interests of virginity. On the whole he regards public opinion, not I admit with great exaggeration, as ill-informed, envious and censorious of diversity, let alone non-conformity, and generally in a state of clinging conventional huddle. Its main virtue from Mill's position is that it can censure, but has no power to punish other than by its disapproval. He appears to regard this as more than sufficiently harsh; nevertheless, since freedom both to hold and to express one's opinions however objectionable to others, or even false, is another inalienable natural right, there is here again no question of governmental intervention to restrain the worst severity. Here our later experience and some contemporary moral novelties give us ground for questioning.

It is true that we have enlarged our conception of individual freedom in the Western world, and in personal matters interference by government has correspondingly lessened. Superficially it might appear that ordinary 'social' opinion has become much more tolerant and that hence we have reached a higher stage of genuinely democratic freedom. But this hardly stands up to examination. So-called 'permissiveness' is both partial and partisan and full of new forms of intolerance and new conventions which may well turn out to be as envious and odious as those they have temporarily driven out.

On a larger scale, too, than even Victorian society achieved we can send our fellow-democrats to coventry; and we are no fonder of the unfortunate victims, for instance, of authoritarian war-mongering or exclusive regimes: perhaps in practice we find them more of a nuisance than ever before. We may wonder whether in the case of intolerant racialism we have not been driven to governmental interference with the 'free' expression of opinion, because we may have a profounder sense and a larger experience of individual viciousness and bloodymindedness than was possible for Mill, somewhat cloistered as he still was in an exclusive class-education.

Mill seems to have been something of an innocent. We cannot expect him to have foreseen, unless in the most generalized way our more disagreeable moral and social developments; but we can hardly help thinking that he would have had a clearer and more authoritative opinion on the difference between disinterested moral leadership and governmental interference if he had known more intimately the social *mores*, their often hypocritical viciousness and cowardly and sadistic exploitation of helplessness, which characterized much of upper Victorian society. Admittedly, of this we have only hindsight and many of us may not be able to be better informed about the more subtle and collusive iniquities of our own society.

It is possible that such an ignorance, rather than insensibility, accounts in Mill for the laissez-faire residuum in his social morality and hence for the signs of wavering in his treatment of borderline cases.

Mill's 'innocence' does not make him a democrat or, in feeling, a believer in Original Virtue although he seems, somewhat inconsistently as we shall see, to have hopes for our moral progress.

Karl Popper, in *The Open Society*, charges Mill with 'psychologism'. That is his way of alluding to Mill's conception of society as an agglomeration of individuals, a compromise (or, we might think, a scrap-heap) of all conflicting individual self-interests or wishes or wills. If it is hard for those unused to philosophic jargon, from which the admirable Popper himself cannot be entirely free, to see why that should be called 'psychologism' the answer is that Popper is contrasting the behaviour of individuals, which appears indeterminate, with the large-scale economic and sociological laws that have been seen e.g. by Marx, to govern society. Of these Mill, according to Popper, is relatively neglectful. Technically 'psychologism' may be the correct philosophical term, but here it is misleading.

One might prefer to say that, in a more common sense, Mill's account of the 'individual' is not 'psychological' enough; that this is a weakness common to most political and sociological thinkers of all complexions; but that in the case of the liberal it is more serious, even perhaps vicious.

As everybody knows, Mill's education was not only ruthlessly forced, it was adapted in its curriculum to the highly abstract and intellectual conception of the cultivated adult as that was understood and accepted at the time and is still not dis-established. Later, after a breakdown, he saw that this education had totally neglected the life of feeling, the subjective individual person: and he put this right by reading Wordsworth. It may have worked; or the mere realization of his lack may have induced a spontaneous release and recovery: we know that later he achieved a steady but perhaps sentimentally exaggerated happiness with Mrs Taylor. Nevertheless the self-treatment has the not uncommon ideological or abstract flavour. The life of feeling cannot be taken intensively in doses or injections.

It did not teach Mill to give his concept of 'the individual' any particular human content. Yet for the liberal more than most, the individual is surely nothing unless he is a concrete universal, someone whose common humanity with ourselves we can recognize and sympathize with, not only in spite of, but partly because of, a welter of diversity, even quirks. Lacking this perceptual imaginative and moral content how can the 'individual' be other than a dogmatic assumption? Or conversely how are we to conceive a society composed of these paper-figments — except perhaps as a politically prejudiced generalization of ways of non-being. How can we come to recognize it as the kind of society, whatever it may be, in which we can really lead our lives?

It will be said, with some reason, that in the context Mill could not be concerned with this kind of description: he was writing not a novel, but a theoretical survey of the frontiers of liberty and intervention. Nevertheless 'individual' is always, however abstractly, conceived as a developmental phenomenon; that this development should not be frustrated must involve the co-operation — that is, the educational intervention — of society. Admittedly Mill's self-discovery should have implied to him that social education itself needed re-educating towards eliciting the life of feeling. But on this Mill has nothing particular to say, not even that this question is integral and must be given detailed treatment. Obviously Mill could not allow government as such to have any say in defining our goals of individual satisfaction. (For example, government has no positive role in education, intellectual or moral, only the limited function of prescribing that it should be universal, and of paying for it where necessary.)

Mill's 'individual' then is also a fiction, but of the wrong kind: the statistical and utilitarian kind favoured by political thinkers of all parties. Mill's limitations, as well as his insights, go some way to persuading one that the liberal thinker, thinking primarily about individual freedom, needs a very particular type of critical sense enabling him to pursue his own subjectivity; to follow his observations, arguments and judgments wherever they may lead; and, the more ruthlessly, into the warrens where his assumptions may lie concealed. Thus if it appears that political thought or the construction of polities cannot get on without fictions, he may have to give up professional political thinking or pass beyond it to some wider or more radically human study: even perhaps, after all, to write novels, autobiographical and biographical fragments, instead of political treatises; though there is nothing to prevent him criticizing, especially from this 'psychologistic' position, the treatises of other political and social thinkers.

Those others, least of all if they are of state-authoritarian inclination, have not been able to get on without their fictions. Indeed they have often got on much better with them, because the ones that they, perhaps unreflectingly, prefer are not inconsistent with their generally abstract dogmatism.

Since the common fictions – e.g. 'state of nature' and 'social contract' – are unhistorical, they lend little to biological or evolutionary argument or explanation, nor hence to the practical utility of the other fiction, 'Man'. But in some examples, notably the 'social contract' they can be used to mitigate crude illiberalism and to soften, and sweeten with apparent reason, the unacceptable face of authoritarianism.

Mill would no doubt have rejected these aetiological fictions if he could have become aware that they were somehow present in ghostly shape outlining his own conceptions of both individual and society. But one fiction, especially when it is assumed and unexamined, leads to another. And it is not only that Mill's 'individual' is to be found only in a fictional 'state of nature', there seems to be no way of providing for his necessary (though minimal) involvement in 'society' except by some equivalent of an equally fictional 'contract': in Mill's case, free assent based on reasoning. For Mill not only believes that it is the duty of an acceptable society to sell itself to 'the individual' – it has no natural claim on his co-operation except what it can pay for in protective advantages by holding the ring between himself and all the other occupants of isolated and defensive areas of *Lebensraum* – he also believes that, whether this has ever happened or not, the sale can take place by means of reasonable suasion. And this is a fictional contract: there is never any positive consent: and if there is passive assent it is never procured by rational argument or even discussion.

Unlike the authoritarians, Mill is under the disadvantage of having to account for a developmental process of the individual, one which is due to follow, once the illegitimate restraints on his potentiality have been released. But it is very difficult to discern, let alone account for, the development – presumably towards greater freedom, morality and rationality – of an abstraction or fiction; or indeed, on such an assumption, to show how any existing educational process, good or bad, really affects individuals, or to plan for another and improved one. For individuality is not just entering into the fulfilment and enjoyment of one's own purposes, interests and powers including one's powers of social criticism: it requires something to exercise them on and even to elicit them.

That is to say that the individual and his society must be complementary realities, not complementary fictions. But the reality must be that of biological, psychological and moral growth; and except for certain aspects here and there and from time to time in history, human beings, including liberals, have not discovered how to create it on the political plane.

The real weakness here, typical as much as anything of liberal thinking, lies in ignoring, or in vagueness towards, the actual cultural 'infrastructure'; the actual ways in which – in families and neighbourhoods, even in nationally standardized school systems and their opportunities; in class-conventions and other stabilized illusions – societies, for good or bad, do in practice educate their members. The process continues until the cultural structure dissolves or is destroyed: cultural societies (if for instance we are to believe Miss Fitzgerald's account of the Vietnam war in *The Fire in the Lake*) sometimes have the toughness and resilience of flexibility, and of 'giving' to political storm and earthquake. Nevertheless, as far as we have seen, the solvent is not the spontaneous upsurge of creative and inventive power in 'free' individuals acting in consonance, but rather is provided by revolutionaries either of the left or the right, who seize power (generally in the name of 'freedom'); who resemble each other, if in nothing else, in being dogmatic theoreticians (that is, authoritarians); and who proceed to impose their own versions of the cultural 'individual'.

Mill, like other liberals, is not very convincing about the best maieutic measures for actually eliciting his free individual. Theoretically at least, the idea that individuals and their social affiliations need a reciprocal definition and are capable of a reciprocal education needs more exploration: particularly by liberals, for the reasons given above, which can be summed up by saying that only they have a vital interest in finding an effective compromise.

Otherwise, the way, for the liberal thinker, lies open to a more dangerous, because more insidious kind of authoritarianism.

This is the case with Mill, not only in his hankering after (or assumption of) a 'clerisy', or intellectual elite, but in his projected Sociological Science which is intended to provide a blueprint for a rational and presumably just and 'free' society: but which is really based on a collectivist, that is statistical, assumption about 'human nature' — (another 'fiction') — or, we suppose, 'the individual'.

These 'practical' developments and proposals all represent some surrender to a social abstraction into which Mill can fit his potentially 'free' individual only by what amounts to a psychological miracle.

For Mill leaves us with a curious doctrine of a moral-social second nature* for which neither he nor our own experience of social existence and its history have prepared us and which our generation, again with its temporal advantage of disillusion, can surely see as flying in the face of common observation: common we may say not only to the authoritarians and Augustinians (i.e. believers in the doctrine of Original Sin) who — partial though we may hope and believe them to be, certainly give a faithful account of the kind of behaviour that has so far predominated in history and hence so far bears the signs of an evolutionary success — but common to each of us who towards the later stages of his short history has learned anything of the probable reactions in typical and inevitable situations, both of his fellow-beings and of himself or herself.

Do we, for example, even those of us who are *relatively* free because competitive economic and social pressures upon us are comparatively light; or because we enjoy our work or because our family lives are not too abrasive; or because we are of uncommonly happy disposition or anything else that makes us a part of a psychological minority — still privileged — do even we so greatly welcome other individualities (even if they share our beliefs about free development, even if they are not painfully better at it; even if they are our own flesh and blood)? Many young liberal-minded

* Not only does all strengthening of social ties and all healthy growth of society give to each individual a stronger interest in practically consulting the welfare of others: it also leads him to identify his feeling more and more with their good [*Utilitarianism*]. See also p. 266.

adults who are in the parental situation, seem to me to do their human best, but more often from ideological duty than joy.

If we are not to have this psychological millennium, and it is hard to believe in it, Mill might be taken as suggesting a particularly insidious example of Mohammed and the mountain (which after all was a defeat for Mohammed). He seems to imply that the individual will come to accept the new sociological society and even to persuade himself that he has really liked it all along.

That this is not unfair is illustrated by another of Mill's examples of the spontaneous development of social feeling in the individual, this time of a highly and significantly specialized kind: he will come to recognize and respect intellectual superiority: and accept, we must suppose, the leadership of the 'clerisy' or elite. People do follow leaders, apparently sometimes willingly, but not usually because of their intellect.

Even if we think that Mill's 'individual' was lacking in substance we have no ground for saying that as a practical politician and administrator he himself lacked knowledge and judgment: or, much more importantly from a liberal point of view, that he fell short in integrity. His work at the India Office is evidence of the one: and his 1865 address to the electors of Westminster, evidence of the other.

This combination of qualities may well have given him confidence in what we might nowadays describe as his 'territorial' admonitions to the state and governmental power: while at the same time they would encourage his expectations for a liberal improvement of society: and Mill did really believe that what has just been described as the 'psychological miracle' – not only the amelioration of society but the willing moral improvement of the species – would come about: by the rational methods of liberalism.

At that time the liberal's grounds, political and other, for self-confidence were unshaken: his good English Conservative tradition stemmed from Locke; private enterprise and Free Trade had not disproved themselves; and British imperialism was spreading the benefits of its customs and law to the lesser breeds without them. This tradition had shown itself successful in the sense of having survived up to the moment; therefore the seeds of progress must be contained within it.

To the philosophical liberal, like Mill, who looked further than political and economic power (or to some extent overlooked them) liberalism was also a real and continuing tradition – but, as we saw an intellectual one; something much more conscious, selective and, one might suggest, artificial than our usual much more haphazard varieties of law, custom, culture and religion. Its apostolic succession came less from either the laying-on or the joining of hands, than from the laying-together of heads: even, one might think, of 'Heads' in the academic or scholastic sense.

It is ironical but perhaps it is also typical of the illusions of liberalism that such confidence and optimism for the future was generated far more by what we can call the conservative and habitual elements in British liberalism than by its progressive ideas and forecasts. Mill attributed his grounds for hope to the wrong tradition.

It is true that in his own terms and according to his available experience some optimism about purely political reform and even about the effect of that on social progress might not have seemed unwarranted. But improvement, moral and social, meant to Mill developing one's individuality by learning to see reason – by a process of rational self-enlightenment: that, coupled with a fairer electoral procedure would enable everyone to take their share in building a juster more rational society. (Philosopher kings by postal vote!)

Again our situation of hindsight is a benefit: we can see that the future of liberalism obviously depended on a combination of moral and economic improvement: it was obvious, too, in Mill's time. But if we classify (and pigeon-hole) this as a 'psychological miracle' we are justified in our language, for Mill's belief is not much more than prophetic. It is not reasonable – something so important for Mill's consistency – that is to say, it is not realistic in the sense that he is able to tell us what the intervening process of human change would be. But although he does not really try to do so, he put a great deal of intellectual labour into justifying his futuristic optimism: some of it directed towards a general Science of Human Nature which he thought was already well on the way to establishment. He also thought that a human ethology could be established.

Ethology petered out. The reason Mill gave for this failure was 'paucity of data'. He admits that individual character cannot be studied by experiment, something that would be required for a scientific ethology, but did not have to give the further reason with which we could supply him today: that Behaviourists can and do experiment on individual character but in doing so run the risk of obliterating the individuality by an adaptive and Procrustean technique. Mill anyway did not surrender the hope that the data of individuality would become more readily available: and there is a paragraph in *A System of Logic* where he foreshadows the psychological and social engineering, just referred to, with optimism and apparent approval and no overweening concern for individuality:

> Ethology is the science which corresponds to the act of education in the widest sense of the term, including the formation of national and collective character as well as individual ... It is enough that we know that certain means have a *tendency* to produce a given effect, and that others have a tendency to frustrate it. When the circumstances of an individual or nation are in any considerable degree under our control, we may, by our knowledge of tendencies, be enabled to shape those circumstances in a manner much more favourable to the ends we desire than the shape they would of themselves assume.

This is a technology: and we can see that it needs to be based on a Scientific Sociology (or Science of Human Nature, or rather of human Behaviour) which Mill thought to be not only possible but desirable. Whether we have such a science today, or the beginnings of such a science, is doubtful. And it is very doubtful whether what we have is by any means wholly desirable. Much of it is more analogous to physical science than to a humane psychology: and it could hardly be the basis for the kind of ethology that Mill would have liked to see: it still suffers greatly and perhaps irremediably from 'paucity of data' about that elusive individual. Sociology studies the statistical behaviour of masses of 'individuals'. But individuality is also a subjective concept. And the predominant school in Western psychology, Behaviourism, has no place for subjectivity or for introspection: the only method by which the 'subject' knows or may get to know about himself or herself; and also about others.

We know from introspection, in so far as we are able to practise it – and it improves with practice – that we are intentional beings, conscious of wishes, purposes and the objects of our environment which we constantly try to make objects *for ourselves*: to appropriate.

That we are often aware, too, of our *failures* in awareness actually strengthens the reality of our individuality, our 'freedom', and the validity of its concept: we are frustrated by causes from outside our immediate scope and also by those which echo and reverberate along our history of existence.

That does not mean that the sense of individual being need be causative in the sense that behavioural observers seem to demand, if they are to admit the reality of human individuality (or 'personality' as we might now begin to call it). An individual's spontaneous feelings and ideas and his own awareness of them, dim or clear, may have no positive role of interference in the course of observable events or even in his own experiences subsequent to that awareness. But they can often account for his inhibitions, withdrawals, reticences and passive resistances, or of course his failures in participation: his avoidances, his goings-to-earth. Those are data no human science can worry out, but they provide a weighty bias to all human cultures and they are the tacit but significant contribution of individuals, all original within their range.

There seems then no alternative for it – the one behaviourism deliberately takes – but to deny the very concept of individual personality: 'Individuals' do not exist because the connection between their subjective awareness of the world and effects and alterations to that world is not 'scientifically' observable: it cannot be described in a scientific language, a language of quantification.

We are generally aware, and Mill himself became aware, that Utilitarian psychology is wholly inadequate as a basis either for individual analysis or psychotherapy or for a human sociology. But the human sciences in so far as they consider either the subject or their own applications at all are still based on a vague utilitarianism – the greatest happiness of the greatest number. That can be at most a pious formula and a rationalized rejection of the consensus of selves that gives the world its human dimensions. We know by now that 'happiness' is an individual, and can never be a statistical, concept: thus to proceed as if it were must be a self-propagating exponential lie.

Sociology, as Mill for one would certainly have wished, cannot do anything to liberate individuality or to help the individual to further liberation and development except in so far as its theories lend support to a humaner economics and to the removal of obviously irrational restrictions.

In sociology and psychology there is admittedly an enormous amount of mass-observation and also what can be called fieldwork among individuals. There is, almost literally, no aspect of individual behaviour however intimate or unconventional that may not be revealed in close-up, or sometimes through the telephoto lens. It looks as if whatever its other shortcomings our scientific sociology or 'human science' does not suffer after all from 'paucity of data'. I myself remember that I used to agree with Mill that a chief source of our misunderstanding of ourselves and of our fellow-individuals was just this. I was being analysed at the time and, being with many another innocent an unshakable Freudian Fundamentalist I rationalized my doubts about the strictly scientific validity of psychoanalysis by advocating the expectant approach: the 'scientific' method was sound enough; but our age's task was to get on with collecting the data: more and more data, endless case-histories, compulsory analysis all round if it could be managed. In about 100 or 1,000 years there it would all be, strewn on the bench, to be put together in an irrefutable and perfectly working theory.

It may very well be that the real data of individuality are indeed available but that we are looking in the wrong direction and moreover are obsessed with methods that will never teach us to unearth them. There seems to be a strong possibility that Mill's individual ethology failed because he did not really care for what he himself thought were the essential defining characteristics of individuality; any more than do the rest of us.

It has already been said that he seems not to have been greatly interested in historical examples or in the biographies of great 'eccentrics'. It is clear that every 'individuality', the more selectively and consciously 'eccentric' the more obviously, can come up against some or any other individual, his beliefs, interests and the laws and customs he accepts and prefers. It is very hard to lay down in advance what anyone can legitimately construe as harm to their rights and interests; we are all of us at some point dogmatic about what is the best social life. It may be identified for us with the only kind which we find tolerable; how can we then agree that it is not better for everyone else?

Moreover 'eccentrics' include amoralists, immoralists, criminals, bullies and even those leaders who can compel a following. Yet it is difficult to see at what degree of eccentricity Mill should in consistency have drawn the line. Mill's moan on our loss of 'diversity', on the sameness that threatens democracy, could have been written even in our own day by any unashamed and reactionary praiser of times past, who secretly resents that opportunities of culture or travel are no longer the exclusive privilege of his class: Waugh's *When the Going was Good* is one example. But I am not denying that one airport or one Hilton is very like another, nor that mass- or pop-culture is in many ways a levelling-down – or out; more seriously, that what we call culture is too often imposed or insinuated rather than elicited.

Tocqueville earlier (*Democracy in America*) said something similar but much better because more realistically than Mill. He also foresaw American social and cultural life seeking its own water-table; but he remained very much aware of, and was able to convey vividly, the cultural, professional, occupational, urban and rural behaviours through which this convergence would have to work. Behind the statistical picture, the calculation of mass-directions, a feeling for a jostling energetic population working out its destiny through its contacts and frictions can be detected; the possibility, in short, of a real diversity of individual lives, many of whom had a minor but indispensable role of ecological significance. Admonishing and perhaps wrong, Tocqueville appears in this comparable piece of prognosis both more hopeful and more consistent (anyway with his own principles) than Mill.

Can it be that Mill did not want to face – he could hardly have failed to glimpse it – the problem of the active original intelligent extravert whom no existing society can satisfy and for whom all societies are composed of rivals; and who also, however much you like or dislike it, has largely made our recorded history? It may be that Mill did not care for the only colouring and details with which he could fill in his diagram of 'individuality'.

There is an odd statement in *On Liberty*. It is near the end; that may partly explain why it reads like a fatigued outburst of petulance.

He is contesting the opinion that we ought to interfere with the sexual and matrimonial habits of the Mormons (then polygamous) for fear that they might influence our own customs:

> I am not aware that any community has a right to force another to be civilized ... if civilization has got the better of

barbarism when barbarism had the world to itself, it is too much to profess to be afraid lest barbarism, after having been fairly got under, should revive and conquer civilization. A civilization that can thus succumb to its vanquished enemy, must first have become so degenerate, that neither its appointed priests and teachers, nor anybody else, has the capacity, or will take the trouble, to stand up for it. If this be so, the sooner such a civilization receives notice to quit the better. It can only go on from bad to worse, until destroyed and regenerated (like the Western Empire) by energetic barbarians.

Probably Mill thought he meant something by his statement which would not be inconsistent with his general utilitarian libertarianism — we have no greater right to interfere with Mormon sexual and matrimonial habits than they have to try and influence our own; and our alarm is therefore a specious and unwarranted excuse for intervention. But still the statement is odd; it appears less consistent with the rational and intellectual tradition we associate with Mill than with that of the Old Testament prophets and others of their generally authoritarian epigones (for example, Hitler, Mussolini and many other 'black' Puritans) who have called for a refining fire upon civilizations too effete or too *effeminate* to stand up for their customs and moral beliefs. Surely to call in the barbarians or merely to invoke their aid would be to put many inoffensive individual lives at risk; astonishing on the part of one who advocated minimal force? Obviously Mill did not approve of our own sexual and marital customs. But he could not seriously have believed that a barbarian inrush would have regenerated them.

Yet I think he would have liked to sweep them away radically and ruthlessly by methods which he himself held to be respectable (e.g. direct reformist legislation) but which were not based on any respect for the gradualism which seems wisest and most humanely natural in many cultural matters. That radical and abstract approach is not really consonant with a diversity of individualities. It fits much better with his intellectual elitism, his 'clerisy' of higher minds (and perhaps know-alls who also know best) and also with his 'Scientific Sociology' or Science of Human Nature (clearly another abstractive assumption or fiction since it is suspiciously like a forecast of our increasingly complex and inter-related structure of 'experts' and of their collective authoritarianism which is beginning to appear ineluctable).

Maurice Cowling, whose little book *Mill and Liberalism* is often unfair and even slanted, has a case, among other examples, when he writes:

> Mill feared democracy and loved individuality, not so much because individuality would induce diversity but because by breaking up existing rigidities, it would make the world safe for 'rational' education, 'rational' thinking and the assured leadership of the 'rational clerisy'.

It is the last phrase that is crucial, if we are discussing, as we must, the *character* of an enlightened rational liberal. It suggests what I think is true, that being born to any degree or kind of recognized or accepted power confers an unquestioned sense of one's right to it: and that liberals, however disinterestedly benevolent, are here no exception.

At the same time it seems unreasonable to blame Mill or anyone else for wanting to put their sincerest convictions into operation. Nevertheless, accepting that their motivation was partly interested, we may still question whether they would have worked protectively for Mill and his type: made the world safe for *his* kind of individual. Or for any other. Individuality need not make the world safe either for democracy or for rational elitism; still less need it include either respect for intellect or social sentiments. On both, as entailments, Mill pinned some of his arguments and much of his hopes. Our hindsight judgment has shown us that the more 'individual' we become the more our respect, if it can so be called, is reserved for performances which are only sometimes 'intellectual' without too much discrimination between skills and values: and/or their mechanics; nor does individuality necessarily respect other individuals – or, in other words, nourish 'social sentiments'.

Mill's kind of individual was supposed to believe not only in the principle of absolutely free discussion, which by definition he was able to undertake, but that endless debate ought to be part of the real structure of social existence: no dialectical or conversational bones should be left in a quiet grave; they should periodically be dug up and gnawed over anew. Both the freedom of the individual and his duty of social contribution demanded that no question should be seen as finally settled.

Obviously all questions if they are treated honestly and realistically must be seen to refer to changing situations; and it is proper to exhume them if they show signs of resurrection or, not less unwelcome, of having been interred alive: this openness is part of a principled and working democracy (a political form which Mill, we must remember, did not favour too greatly). Yet it is doubtful whether endless debate, totally uninhibited 'free' discussion is the best practical method, even of establishing or airing the natural rights of real individuals, let alone of solving problems or illuminating paths that may lead to their solution.

It is not only because debate may indeed be endless, may never lead to any satisfactory change in understanding and its application, that one may look upon the ideal of 'free' discussion as largely another fiction, and an act of mere piety towards another liberal abstraction. Most of the dialectic that Mill had in mind belonged to the public and objective sphere; where anyway chairmen and the guillotine commonly operate. But there is no reason to suppose that he would not have wished it to flourish in everyone's private life, the very hearth and home of the individual — and in his or her most intimate and delicate dealings with fellow-beings. Most people know by now anyway that this does not work: personal problems, *pace* all the psycho-therapists, are not solved by talking; more likely, if at all by solitary walking — or by wordless mutual patience.

Mill may not have thought this out. But though he no doubt honestly believed that he welcomed the expression of all opinion, however much opposed to his own, it is not readily conceivable that he did not foresee that in the most relaxed social conditions possible a great deal of it would be stupid, bloodyminded or, in the mere expressing, actually harmful or dangerous. ('I detest your views, etc.' enunciates one of liberalism's unavoidable dilemmas.)

Then Mill must have observed that even when feeling their way towards sense, simple or profound, people argue badly: and if they are trained to some degree of skill (Mill was technically in favour of something like the medieval practice of 'disputation') they will often enough argue much more cleverly but much more sophistically and even fraudulently, thus rousing anger and revengefulness in those they appear likely to defeat. An intellectualist, the more if he has great resources of exact knowledge, practical experience and dialectical skill, must always remind himself that people argue to win. An elitist, further, has even greater cause for deliberate exercise in humility; he has to see for himself not only that *he* wants to win but that he wants the cup for keeps—the higher minds seldom intend to come any lower; or even down from the pedestal they have probably allotted themselves. An intellectual, says Mill, with amusing pompousness in *Autobiography*, should not even go into ordinary lowbrow society, *except as an apostle*.

It appears that Mill didn't altogether trust his 'individual'—either as generalized concept or as the phenomenon he/she was likely to present after the fullest opportunities for emancipation and development had filtered down to him/her by way of the apostleship of higher thinking. Or could it be that Mill didn't entirely trust his own understanding and conception of human nature and the individual human beings through whom we experience it? Such elitism is inevitably paternalistic; and papas, spiritual and otherwise, are always half prepared to be disappointed in their offspring; not least those who are persuaded that they are working only for the emancipation of the next generation, because this is almost invariably if tacitly 'according to my ideas'. The last freedom that fathers, Fathers in God, or Platonic Guardians hand over to their children and pupils is the freedom to make up their own minds; and a mess of their own lives if they so prefer.

It may sound paradoxical but may still be true that we detect 'individuals' only in their immediate social or family setting, particularly the latter. If that is so it is in considerable part for the reason I gave earlier which applies also to the historical individual: self-realization as we understand it in modern times arises in conflict. If individuality is in the first place a familial or cultural concept—a belief I shall have to justify—its recognition and detection is likely to be intuitional, to depend on immediate and personal contacts, *a relational texture of individuals disposed to welcome their like*, rather than on macroscopic and detached observation; and on an imaginative and sympathetic, even perhaps an artistic, eye and an involved curiosity rather than on a training in tabulation or even a gift for it. I have suggested that the 'individual' of the social and political thinkers is anyway a fiction and that we should have better fictions no doubt from fictional experts.

I think that Mill did not have the necessary qualifications; not less than other people, especially other intellectuals, but certainly not more; that no amount of intellectual honesty and openness of discussion could make up for limitations of perception imposed by his own origins of class and education, which were traditional as well as peculiar.

Mill thought that a Science of Human Nature and an individual ethology were both necessary. The first he continued to believe was feasible. But the second, as far as he was concerned, evaporated; and perhaps now it is possible to see some good reasons why it did so.

Nowadays it is claimed that we have or anyway are beginning to have the 'Science' at least of Human Behaviour: but we might think that an 'individual ethology' — provided it really were a genuine study of genuine and subjective individuals — is more necessary than ever, and that it is still lacking. A social *sentiment* (which, it must be emphasized is different from 'social nature' or being a 'social animal') was invented by Mill and of course others, including Rousseau,* as the only possible adhesive which would bring the individual and any society into harmonious conjunction. Somehow the 'individual' has really got to be brought to the conviction that he *likes* his society and his social relations. That is where a science of human nature came in: and comes in, because it perhaps inevitably operates as human engineering: which it can do the more readily in being statistical and not individualistic: and therefore both authoritarian and abstract.

Continuing to take Mill as our example, his 'religion of humanity' (likewise Comte's, with which it agreed) is a concept evading the requisite of individual authenticity and is itself therefore inauthentic. Indeed we have reason to suspect his 'utility-religion' of being much the same as the kind often favoured by the open authoritarians, such as Machiavelli and Hobbes; or by the disguised authoritarians and collectivists, such as Rousseau. It is good for the people rather than for its inventors.

---

* Rousseau has 'pitié', 'compassion' — meant to imply a dislike at least of *seeing* one's fellow-human being in pain or suffering, and he regards it as innate and universal. See *Discours de l'Inégalité*.

6

The New Machiavellianism

That the direct influence of ideas is small and generally distorted has been more than once repeated: rather as a theme with variations than as a slogan. One aspect of this is that new ideas are themselves very repetitive: they are old ideas turning up in new forms; and need again and again to be stripped of their personified disguises in every new generation, so that the underlying structure, or skeleton, as it often literally is, may be laid bare. This is one of the hardest and most necessary lessons for the liberal mind. The liberal has to believe both in the power and the corrigibility of ideas because he has to believe that his often irrationally trusted methods of persuasion and rational argument, whose function is in practice to prove that his own ideas are right, will actually work to bring about the change in average human outlook and relations which he foresees as necessary for survival (or to make liberalism possible).

The supporters of order and discipline do not have to share either his hopes or his fears because they do not rely on persuasion and argument: at least not as a final resort. They do not share the liberal's gloomy conviction (or anyway his moral doubt) that he ought not to establish his beliefs by force, about whose nature and use, in particular situations, they are often much clearer. If temperamentally they prefer to dominate or to belong to the ruling party, they are not often merely cruel, or seldom irrationally so; they simply prefer to be obeyed rather than to be argued with. Here there is some small, rather theoretical, consolation for the liberal; they also, or rather their respected professional (if unread) thinkers, have to work or try to work through ideas; but they do so by rationalization and emotive hortation just as much as any liberal, while the ideas themselves are as little formative and mostly as unheard of as his own: moreover, comparing purely intellectual capacity, he is quite likely to understand ideas better than they.

Machiavelli might suggest a contradiction or at least a paradox in relation to my generalization. That his ideas have diffused themselves through the human mental atmosphere with much more than the usual deviousness and distortion cannot be denied: on the other hand they have *arrived* as far as the modern world in a form which still tallies with their original conception.

Machiavellians today are at least as 'Machiavellian' as anyone has been in the intervening centuries, including no doubt Machiavelli himself. Yet those principles, theories and concepts about the art of governing Man in political societies which can be found in Machiavelli, which are characteristic of his thoughts and beliefs, which form anything like a coherent system, and which also appear to have been put recognizably into political practice, are few. The most important is that the preservation of the state has an absolute priority. This can be phrased in a number of ways with a variety of moral and social implications. With his passionate interest in history (and willingness to slant it for his own ideal ends) Machiavelli may have intended to be merely descriptive: to tell us what powers and what kinds of rule had successfully maintained themselves or otherwise and what causes had apparently contributed to their rise or fall. Like Vico later, Machiavelli took the organic view of states and civilizations and believed that they were mortal, at varying degrees of longevity. This passionate historicism might appear to leave the comparative value – to the people who composed them – of different kinds of polity, an open question: if a genuine democracy could bring it off it would qualify for the Machiavellian definition of successful rule: but in terms of his time that is something Machiavelli could hardly envisage.

It is clear that Machiavelli believed in a *Führer-Prinzip* or perhaps rather, in terms of his age, in a Renaissance individualistic genius, military and political. But even in his day this may have expressed a romantic enthusiasm at least as much as judgment. What mattered and what Machiavelli was always concerned with was power and who actually wielded it: and the possession of power entails the natural desire and need for self-perpetuation. The notion of what is natural slid then and still slides very easily into the notion of 'right'. (We should, perhaps most of us nowadays agree without much difficulty with the negative converse belief that we have no *right* to compel a considerable body of people, perhaps a majority, to go against their *nature*; and if the murderers and the rapists ever form a clear majority or even a large minority may heaven help the liberal conscience: as also its understanding, occupied for a few remaining years with the additional torture of redeciding the nature of Nature.)

There seems no doubt that Machiavelli (who certainly held moral or at least moralizing views) believed that successful Might *was* right — *What you can do that you may.* Neither the practice nor this kind of justification of it, is unfamiliar in history or unfortunately in our century: and thus there seems no good reason for holding Machiavelli responsible for an idea which a number of people have shown themselves capable of thinking up for themselves.

What does require explanation is the Machiavelli-rehabilitation industry which has now continued for some years; and which a liberal moralist might reasonably find sinister — long before he discovered that unconscious identification accounts for much justificatory theory.

Both in literature and in historical and social studies, the research industry itself invites a general question: Why does a figure of the past, major or minor, incite the commentators to buzzing convergence? The reasons, even if they can be to some extent generalized, are various. There may be a commercially valuable chance of illustration to a possibly pedestrian thesis because lapse of copyright has made it worth some publisher's while to reissue. Or it may be just because the figure *is* minor and has therefore been so far overlooked by the research- and fatigue-parties. With a major figure, Machiavelli, the competition is likely to be more distinguished and the reasons therefore more complex. Sidney Anglo (whose book *Machiavelli: A Dissection* is one of the most commonsensical and balanced, as well as the most agreeably caustic that I have read) refers to this variety of concentration in research in a phrase of general as well as particular utility — '*the law of diminishing fleas*'.

But Machiavelli is, nevertheless, a special case: there can be no doubt that he poses a real problem whose significance goes far beyond his own opinions and historical conditions and well into our own, present and to come, and even beyond the truth or verificability of his arguments. It seems likely that the research-antennae, not always tuned to the intimate and perennial implications of their objective studies, would not have been able to help picking up a fundamental question so pervasive of the moral ether.

It is still, fortunately, a question: when I said earlier that Machiavelli, whatever his capacity for moralizing, believed that *Might* was right, and moreover that this was not a novel contribution but a notion that history had made all too familiar, I did not imply either that the belief itself could go unchallenged or even that it was something we necessarily have to live with. On the contrary I should say that it demands from a committed liberal — thus putting him as to his principles in a paradoxical situation — both the most unbiased examination, whatever the conceptual results in his own mind, and the most determined resistance to its practical consequences of which he is capable.

As a descriptive summary of the way most people have behaved and felt obliged to behave throughout recorded history, the slogan *Might is right* looks warranted. Moreover, weighing the effects of education and correction which have been recorded one might well conclude that both in belief and practice human nature has generally accepted itself as in this all-important respect, incorrigible: force and its Machiavellian auxiliaries will always win and have even created a moral and psychological feedback: force has made us the kind of beings we are and thus in a sense to be so impracticably self-critical is a kind of racial and specific *hara-kiri*.

We have to remind ourselves that it is still a question and still very much a matter of 'sides'. Even as regards human behaviour, not merely the more nebulous 'human nature', it is still only a hypothesis, an ascription, that looks alarmingly general but has not been and possibly cannot be inductively tested. We are not and may never be in a position to say how far those who really prefer freedom and creative peace for themselves and everyone else could make those a possible and acceptable universal goal, for we do not know how to make a favourable variation in the psychological conditions.

We may even believe that the other side, the side dominated by concepts of order, authority, probably Original Sin — and force — may contain those who are simply and sincerely resigned to human iniquity, and only to making the best of the bad job that we are, while they mourn over the Garden of Eden and our innocence eternally lost, at least as much as ourselves. Still what they do is to settle the question out of hand: even *trancher la question*. But then as a theoretical question it isn't settled and like all really significant theoretical questions this one has practical consequences which, if you regard it as settled, will emerge as misled and misleading.

Whether in authenticity or not Machiavelli posed the question as a dichotomy, even perhaps a dilemma. What is important for us is that in his opinion of human possibility he divided power from right, not that he identified them. That we regard private and public morality, on the one hand, as distinct or, on the other, as continuous, provides another crucial political and social classification. In the Western democracies and those that derive their structure from the West, the customary private morality, at least overtly and formally, is still taken as the standard: in public affairs, business or political, I am not in theory, even in legal theory, generally allowed to do what I am forbidden to do, by custom or law, as a private citizen. Clearly, as the recent experiences of Watergate have shown us, that does not prevent habitual corruption, which now appears to infest the democratic structure to an alarming extent. There can now be little doubt that in all the Western democracies a moral pest-control needs to be maintained.

In some, bureaucratic and administrative corruption is endemic and one may say that the population has learned to live with it, although it is still a question how nearly the social effects border on the intolerable or, in other words, what is meant by 'living' for those who are the victims of the worst type of infestation. Even in those countries where democratic institutions are best established and most powerful, the methods of running the community in economic and civil life, to put the matter as mildly as possible, are often designed to benefit factions, enterprises, pressure groups and dominating individuals, rather than the just and natural interests of the average (legal) person: and some of this is inevitable while human beings remain so often nepotic, insular, partisan and prejudiced. In many of these cases 'the law is silent'.* And when the law is positive *against*, the laws (as in the cases of racial and sexual discrimination) are hard put to it to become effectual. We

* Hobbes, *Leviathan*.

E

see moreover in recent civic scandals in England that constitution-
ally illegal corruption can flourish for a long time without retribu-
tion and with plenty of financial padding to cushion its after-effects
when it has collapsed.

But the theoretical *principle* is so far little affected, at least in
America and Britain (and many other countries not so much in the
global eye). Private individuals are generally forbidden both by
law and accepted custom as well as by continuing norms of behaviour to murder, rob, commit violence, even to lie, where the practical effects on others of mendacity and distortion are harmful and
can be estimated: and here too in theory at least all are equal before
judgment. In America and England (and many other countries)
offenders can be brought to book and occasionally this even
happens. In those countries, the private morality, not perhaps very
subtle or discriminative or psychologically humane, which has
been taught to their citizens throughout the history of their
civilizations and from their earliest days, is still the standard: on
the whole they have (ideally) rejected the *raison d'état* endorsed by
Machiavelli and Hobbes (and many others).*

It is at least arguable that even under the authoritarian regimes,
the principle of continuity of private with public morality, though
in practice rejected and buried, has not been entirely forgotten:
that some of its archaeological outlines remain, even in the minds
of the rulers, many of whom in early life must have been tainted
by the personal morality of religion and of most of the great
examples of their literature. (Among dissidents, even those who
still adhere to the communist or totalitarian faith, it is clearly still
very much alive.) At least we can say that the authoritarian leaders
and the local orthodox, while both in theory and in practice denying

* It must be noted that I am not being 'psychologistic'; I think there is nothing
morally special about the individual citizen of our democracies: our democratic
structure *allows* them to behave fairly decently. This asserts no generalization
about how they individually prefer to behave; nor about how they would
behave if moral opportunity were sharply diminished; or conversely if moral
temptation were sharply increased by political change. This is a subsidiary
reflexion on a more general question which considerably motivates the writing
of this book: liberals may come to certain agreed conclusions about both our
moral potentialities and the desirability or even the necessity of fulfilling them;
but they still have to find an answer to the question: What if anything are we
to do about it, having first decided that it is worth trying? That must be
understood as a permanent marginal comment.

the principle, have to try to make out that they have substituted one that is superior; that the rights of individuals or 'democratic freedom', respect for which is the essence of private morality, are actually better preserved and protected under their kind of authoritarian rule. (This can only be logically maintained by some preliminary and biased division into sheep and goats.)

Sometimes the paternalism is genuine or at least genuinely self-deceived. Father really does believe that he knows what is best for the children, forgetting of course, as all fathers sometimes do, that democratic procedure has to pretend to assume that the children have grown up, or ought to have and must be helped to do so. To maintain the authoritarian system among moral and political adults, however few they may be, requires at least (twisted) lip-service to personal standards of morality and must include the belief (real or assumed) that all people are potentially persons. Thus what these regimes have taken over from a Machiavellian-type psychology is fraud rather than force (although the force is there not far in the background, as we see, and although indeed fraud is only another kind of force, merely less easy to detect and oppose).

A cynic might be tempted to say that fraud and deception, including self-deception on a mass-scale, are the permissible pseudo-democratic substitute for straightforward *Realpolitik*. Injustice must not only be done, it must not be seen to be done.

Raison d'état (the right or rather the capacity of governments or rulers to set aside ordinary moral codes for the alleged benefit of those they govern), anyway in its Machiavellian form, does not claim to be 'value-free'.* Machiavelli was much more like a

---

* It is worth while commenting here on a possible complication to modern Machiavellianism. Science, anyway as an investigation and study, if not in application outside those fields, claims to be 'value-free': to be intellectually impersonal, to be not directly concerned with individuals or with the specifi-cally human and its human needs (except according to legal and practical limitations); nor therefore with choices and preferences—including those of scientists as members of our species. The reason given is that this unconcern or detachment provides the only mental climate in which science can do its work with proper precision. Yet in fact science establishes for itself an absolute hierarchy of values, and hence a claim to moral rights, beginning with the right to unlimited curiosity; thus of taking, on or against our behalf, the risk of completely altering our mental and cultural climate—intellectual pollution.

political moralist than a political scientist. If his doctrine implies *Might is right* then that means, in his logically justifiable definition, what it appears to say: it is right — as also with Hobbes — because the preservation of state order has overwhelming priority. Or has been seen and at any rate tacitly defined as of prime and universal *value*.

This has applied in the paternal home as well as in the state: no political social or family system has worked successfully for any length of time where the rulers, leaders, or seniors were seriously unsure of their righteousness or were probably even able to see the opposite point of view. Thus *raison d'état* always includes the institution of an absolute hierarchy of values which in our time — that is, since the democratic idea was established anywhere and states have had at least to pretend to be identified with the interests of all the people who compose them — claims to be for the ultimate benefit of the community conceived as a whole, and the best that can be done for the majority of its individual members.

Often, perhaps in most cases, this is sincerely felt, as it has always been throughout history: there is nothing emotionally more convincing or more satisfying or inspiring to confidence than a set of absolute values, unless it be another. And it only works, whatever it is, if held uncritically and thus probably abstractly.

It is certain that in their time Mr Heath, Mr Wilson, Mr Nixon, M. Giscard d'Estaing, Mr Brezhnev and Chairman Mao have *wanted* power not as the Good do, but in the sense that they are *ab initio* absolved from the discomfort of self-criticism — they don't have to think about it. They all believe that they have a right to it: and a 'right' right: they all believe, even 'know', that they are carrying on the 'Great Tradition' (as in the case of Dr Leavis, from whom I take the slogan — a very selective one, though this is not admitted). I have no acceptable analytic grounds for this generalization with its association of examples, except my own

---

Individuals become the targets of intensive authoritarian education into 'scientific' (including 'sociological') values.

This is also a case of *Might is right*, for the majority of individuals is powerless to criticize or even be aware of what is happening, nor therefore to intervene. Even here the instrument is often unconscious deception rather than fraud and something that resembles the official piety of those who operate *raison d'état* — in moral ruminations, scientists too often claim, not always with justification, to produce long-term 'values' which, as a by-product, *will* benefit us all, as individuals — if we can only get round to knowing what is good for us.

sampling of human behaviour combined with a slowly developing self-knowledge. Dominant (or what Robert Ardrey calls 'alpha'-) types, especially when they are successful in their chosen fields — when, that is, like good artists, they themselves are dominated by their medium — are extremely idealistic: they are not over-concerned with the material embodiments of power; one might almost guess that they have, as it were instinctively, absorbed the sumptuary lessons of the Graeco-Christian tradition, and accept that possessions, to a man stripped for action, are a great bore (he may have to depart in a hurry). My guess is that these 'alpha-types' have made only a marriage of convenience with the material perquisites of power: in a technological and 'affluent' age, they want for themselves only those material instruments which they can use with economy and without undermining the dignity that supports their (O so necessary) dominant self-confidence.

I do not believe that they are 'value-free': they sincerely believe that they are called to maintain some long, though hazily defined tradition based on 'human nature' (according to their own partial, though absolute, but hazily defined, definition). This means that they are in the paradoxical situation of believing that what is essentially a caste system can or must be good for everyone. But in our time this obviously has to be insinuated, not openly enforced. Hence the importance of fraud to a democratic education.

All this they seldom directly, consciously, or academically learn from Machiavelli, although he was well aware of it all and was able to be more candid about it. They have usually not even learned any clear-cut conception of his definition of human nature, although it tallies with their own unreflected and therefore unargued assumptions, and probably with those of a large part of our species to date.

Particularly in England but elsewhere too, Machiavelli has been abhorred. (That accounts for the rehabilitation industry but it is not certain that the rehabilitation industry accounts for the dislike, or even gives the question the attention it deserves.) One may think that the original 'Machiavellian' was identified with the Anti-Christ and thus Machiavelli himself with a deliberate attack on traditional Christianity and its respect for the person and the individual soul.

In English history, where the horror and condemnation have been unusually marked, it might well be a case of *'perfide Albion'*.

A not wholly unprejudiced quotation from Giovanni Prezzolini's *Machiavelli* sums it up adequately:

> Fundamentally English opinion of Machiavelli consists of verbal condemnation of Machiavellianism accompanied by its practical application behind a mask of hypocrisy. With a few exceptions this has continued from the moment of the first relations between England and Italy to the present day.

Of late the rehabilitation industry may be very largely accounted for by the condition of simple reversal which in all areas offers one of the most profitable veins of exploitation. (If you wait long enough – but only if so, and with the tricky proviso that you must judge how not to wait too long – people will be ready to hear if not to heed the other side of the question whatever it may be, the more if the plugging has been long and consistently monodic.)

Even so that is not the whole explanation. The horrified dislike of Machiavelli was disseminated chiefly through literature and language: the thought of Machiavelli affected the imagination, it worked through the emotions and the poetic and colourful usage of language, not by argued polemic.

It is not unreasonable to believe that redressing the balance in favour of Machiavelli is at least in part explained by a psychological phenomenon which Freud might have included under 'the return of the repressed'. Machiavelli's latterday champions may recognize something of themselves (Morley thought Machiavelli had got *half* of human nature* in his description of human emotions and behaviour). They may suspect that that half, even in their own case, really belongs to the party of order and power. Sometimes, too, of the aggressors. But the recognition remains unwelcome, because most of them were born into a world where it was thought that naked power was not quite respectable and ought at least to clothe itself. They may half believe, with Eliot, that they themselves, however soon and willingly disinherited, were *rentiers* on the moral (and sometimes humane and liberal) values of Graeco-Judaeo-Christianity: and that meant among

---

* T. S. Eliot, in 'Essay on Machiavelli' in *For Lancelot Andrewes*, comments on the other half of human nature that Machiavelli 'did not see' – 'the myth of human goodness which for liberal thought replaced Divine Grace'. It is possible that Machiavelli was even more Augustinian than that—he did not see perhaps even the myth of Divine Grace.

other things that they needed to be right (and righteous): and therefore further that Machiavelli was *right*, too, after all: *love me, love my devil.**

At present perhaps, in the commonest case, the rehabilitation is carried out by a special interpretation of Machiavelli's ideas, and very often of his actual employment of the language which embodied them—which shows that he was *right* because those concepts, reinterpreted, and linguistically analysed, really agree with the researcher's own acceptances about morality, private and public. Machiavelli was *right* because he really meant what they prefer to think he meant. That considerably accounts for scores of analyses of how to translate *'virtù'*—the most important qualification, according to Machiavelli, for the Prince or Great Man of Action.

To me anyway it seems fairly clear that Machiavelli meant the ability to succeed in what one was up to, and included some strong implications of charisma (which can, as Hitler taught us, be evil as well as good), meaning both the gift and the technique of putting it across. But Machiavelli never made it clear, possibly because he found the ambiguity more profitable, how if at all, this *virtù* (which even in the case of Jesus when he said it 'has gone out of me'—something a black magician might also have said—) should be compared or identified with, or on the other hand distinguished from, 'virtue' of the sort we claim to approve: virtuous conduct, public or private.

It has been possible to subsume all the ambiguities under the sole (and misleading) concept of civic or public virtue: respectable self-sacrificing, dedicated and patriotic citizenry; and this was done by Eliot, in his comparatively early essay of rehabilitation.

It must be admitted that Eliot was both uncompromising and honest according to his lights: he thought that Machiavelli was *right*, and full moreover of 'public virtue': but for one essential and indeed overriding reason—because he was implicitly and perhaps unconsciously 'orthodox'. This was according to the defini-

---

* Eliot has made something like the same point in more figurative and no doubt more rhetorical language. He explains the dominant particularly Elizabethan 'love-hate' attitude towards Machiavelli as the effect of a widespread and heretical Manichaeism: we must have our devil. (The persistent preference for Milton's Satan, quite possibly shared by Milton himself, is typical.)

tion of 'orthodoxy' which Eliot was repeatedly to give in other writings. Or rather, repeatedly to allude to, for it is far from clear and does not appear to be certainly consistent with the orthodox view of orthodoxy (if there is one), or even consistent with itself. What is clear is that it is anti-liberal. For Eliot largely identifies heresy with what he calls 'the liberal myth of human goodness' — from which, as we saw, Machiavelli was chemically pure.

But taken together the two 'myths' — of Original Virtue and Original Sin — provide a classic Either-Or: and we need not assume either of them.

If Machiavelli did subscribe to any belief in Original Sin, it was in a very secular form, and certainly without even a speculative interest in theological niceties. (On the other hand, with Hobbes and Rousseau, he prescribed religious conformism; but in the interest of power, not of moral education. Most human beings were 'bad' and needed keeping in their place.)

Nevertheless that, too, may help to bolster a belief in the *righteousness* of successful power: and those latter-day authoritarians who with, for instance, Geoffrey Woodhead (*Thucydides on the Nature of Power*) hold that power is morally neutral can easily accommodate themselves to this faith ('Justice is successful power in action' says Woodhead).

But though they commonly mean that governmental power in any of its variants is morally neutral (or 'value-free') they do not necessarily or commonly mean that the state is not, in some sense, a moral agency. Certainly we may agree that it sets up moral standards and attitudes, whether altogether intentionally or not, and whether they would be recognized or not by those who retain anything of the individual-personalistic tradition, as definably moral. But it seems safe, because history appears to confirm it, to say that even the most authoritarian or even tyrannical state-systems have been obliged to treat their citizens or members as if they were in some quite practical sense moral beings with rights and duties, though the first may be minimal and the second exorbitant, and though this moral status has usually depended on an original divisive classification not only of membership of the state, but even of humanity. The forms of absolutism we have witnessed in our time have often shown themselves obliged to pay lip-service to older and more personal values, and this has clearly often been the only practical way of reinterpreting them and tailoring them to long-term totalitarian ends. At bottom, though among other purposes, a liberal in a totalitarian state is being re-educated. He is being shown where he was wrong in behaviour and conception and the language he uses to refer to either. That even recantation does not obviate drastic punishment does not mean that the state is of necessity acting immorally, according to its lights; or even neutrally: it is more likely acting in a righteous imitation of 'Nature', who in the long run punishes our crimes against her — which to us may seem not worse than foolishnesses — with ruthless severity; the wages either of sin or of stupidity *is* death. Absolute and arbitrary power too, as we saw, in the Nazi death camps, and as we continue to see in some of the Soviet trials, often works, and most successfully, through irrational guilt: the victims or offenders really come to believe that they have done wrong (you can do the same thing with dogs) or are in some similar way outside the pale of a moral system which they have come to recognize if not to accept.

The liberal conceives the individual person as both the source and the instrument of authentic morality: and moreover the individual's development including his self-development, as its objective. Hence a theoretical distinction between private morality and a public morality, even if that public morality dictated acts that were acceptable, must strike him as not only iniquitous but absurd, a contradiction in terms; and as still more absurd the attempt to maintain the distinction in practice: he will find it hard to believe that Himmler was after all a domestic model.

Yet he cannot easily dismiss the likelihood that Machiavelli was right in description of human behaviour (or at least 'the half of it' — *that* covers the public half): but not in prescription. It is not what *ought* to be: and politicians, statesmen and other organizers of power still fulfil Acton's formula.

Thus especially in our present conditions he may not unreasonably regard as sinister the resurgence of Machiavellian sympathies even though they seem intellectually objective or academic: not least because the privilege of moral neutrality is at the same time being claimed in many other fields and studies which may at present seem fairly remote from practical or anyway social activity.

To accept the descriptive accuracy of Machiavelli's moral view no doubt opens up alarming possibilities of depression and helplessness for the liberal. If statesmen, politicians, businessmen and whole governments (with plenty of lesser cogs) are in fact parts of a machinery of power which compels them to think with collective amorality, and thus to discount even their own individual moral preferences (while those persist), the liberal's hope of purifying public life in the interests of individual morality appears as improbable as any other expectation of dramatic conversion.

But there might be one good reason why liberals could be thankful if governments and authorities were able to maintain the distinction between private and public morality: although that might depend on whether or not they were mature enough to do so openly, if not cynically. The liberal might after all still learn to be glad of a policy of moral laissez-faire.

Nevertheless, as we have seen in our own day, the distinction is not maintained but confounded, and the most authoritarian states still pay some lip-service to at least the language of private moral maxims. In social democracies what is likely to happen is that the private moral sector becomes eroded by a public morality apparently democratic but actually self-deceiving or hypocritical.

Democracy is after all a moral opinion which claims to serve the moral individual: but in practice tends more and more to prescribe him a pattern. This may well be most marked, however unintentionally, in education, a field of peculiar interest to the liberal and where he is increasingly likely to look for the only real influence that is within his grasp. He must still probably agree with Mill that the business of the state is to pay for education, but keep out of it. (He is often inconsistent about this – demanding that the state or society in its educational and social institutions *should* be a moral agency; but according to *his* conception, which despises mass methods: the almost Robinson Crusoe situation of Rousseau's *Emile* still seems to haunt the educational ideal of liberalism, which therefore again fails to face a real dilemma.)

The current argument about comprehensive versus grammar school is in part, but essentially, an argument about social and moral attitudes, about what I later call 'privileged moral minorities': and about 'justice' and what the individual either ought or can be made to accept as 'just'.

But it is also an argument about the self-perpetuation of a certain kind of polity and society. Our social democracies, like our conservative democracies (and like most of the organizations we construct) not only desire their own infinite survival but wish to convince themselves, ourselves and all our immediate heirs that this desire for immortality is good in itself: and acceptable unto all generations.

Both openly and insidiously (or fraudulently) authoritarian states are at an advantage here. They do not have to think too much about the future because they feel able either to prescribe it or breed it. His developmental individualism would oblige the liberal in any circumstances to think about the future, but if he were thinking realistically, only as far as he could see in the round; that is, through the immediate familial generations. In fact, his futurism is more often an evasion than a projection of these concrete realities. He cannot think more realistically than anyone else about the real people, the real individuals, that will come to be. Thus he is driven to the inconsistency of thinking about the future of societies, his own in particular: and therefore to think about society as a moral being with a moral future, i.e. that it is capable of self-improvement or moral evolution.

The authoritarian social thinker does not have this difficulty or reveal this inconsistency. If he is theocratic the future is by definition taken care of. If he is in practice secular, like Machiavelli and Hobbes, all that matters to him is the preservation of the polity that he approves of and prefers.

But in any case, self-perpetuation is and has been the 'morality' of authoritarian societies or indeed of those organizations, either political or social (or cultural), which do not feel any call to be genuinely democratic: in practice most organizations.

It might seem paradoxical at first glance that a preoccupation with survival had so little concern with prognostication, with the actual concrete and detailed forms in which that survival might be embodied. In the first place most political thought, not only that of the liberals, is inclined to over-abstraction; and where it is not, it may be realistic for its time, but is partly for that reason too immediate and personal. What is slightly more surprising is that both Machiavelli and Hobbes, if they thought — in their rather generalized terms — about the future of their societies, or any society, did not think much of it: they were pessimistic. This reflects their sense of an embattled position. They both believed that their societies were faced with imminent destruction. Machiavelli's society appears as running hard or battling hard to keep on the same spot, without stable institutions except for the military and state religion. Machiavelli's Prince had his thumb in the dyke. Moreover Machiavelli cannot have believed that his state control, however successful, was really more than a patched-up job; for he believed as Vico was to do, let along Spengler and Toynbee, in the mortality of states and civilizations; whatever you did they came to dust.

Whatever Hobbes believed or not about inevitable decline, his political edifice was much more logically and consistently constructed than Machiavelli's as well as more artfully. Machiavelli's society was a temporary refuge against the other tribes of one's kind. Hobbes's was a stout kraal, certainly against human aggression and dissidence but also against the natural and elemental enemies of all humankind considered as a side. A home from homelessness.

Part Three
Contractualism
From Rousseau to Rawls

7

Old Pigs in New Pokes

We can see that it is relatively easy for authoritarians to reconcile private and public morality by identifying them. The liberal's task is harder. While he remains recognizably a liberal, he is under the obligation to try and give some real moral and psychological content to individuality – for instance his individual has to be authentic and motivated by the impulse and will to freedom – but the good society has to be constructed round this individual, otherwise the world is morally inside-out. If – as often in later life – he is driven to compromise, and sometimes further, this sense of a natural and proper order of priority still dies hard, if ever: and the fairly reasonable generalization that 'Society is made for man, not man for society' can become rather wishfully transformed into 'Society was really made by individual men for their own benefit – not the other way about'.

It is not uncommon with optimists – one cannot remain a liberal without also remaining an optimist – to accept situations and solutions which they have persistently and consistently rejected, sometimes even abhorred; and to do so with a bright smile as if it had all along been their own idea, rather than admit that they have been defeated. This attitude the liberal has often, and characteristically, projected on to his 'free individual'. Like Saul-Paul to the martyrdom of Stephen, he is 'consenting unto' his incorporation into collective society. Another logical fiction has to be devised and established both to account for and to justify the (fictional) individual's 'willing' surrender of his (fictional) perfect liberty to opt out – or to refuse to accept what is better – or possibly even good for him.

Contractualism, or the doctrine of individual consent, is a fiction and in the form we have known it, since roughly the beginning of the industrial age, a liberal invention.

Contractualism might also be regarded as a liberal compromise not only with an unwelcome conception of society, but possibly even with liberal principle. This view is supported by the fact that, chiefly in its form the 'Social Contract', it has been and still is significantly useful to people who could by no means be described as liberals. For instance, Hobbes, and in our own day Robert Ardrey and other popular ethologists.

The Social Contract, we accept, is not a historical fact or situation. I have just said that contractualism in all its forms is a legal fiction, but that is not quite saying the same thing. It means only that no individual in his social (including economic, and personal) relations is ever in the position of total enlightened consent. That is obviously true of the Labour Party's usage and version of the term; but as a fiction it is representative rather than metaphoric: roughly representative, like all the rest of political democracy.

The metaphoric usages — in which I include, however much they may appear to differ, those of Hobbes, Locke, Rousseau and the dramatic ethologist, Robert Ardrey — are also unhistorical, a fact which it is easy to misinterpret: or even to underestimate, as structurally significant in human psychology and thought.

There never has been a real Social Contract. In one sense the historicity or lack of it is of no importance: it is the kind of history it implies or which has been imagined or projected as its background that is significant, for that depends on a standard and structural psychology many of whose 'fictions' have already been referred to — such absolute attributes of an absolute 'human nature' as Original Sin, the State of Nature: and in our day the 'aggressiveness' diagnosed by the ethological psychologists which needs to be contained by 'contractual' arrangements learned from the social animals (as if the goats could be put in pastoral care of the sheep).

That 'innate aggressiveness' is a historical conception (it depends on evolutionary history); but there may be some doubt whether the conception and its interpretation have total historicity or are not in some versions projected, slanted, exaggerated or plain imaginary. Of this more must be said in a later section.

It may be said that the earlier contractualists could not have been historically minded because they wrote before the days of proper scholarly historiography. It is true that that may partly account for the lack of interest in ordinary subjective individuals whose very existence needs discovery by minute and complex research and on whose behaviour and idiosyncrasies a fully concrete and realistic and, I suppose, 'scientific' history must be based. But we should not therefore allow ourselves to assume that Hobbes or even Locke or for that matter Rousseau would have been historically minded in the sense indicated, if only they had been given the chance. Possibly the contrary is the case; and it is only because the documents have been lacking that the social-contractualist either of the older or the metaphoric kind is in the fortunate situation of being able to assume a supporting history: or of believing that he is so able. He needs this support for what has been called structural reasons. This has two aspects, the one particular and the other pointing to a more general characteristic of human thinking. In the particular aspect, the 'Social Contract' has in fact been treated as if it were historical. All contractualists, no doubt for obvious reasons, are moralists—this is almost tautologous—of one kind or another. In all of them consent must be regarded as *owed*: it is not enough that it should be expedient or realistic or 'natural', as logically entailed by the conception, whatever form it takes, of the state of 'nature' and the 'nature' of 'Man'. It is seen as a duty between the contracting parties—although generally in unequal proportions, like the reciprocal duties of man and wife. Or in other words, perhaps, consent is not consent unless it is free: since their beginnings contractualists have been uneasily if dimly aware that in political and social life it is never so; hence their historical need which, in the dearth of sufficient historical content, works out as a doctrine of origins.

Thoroughly documented history has not cured the human mind of its aetiological preferences. In all studies which have not moved, or perhaps cannot move entirely free of the hypothetical stage, there is always a danger that the past may be conceived as a *cause*, a moral one as well as a logical. This is seen as well in 'subjective' Freudianism as in the 'objective' class-theory of Marxism.

The doctrine of the Social Contract fits into this structural category whoever may hold it and in whatever way they may do so. But those of the more liberal inclination are more in need of an explicit historical justification than the authoritarians or those who are primarily parties of order. I mean that their need of this justification is one of logical or moral consistency, not that they are always or usually aware that it would be necessary or even useful to them. The liberal has to believe not only that the development of the individual person is the true aim of societies, but that the individual in this sense, if only potentially, is a historical phenomenon: history was always moving in that direction. The individual is 'born free'; that is, in merely being born he inherited certain potentialities and the right to develop them—for example authenticity and the respect due to it—and to defence against its infringement. He is born free—but mostly weak: and of course weaker in the past than in the present just to the extent that his society did not realize its protective role, among other things auxiliary to his development. The process of history, as assumed by the liberal, is or anyway ought to be the realization of their reciprocal roles by individuals and their societies. The Social Contract is a true or just bargain in so far as it is between real identifiable parties. Nevertheless the individual in this liberal sense, if he is to be often or readily identified, is more probably a modern phenomenon and even largely an accidental one. He had in himself no historical driving force: and there is obviously no evidence that great 'individualists' or 'Great Men'—this has already been remarked—were concerned with the principle of individuality or the right to freedom as such and with building society around it. History fails the liberal contractualist and he has to fall back upon some philosophic generalization, more or less 'psychologistic': generally an abstract account of human behaviour based on an equally abstract but favourably and optimistically slanted account of human motives. This can be seen in the case of Rousseau: and I believe it is also true of at least one modern contractualist, whom I shall discuss: John Rawls, author of *A Theory of Justice* (see p. 152). Obviously the society which Rousseau projected for the necessary preservation, protection and *development* of his 'born free' individual was, whatever his original intention, very far from liberal. Or in other words, in this context, his Social Contract was not a true bargain between real contracting parties, it was more like a confidence trick. I shall suggest that the same charge of unrealism, both psychological and social, applies to contractualism in its modern form.

Even if the other outstanding contractualists, Hobbes and Locke, also belong to the same structural category they were, within their limits, less unrealistic. In both cases, in their versions of the Social Contract they offered a real, if limited, bargain. Neither Hobbes nor Locke could afford to be so abstract: in both cases, the need for stability, security and peace was seen to be paramount; Hobbes had uncomfortably survived the Civil War: Locke saw it as his duty, to which he was sincerely committed, to justify the ways of the subsequent English Revolution to its heirs.

Moreover whatever either of them thought about 'freedom' in the abstract neither of them totally lacked concern with personal and civil liberties. Probably with the increasing secularity of protestant culture, it could not have been otherwise. The official philosophy of Machiavelli's world was still theocratically centred: the social bargain if it could be conceived at all was basically or originally between God and man — two abstractions; therefore in any discussion or analysis of the relations of actual power it did not have to be mentioned. (Of course Christianity is based on the notion of a serial bargain, God with the Son and the Son with Man. However it is not based on consent.)

Locke, commonly regarded as typical of English liberalism, certainly had a wider view of those personal liberties than Hobbes, the authoritarian; that some, if circumscribed, rights of the individual against the state were inalienable — part of his moral contents, we might say. Locke's conception of that 'individual' as constituting a recognizable person, if only in the legal sense, was chiefly more urbane than Hobbes's, and less emotional: a matter, no doubt, both of historical circumstances and of temperament.

Hobbes, feeling the advantages of having come in from the cold, had no use at all for that 'state of nature' which with Locke and Rousseau he assumed, or of 'Natural Man' — in Hobbes's conception 'free' only of the benefits of order: of what alone made human existence decent, safe and tolerable. He roundly repudiated this 'freedom' in words now familiar to schoolchildren; for him the Social Contract rescued mankind from its instinctive propensity to evil behaviour and its condition of permanent warfare. It seems clear that Hobbes conceives 'Man' as a profoundly irrational animal, and a naturally poor judge of his own interest, unless in the shortest term: it is therefore surprising, since Hobbes also conceived of the Social Contract as a collective act of the highest and wisest common sense amounting to a providential salvation, that it could ever be achieved by such brutish creatures.*

In Hobbes's interpretation the Social Contract demanded an

* Commented by Vico (1668–1744) as well as by Rousseau.

absolute surrender to sovereign power which was to all intents and purposes irreversible.* Michael Oakeshott in his Introduction to *Leviathan* has said that there are more grounds for calling Hobbes a liberal than many who have claimed the name. It is true that, while he was contemptuous of 'freedom' in the anarchistic, the only, sense in which he understood it, he conceives of power as limited by the laws which admittedly it has made itself, and can therefore also conceive of not negligible areas where the individual is left alone—wholesome neglect which, as some educators say, in the case of children is *not* negligible. All law is conceived as positive and initiative, and where 'the law is silent' the subject can please himself. Nevertheless the rent for these plots of privacy is a total superficial conformity to the religious and cultural establishment, whatever that may be; and dangerous thoughts if they lead to dangerous expression, as they must if civil liberties are to have any recognition, are effectually proscribed. (Hobbes didn't think much of the students of his day, blaming their Liberation fantasies on the classical education.)

But Locke, too, though he did not think of the human individual as by nature a poor savage, wretched or brutal, resembled Hobbes in not thinking about him at all in the way that since Mill at least we have come to understand, and often and uncritically to accept. Both really assumed human beings as already socialized both politically and economically and could not think outside this assumption; this may only be another way of saying that they were preoccupied with justifying, as the best of all possible societies, the form of social organization they each preferred.

Locke's 'individual' in short, was cooked rather than raw; not in any 'state of nature': he is in fact already the potentially successful individual with a start in the race of life, equipped already with a property qualification (which qualifies him to obtain more).** Individuality and its freedom (to make the most of itself) is in

* This must be qualified to some extent: the sovereign power had a job to do —by the promulgation and maintenance of law to provide its subjects with protection against internal anarchy and external war—and clearly if this broke down it was no longer sovereign: but where its law held and spoke, its word was final.

** It is true that by 'property' Locke means not only the amount of land and other material wealth that a man can legitimately acquire by the amount of work he can carry out to appropriate and develop them, but also a man's own life. 'Property' then, in this interpretation, has a clear and strong bearing on the

Locke's conception exclusivist, and leads, one would say, to a self-elective elite or to maintaining one. Indeed the free man in Locke's simplification is much as he would have been if he were an Athenian citizen: equal in freedom before the law with those who were his equals in property and power; and not even particularly aware that the price of his freedom and equality was slavery for the majority.

We must remember that not only limited concern with humanity as a whole, but limited experience of it, must have been characteristic of political thinkers almost up to our own times, because they almost inevitably belonged to the classes that possessed power, including wealth and education (I prefer this circumlocution to 'bourgeois' because of the both abstract and now proprietary quality of that term). Their acquaintanceship where it was at all intimate lay among the successful and powerful or those who were —and still are—taking the right road to success and power: these were not only more likely to be extraverted and self-assertive, if not actually bloodyminded; they were extremely unlikely to be meek, passive or sensitively and intelligently imaginative. We must also remember at the same time, I suppose, that here too, as with Machiavelli, we have 'the half of human nature'.

Nevertheless we can at least say that not only Locke the liberal but Hobbes the authoritarian saw that they ought to offer us something for our money or rather for our liberty, as they conceived it, and its surrender. They made some attempt, that is, to estimate the needs and interests of some men, as they understood men, and to show how these were better served in societies than in an unsocial or anarchical condition. They both, that is, were putting forward formulae for some kind of genuine bargain. Even if we regard it as a pig in a poke (like many bargains) the offer in both cases was not only as far as it went genuine and honest, it was partly reasonable and even showed some sense of justice (or at least fairness, for justice in the universal-human sense, which haunts the liberal, is something of a stumbling block to any kind of contractualist or social bargain-driver, even when he is a liberal).

This is particularly to be remarked in the case of Hobbes. His conception of human nature and its situation was, unlike Locke's,

---

possibilities of a liberal philosophy of human existence. See the discussion (p. 252) of MacPherson's 'possessive individualism'. Some comparison can also be borne (if with difficulty) with Robert Ardrey's account of instinctual territorialism in Man and the dangers of frustrating it.

in a sense egalitarian: it applied to everyone, for we were seen as all
equally at the mercy of our fellow-men. In that hypothetical state of
nature we were all equal in misery. And in the state of society
according to Hobbes, we are all equal before absolute sovereignty.
It is true that with Hobbes, even in his chosen form of absolute
monarchy, sovereignty expresses itself as the rule of law and this
leaves some latitude for individual choice—in matters where 'the
law is silent'. But Hobbes's conception of law is positive: the sovereign can always extend his powers in any direction where he or it
feels a challenge, without consultation or consent. Thus the sovereign once established, whether by institution or *acquisition*, is not
really a party to any contract or bargain. It is all, as with Machiavelli, a matter of power: *what you can do that you may*. If we assume
the state of nature—and that it was as Hobbes described it, but only
so—it is possible to see the logic in such an absolute surrender on the
part of the governed to absolutism: we must remember that this
'equality' before the sovereign law applies to all groups of organizations as well as individuals, and thus to any notion of combination,
which must constitute an impermissible challenge. Absolute sovereignty with absolute command over all the means, kinds and
sources, both actual and potential, of power was the only way,
as Hobbes conceived it, for the state to fulfil its function of protect-
ing this unsocialized individual from his own helplessness and the
predatoriness of all others.

We can see then that both Hobbes and Locke offer us some things
that are necessary not only to our survival, but to our well-being:
peace, security, minimal property and order (which to make the
social offer look as liberal as possible can be taken to imply some
social arrangement for the distribution of wealth and other communal utilities and services); and in Locke's case, too, certain civil
rights to toleration and freedom from unnecessary state interference; though, as Hobbes saw, states are in the habit of defining
what is necessary. However, there is nothing even in the Lockian
view of the Social Contract which is certainly in the direct line of
our contemporary idea of liberalism depending on the free play of
individuality: it is quite as compatible if not more so with a benevolently intentioned or anyway benevolently defined collectivism.

Moreover with both Hobbes and Locke and, as we may come
to think, in any other interpretation, including some modern
forms, the Social Contract presents an odd idea of a bargain. A

bargain ought surely to be fair and undertaken with one's eyes open and, for the advantage of both sides even if in differing degrees, without pressure either of fraud or force. (Fraud includes the withholding of feasible enlightenment.)

The test obviously of a free (that is, a genuine) bargain, the only one that an orthodox liberal can or even perhaps ought to accept, is: *What do I do if the other party doesn't keep its bargain?* Speaking here as the individual, what do I do if the state I have helped by acquiescence, if not by overt consent, having originally absconded with my individual freedom of action and judgment proceeds to encroach on them still further and arbitrarily: and thus of necessity doesn't provide me with peace, order and security (still less, as so many philosophic liberals have hoped, with the positive opportunities to develop my own creative and personal satisfaction)? Perhaps even more importantly in our latter-day conditions, *When* do I do something? That decision, and the ability to make it, implies that I have all along been developing the moral and intellectual critical power to assess both the justice of the social bargain in its particular form and its place in the establishment of a general principle of human justice.

Within their own differing terms, both Hobbes and Locke 'solve' the problem consistently. If the bargain from the state's side can be seen to have irretrievably broken down, if, that is, the state machinery can no longer supply peace, security and protection against predators, within and without, divorce, as in contemporary marriage, is allowed; much more grudgingly by Hobbes than by Locke, for the obvious reason that Hobbes had only to justify a return to another and he would have hoped, more successfully absolute authority: the ground had only to be cleared for a more efficient edifice of power. Locke had also to justify a recent revolution of an approved type, which, we admitted, established some 'liberties' for some people.

Hobbes wanted to justify any state in power: Locke wanted to justify one particular one. In either case, the *right* of rebellion — that is, the right to reject an unfulfilled bargain — is not seriously envisaged as part of the historical and social logic of that bargain. It is a necessary clause in the legal document put in to justify the theory of 'consent' and perhaps to disguise its abstract and fictional nature and its lack of connection with freedom, as anyone realizes or experiences it, as something that must include free and informed decision-making or genuine participation in decisions. (I am really only saying that in practice the dividing line between 'liberals' and authoritarians has been and still is narrow: and that even the 'Fathers of Liberalism' such as Locke and Mill have not been free of paternalism.)

In general the weakness of contractualism, even of the most liberal and moral kind, is that the contract is in practice not a bargain but a pig-in-a-poke.*

The leading contractualists have not been liberals, at least not in the modern sense of the word, however vague that may be. The Social Contract, in whatever version, implies consent, and consent must be free. At heart the liberal cannot see how consent can be freely and consciously given except by individuals. At heart he also believes that our individual freedom cannot be wholly alienated. (I mean that he *feels* these things, often inarticulately: they are part of his definition of being a liberal, often not more than semi-conscious.) But consent, whether as a contract or as mere average acquiescence, is consenting to the surrender of a portion of that individual liberty that ought to be inalienable. Indeed the radical liberal has to compromise not only with his feelings but to some extent with his principles to accept a sovereign society at all, even the most democratic: consent in this individualistic sense is, as a concept, perhaps more meaningless in contemporary democratic societies even than in authoritarian states, where at least it can be consciously if tacitly withheld.

The radical liberal, like Mill, does not believe that anyone else

---

* In at least one distinguished modern version the poke is enclosed in another poke. The practice of acquiescence or even 'assent' can be a perfectly fair description of the ways in which people actually get into groups to organize any common purpose whose fulfilment must be of long continuation and therefore cannot be wholly foreseen or predicted. Nevertheless this cannot be described as a contract or bargain: rather as a one-sided agreement not to ask difficult questions and therefore not to keep one's eyes open. In *A Theory of Justice*, John Rawls has sought to re-establish a version of the Social Contract which elevates the pig-in-a-poke not only into a necessity but on to a pedestal: for in order to enter into a just society with free consent we must be ignorant of or have wiped out of our minds any knowledge or speculation of the way it might suit our private interests: or any expectation, one must add, that this or any other bargain ought to be fair—otherwise it is not a bargain. An extremely abstract example of liberal high-mindedness.

can effect consent — or surrender of natural liberty — in his (or my) name. That means not only that the contractual fiction is out, but that in strict logic and even strict social morality, any representation, however democratically elected, must be regarded as another fiction: for by functioning through a mere majority, my elected 'representatives' can cease to represent or can even obstruct my minority views.

The liberal often tries to deal with this very real obstacle to political and social justice by a political mechanism: some form of proportional representation. Indeed this is fairer and more reasonable than straight majority rule but it goes very little way towards solving the human and social problem of the just relation of freedom and power: in our industrial democracies even the definition of the problem is nebulous and stops far short of the minimal information — to be summed up as the answer to the question: *Who is manipulating whom and to what end?* — which would begin to give any political or moral significance to individual judgment and preferences. In other words, proportional representation is also a kind of fiction: whose outlines can be most clearly discerned in the representational theory of the most famous of all contractualists, Rousseau.

Contractualists of all sorts have to sell the benefits of society to those who compose it or may enter into it. The authoritarian usually does not have to try to sell it to everybody and it may be that he is not obliged to do more than fit the Contract or 'bargain' into a conception of human society which he himself regards as ideal — perhaps, like Hobbes, as scientifically accurate. In that case he knows that he is right and those who disagree with him are wrong. The more inclined to liberalism, the more the social contractualist has to take his market into account — and produce a good product: and the more difficult the sell. Those who are on the buyer's side of the counter have to be convinced that they are actually better off if they accept the purchase, even the pig-in-the-poke: because the would-be seller has first to convince himself: and of this the liberal, the pro-liberal and the would-be liberal, almost by definition, have doubts which are never wholly eradicated.

Rousseau undertook, with or without reflection, the hardest sell of all: and we may gravely doubt whether there was ever any pig in the poke at all.

Of all the contractualists he alone had an original myth to put across: a myth being different from a fantasy or a fairy story in requiring the support of history or anyway in being destroyed by demonstrable history. And though he does not fill in the details, no doubt because this was not possible, Rousseau makes in effect a kind of historical appeal. His myth refers to a natural superior Man, the inhabitant of a Golden Age, thus of a better past in actual if not measurable time. All this is included in being 'born free'. Like most myths it is essentially psychological or subjective, although it may represent the convergence of many psyches: it reflects the psychological fact that we can feel free anyway some of the time or that we feel we ought to feel or be free.

Not all liberals, and not all contractualists by any means, have to construct their political and social theories in such a fashion as to justify or rationalize, and maintain, this feeling. Locke, for instance, or Mill, may have had rather negative notions of personal liberty; of that their preoccupation with the details of possible infringement is even some evidence: they can both refer to 'freedom' or 'liberty' or 'liberties' on the one hand, or 'restraint' or 'restraints' on the other, and of course to these conditions as affecting 'Man' or 'Mankind'. But neither gives you the impression that he feels imprisoned by social life or can enter imaginatively into the condition of those who do.

Of the three contractualists probably only Rousseau was of this predominantly subjective type, with a personal and Romantic conception of freedom which he projected into theory — essentially Romantic behaviour. It did not prevent him from constructing some very illiberal doctrines which had some very illiberal implications and indeed consequences.

Russell wrote in 1946:

> Much of the Social Contract's philosophy could be appropriated by Hegel in his defence of the Prussian autocracy. Its first fruits in practice were the reign of Robespierre; the dictatorships of Russia and Germany (especially the latter) are in part an outcome of Rousseau's teaching. What further triumphs the future has to offer his ghost I do not venture to predict [*History of Western Philosophy*].

Romanticism, in so far as we are obliged to regard it as an intellectual and moral weakness, may almost be defined as this kind of projection of subjectivity; as the wilful disregard, in the interests of abstract theorization, of the natural laws and limitations which prescribe practice and implementation of the real and therefore the possible. This, in the event, either in private or public relations is a main cause of insensibility towards either rights or feelings, and therefore of actual inhumanity and cruelty. By that I mean to attack not liberal aspirations, nor the naturalness of the desire and the feeling of freedom, but to some extent its critical immaturity; in short, liberal *unconsciousness*. The price of liberty *is* eternal vigilance, not only in observing public measures and being ready to help resist those which are stupidly excessive, but in observing oneself and the uncomfortable demands of one's irremovable lodger, principle.

It is this Romanticism which has been confused for us by Rousseau with liberalism: a cruel Romanticism which has been responsible for the wild and tangential deviations of liberal thought and for much of its ineffectuality.

If we first consider the political doctrines of Rousseau in this subjective light, we can take into account the preciousness implied for him in the mere notion of 'freedom': and thus understand how it made him less rather than more able than other thinkers about human beings in society to come down to earth and practical measures. It may also help us to detect some of the more common parallels of this romanticism in human structures which are not strictly or mainly political. To put it as shortly and crudely as possible, Rousseau's attitude to freedom resembles that of the average man to his virility: it is inalienable, at least it ought to be, and therefore it has to be thought so. Nothing is more common surely than to assume that the beliefs and associations in which we have deposited our main treasure of dignity, either as egos or samples of humanity, are indestructible: that is, that their destruction is unthinkable; and therefore that their destruction does not happen (this though we have witnessed their destruction again and again, so that our only refuge from either reality or logic is fantasy, or rationalization of these unwelcome facts).

That means a paradox: Rousseau, who must have known and seen that most human societies to date had been very little concerned with human freedom—if by that we mean the enlargement of individual powers so that people actually have the feeling of discovering, using, and being encouraged to use them—had without meaning to do so, set himself the awkward task of showing us convincingly that we remain not only just as free in society as in the state of nature but more so. It is not true to say what is often believed that Rousseau — like Mill, at least at one stage — looked on society merely as a necessary evil: in fact the benefits of the bargain have been calculated with an almost mathematically precise justice: a conclusion totally inconsistent with his initial assumption about human nature and need, about the 'freedom' we were 'born' to.

Rousseau's conception of the 'state of nature' though not as in the case of Hobbes nasty and vile, was not on the other hand paradisal: it was rather, childish and undeveloped. Natural man was conceived as a somewhat Micawberish figure waiting for something to turn up, although not with the degree of consciousness implied by so much expectation; 'good' chiefly in the sense that he was not smart enough to grasp either the alarming or the stimulating possibilities of organizing for competition. Admittedly it was the seizure and institution of property that taught him to be positively bad. Even so, Rousseau seems to ignore the possibility, taken for fact by socialism and communism, that social forms have been instituted mainly to confirm the security of property* — certainly much more than that of people. He seems indeed to have had little idea of, or anyway no practical interest in, the varying economic structures of societies either existent or of the past. He thinks of slavery as social or political, not economic, one reason maybe why he thought it was only the dark side of 'liberty' — as of course it is — for some people.

Rousseau had to save freedom as a whole unsullied conception, an ideal abstraction: and the form of society which

---

* In *The Social Contract* there are two fleeting allusions. The first is in the chapter on 'Real Property', which concludes: 'instead of destroying natural equality, the fundamental compact substitutes ... an equality that is moral and legitimate and men who may be unequal in strength or intelligence, become every one equal by convention and legal right'. The second occurs as a footnote within the same chapter:

Under bad governments, this equality is only apparent and illusory; it serves only to keep the pauper in his poverty and the rich man in the position he has usurped. In fact laws are always of use only to those who possess, and harmful to those who have nothing: from which it follows that the social state is advantageous to men only when all have something and none too much.

can even partially preserve it is likely to be an abstraction too.

He is hardly to be blamed for not thinking directly in economic and social terms any more than he was able at the time to think historically. Political philosophers did not cease to be largely 'philosophical' until the time of Marx — neither the material nor the eye for observation was so far readily available for them. Yet as we see from his other writings, expecially *Discours de l'Inégalité*, Rousseau knew that inequality was a matter of real disadvantages and disabilities. One may have more than a suspicion that his preposterous formula the 'General Will' is both an over-compensation for a wilful blindness to psychological and historical fact and a rationalization to disguise, among other things, that his 'freedom' and his 'equality' are abstractions; collectivistic abstractions moreover, which reify society and are peculiarly favoured by authoritarians in disguise. Like most of us Rousseau sees that in the world as we have so far made it there is bound to be someone running the show; there is a ruling 'side'; and for subjective reasons — which, as with most of us, include an inability to imagine how this can be changed — he prefers to be on it. But his real underlying purpose to justify rule of domination is complicated by his theoretical commitment to individual liberty. The 'General Will' is a formula to save both these Janus-faces.

Rousseau distinguishes between the General Will and the Will of All. The will of all is the sum of individual wills which make up the milling floor of society; necessarily conflicting and therefore one would think better referred to as the 'Wills of All'. The General Will on the other hand, while still conceived as *my* will, is my will as an inseparable part of that Society (conceived as a legal — and superior — Person). By my voluntary participation in the Social Contract I helped to create that society as an enlarged ME. The General Will can therefore never will anything that is harmful to my interests (or that fails to express my real will). This harmonious condition arises from what I did (as a member of the People, an initial abstraction for the total multitude of Me's) in making the Contract: I/The People embodied Myself/Ourselves as the Sovereign Power — which is absolute, while it exists, but only as Me/Us. We traded, that is, our individual wills, freedoms, to form a General Will, or an absolute freedom* But there was a bargain.

* This is in fact what has happened in the present conception of the new Nation States which are only 'free' in an international Free-for-All.

We all surrender our freedoms and wills but we get back in exchange the freedoms of everybody else, of all the other parties to the Contract. We all obtain an equal share of this 'Freedom': which means in effect that we are all equal before 'the Lord' — or flat on our faces before the Sovereign, whoever or whatever in practice that may be.

At this point we might ask ourselves what sort of concept the General Will belongs to: it is not descriptive either as history or science; it is not psychological, for it does not describe the thoughts, wishes or behaviour of anyone we have ever met or are likely to meet, nor is there any reason to suppose that Rousseau himself thought that it could be classified in any of these ways; it would hardly be admitted as philosophical by the majority of contemporary philosophers, anyway of the dominant Anglo-American schools, because it is not critical or analytic. There is a case for including it in the Idealist tradition of philosophy — it certainly looks back towards Plato and points onwards towards Hegel and the neo-Hegelians who also personified and even hypostatized the state. But it appears that Rousseau, even if he was not being at all sociological, even if he was not describing what people are actually doing when they exist in or form or carry on a state, wanted something a little more realistic than that at least in the sense that it satisfied the desires of his own mind. He wanted to make sense of the social and political impulse: to justify or at least to rationalize government, even existing governments no doubt, and submission to government; but also to account for it to his own feelings. Like a spoilt rebellious child, unable to admit that he cannot get what he likes and is by no means the conqueror of the thwarting facts of existence, he must lecture us all into liking what we have got.

The doctrine of the General Will is meant to be something which the ordinary individual, if he could understand and see it, would accept as explaining what he himself wants, and what, although in the main unconsciously, he is actually doing (and in this way resembles other theories of motivation — that whatever you think you are doing you are actually doing something else — something which the theorist naturally prefers* as interpretation).

Rousseau's *Social Contract* is a continuous gloss on some of the essential implications of the General Will. It is infallible. This

* For example the Freudian theory of the Unconscious and extreme Behaviourist doctrine.

infallibility, like the Pope's, is more restricted than is popularly supposed; but it is also intended as ideological reassurance and perhaps even consolation: the individual member who voices himself in the General Will can see confidently, in retrospect upon all its enactments, that he couldn't have done anything different, even if what was enacted was something so apparently chancy as the barter of his own freedom of choice.

But it appears that the General Will is only infallible once it has revealed itself, when we or the willers have found out what it is. We do not know in advance; nor is there any evidence in advance that it is infallible. In fact it looks as if the General Will, which is also *my* will, is what no one knows except retrospectively and as revealed by the verdict of a simple majority. That is particularly awkward for Rousseau, who favoured the old City State to flatter his old homeland Switzerland, and partly through nostalgia for Rome: and believed in government by direct voice of all the citizens, already by his time a regrettable impossibility. It is after the majority vote is cast that the minority see that they were wrong; they did not know what their real will was. But how this can come about if the Will is really General *ab initio* and at the same time infallible is difficult to follow.

Rousseau's problem is representation, which he has already ruled out as invalid: indeed impossible. In my contract to exchange my individual native freedom for the necessities and advantages of society, no one can stand in for me or act as my plenipotentiary agent; I cannot alienate my own freedom. And the General Will, therefore, one would deduce, since it is also my will, cannot be expressed or enacted by majority rule. Rousseau to some extent covers himself logically by saying that the representativeness of a majority is guaranteed by some prior convention to accept it as such. (The law of majority voting is itself something established by convention, and presupposes unanimity on one occasion at least: the mythical date of the original Social Contract.) But this seems to be begging the question. And moreover the infallibility of the General Will, thus only retrospectively revealed by the mechanism of a majority vote, in whatever way that may be described, does not prevent people choosing — and so willing — a bad government, one which according to Rousseau can render the equality and the guaranteed mass-freedom for which General Willers have bartered their freedom as individuals, 'illusory'.

It appears then that the General Will is infallible as long as it risks no fallacies — something which is not the natural or even the possible way that either thought or practice operates in the real lives of either legislators or ordinary people. This difficulty is covered to Rousseau's satisfaction at least, when he makes it clear that the General Will is general because it is not particular: the General Will does not will any particular objects, decisions or applications — this we must assume is the job of the banausic branches of actual executive government. But that is not much more than a shift in naming: when the voters go to the polls they go with particular issues in mind, however muddled they may be, or however much they may have been muddled by candidates either of the government or of the opposition and, however inconfident they may be that their solitary vote will in the event bear upon these issues at all. The majority verdict is in effect the victory of another set of particular interests. If for the moment we accept Rousseau's formula of the General Will which reveals, we must remember, after the electoral event, that the minority or minorities were after all mistaken, how are we to interpret the case in point: that the minority were wrong in having any particular interests or in thinking that they had particular interests? Or — what is more plausible — in believing or hoping that these particular interests would be or could be served by the electoral result they imagined they preferred, or Willed.

This defence by which Rousseau saves the generality of his concept of General Will is an important link with later contractualism; and also, since most contractualists are in the general stream of liberalism, it bears on the conceptual difficulties and commitments of a liberal. For though most of them have not favoured the formula in itself, liberals and self-styled liberals, politically concerned or non-political, have a penchant, perhaps nostalgia, for the noumenal world which makes it hard for them to distinguish among fictions, legal fictions, useful or constructive fictions, and fictional distortions. That further makes it difficult for them to understand that generalizations about human behaviour or conditions can only be valid or useful if they are based on real experience of those conditions and that behaviour: generalizations do generalize particulars, and for that reason accurate and meaningful generalizations are hard to come by; but justice, which is not an abstraction but also entails the effort of accurate realization, demands that we, or at least the liberal, should try.

Obviously for the liberal the doctrine of contractualism is meaningless unless it bases itself on the meaningful consent of mature, free individuals. (In other words, it is either meaningless or fraudulent.) He cannot extract this consent from Rousseau's General Will whose plausibility he must even reject as a way of justifying or rationalizing the desired social arrangements of authoritarians, who often use an analogous mysticism for this end, distilled from the historical tradition of thought to which Rousseau really belongs and which, it was said, links him to Plato and Hegel and the neo-Hegelians. In this intellectual sense alone the historicity of the Social Contract can be said to matter: in modern political philosophizing it lingers or recurs chiefly as a metaphor or – in the doctrine of consent – as a structural abstraction. But the tradition recurs or re-emerges parallel to other forms of bad 'history' – anthropological or evolutionary and ethological – many, though not all, of recognizably authoritarian colour.* These are important to a liberal, relying for much of his human content on 'scientific' research and not by any means always able to draw the line between science and ideology.

With some of these authoritarians, lip-service to 'consent' is seen as a requirement or an equipment. They have to posit a 'social instinct' which includes an instinct of submission or a pecking-order. You 'consent' not only to the loss of individual freedom but to being kicked around – in an orderly way for your own good.

Contractualism, among other things, is the liberal's apologia: in its historical or semi-historical version it defends the notion that he, we or some of us did at some time start off to grow freedom even if the crop withered: and in its psychological or symbolic form it suggests that freedom is in our nature, given a chance.

So liberal political philosophy is generally justificatory; as opposed to the practical authoritarians it remains affected by the emotional tradition of Rousseau that begins with the assumptive axiom that we are 'born free' and the feeling that this sacrifice of natural freedom has to be compensated. That feeling, if allowed

---

* Freud's imaginary anthropology of the primal horde and the memory-traces of racial guilt for murdering the sexually all-powerful old man of the tribe, is a case in point. See *Moses and Monotheism.*

F

to function consistently, puts all collective authority if not in the dock at least in the witness box, and calls upon it to justify itself.

Notwithstanding, liberal theory has strongly inclined to do this work for it – to justify government, the state, the rule of majorities (democracy) often in terms of abstract principles and reification of institutions which neglect the actual private and social needs either of minorities or individuals.*

It may be said that the liberal political philosopher is not a sociologist and it may well be replied that probably he ought to be; at least to the extent of studying the ethics of economic life which involves the actual distribution of real power, economic, social, and cultural, among competing groups; the realization that we live in a market society; and the confession that that is where liberal philosophy began: at the point when a new concentration and stabilization of power had to be justified, generally by the rationalization, in some form or another, that that special concentration was for the greater good of everybody, including all the others who resist it. Contractualism in short is typical liberal theory just because it is a market theory, a theory of the fair bargain. But the fair bargain is supremely difficult to decide upon in the abstract: simple observation shows us that social fairness must at least be struggling to accommodate and balance the actual needs of the actual individuals (rooted in the real complications of their initial families and groups) with whom functionaries and administrators are in intimate contact. A system which is trying to be democratic may be excused if it runs by rule-of-thumb methods, including case-precedents – even if as a political and legal system it is less than totally efficient for everybody, instead of only for some, probably the comparatively few. The benefits of this natural muddle accrue from the dim (or democratic) recognition that the principles of justice are embedded in actual situations, public and private, of conflicting interests; and are revealed, one hopes, as precedents for future (and improved) use, in the attempts of parties concerned to straighten them out.

All that means admitting the sway of the market – in its widest sense, admission that in all our relations with others we propose some exchange which we intend to be of benefit to ourselves. That

---

* The neo-Hegelian T. H. Green (1836–82) rejected on stoutly individualistic liberal principle, the totalitarianism and state-worship implicit in Hegel's thought but inconsistently compromises with *social* authority.

need not preclude the benefit (though often indirect and even subsidiary) of others: the admission also may be done with regret and even disapproval and, in so far as it is real, not without hope of grace for ourselves and all.

The liberal thinker often lacks or evades this recognition (as of his actual market origins) and inclines to withdraw into the abstract contemplation first of freedom and then of justice: and, in so far as he is a contractualist, of what would constitute the per-fectly fair bargain in the distribution of all the powers between people, and those who are running the show and supposed to be representing, not competing, with their interests.

That political societies which a liberal, vague or philosophical, would recognize as democratic, are based on an assumed or theor-etical consent, may then be taken as an axiom of liberal discourse: and, as an axiom of the conceptual criticism of liberalism, that 'consent' itself is a Pickwickian legalistic fiction. It can be left aside at the moment, as a problem of liberal political theory: with its perennial scandal (or one of them) with which it from time to time has done its best to deal, often in ways — for instance propor-tional representation — which are not impractical as *ad hoc* methods but which leave the theoretical, and moral, dilemma unresolved: in a total opposition, either of majority versus minority, or of competing minorities.

'Consent' in fact strongly resembles Rousseau's hypostatic con-cept of a 'General Will' (which is no particular person's will); among other things, in the mystical-idealistic implication that where it is invisible it is still somehow potential; it can, as it were, be realized on one's behalf, by communal convention, over one's unconscious or unenlightened or even *unwilling* head: dissenting, as part of a minority, one is really consenting without knowing it.

What we have to ask ourselves here is what consent, especially consent in advance, ought to be expected to consent to. For the liberal this must surely mean that he rejects the Rousseauvian generality, the pig-in-the-poke.

If we can suppose that we were or could ever be in a position to 'consent' we should still not, while remaining human beings of average intelligence, feel called upon to sign a blank cheque: and in fact we do not do so; and the more intelligent among us do for a good part of the time demand particular and precise information at least about what is relevant to our own concerns more or less generously defined. That we do not get it is another matter: although that frustration may easily reduce us to the level of the bewildered majority who do not know what particulars they should be looking for, and for that very reason, cannot be said to 'consent' to anything.

A recent book of marked intellectual skill which has already achieved considerable reputation in philosophical circles is *A Theory of Justice* by John Rawls. Strictly, as its title suggests, this is a work of ethical philosophy, but the dividing line between political and ethical philosophy is often difficult to draw.

The book is deliberately and conscientiously abstract; as an ethical philosopher, Mr Rawls, one would say, belongs to what is sometimes called the 'Objectivist School' — his long-term aim is to try and establish moral principles of 'absolute' or universal validity. It may therefore seem legitimate that he should begin by purifying his argument as much as possible from extraneous particulars of a personalistic kind or from actual descriptive applications; or, as already referred to, from what philosophers call 'psychologism' — consideration of the actual contingencies of human conduct, which may seem to some of us to demand understanding in their own right rather than to be immediately brought under some rule of generalization or classification which has to ignore their indestructible nobbliness.

The book admittedly is about the *principles* of justice: but as a sophisticated version of the Social Contract it has not only to try and define what would be the conditions of general agreement on the principles of justice, but also how a social and political organization could be acceptably constructed to embody those just principles. But Mr Rawls seems to believe, with other philosophers of conceptual analysis, that it is both possible and proper to isolate the structure of concepts from their usage and practice.

His method, in this case, is to postulate an 'original position', for his contracting parties, of primal innocence. They are conceived, that is, as free from any particular qualifications. Nevertheless, in this totally negative situation they have to be capable of agreeing on two sets of characteristics which would essentially qualify an acceptable principle of justice:

First: each person is to have an equal right to the most extensive basic liberty compatible with a similar liberty for others.

Second: social and economic inequalities are to be arranged so that they are both (a) reasonably expected to be to everyone's advantage, and (b) attached to positions and offices open to all.

This limited presumption of a conceptual and experiential blankness seems to be inconsistent and even to beg the important question: in the first place it appears that the parties can be conceived as equal only *because* they had also been conceived as ignorant; because all the things — goods, goals, events, classifications — which would make them know about the nature of inequality had been ruled out for a start. This ignorance would apply to the whole of history (which, as history, and as a continuing thread, if not in all its branches and aspects, is the history of injustices). We may be willing even to accept that public history is not necessary to the construction of Mr Rawls's initial position, which is purposely Ideal. On the other hand, private or personal history is also ruled out. The parties to this ideal contractual commission on justice maintain the state of innocence also about their own individual selves, their own interests and needs, their own status in relation to potential justice or injustice, and hence even their own identity as it would be located by their standing and connection with other human beings.

Mr Rawls does not describe this theoretical initial position as 'innocence', as I have done; he uses the term 'ignorance' — the parties seeking to establish an agreed theory of justice do so 'behind a veil of ignorance'. When we remember that his intention is logical and analytical — to be able to say what is comprised in the pure conception of justice and what is excluded from it; what we can be said to know *a priori* about 'justice'; and what, on advance theoretical grounds we cannot claim to know — ignorance seems a better word. I chose 'innocence', deliberately and tendentiously to indicate that Mr Rawls has already got into Utopia: his initial contractual situation is none the less Utopian because it offers a strictly logical construct; all Utopias are constructs and they all in effect claim to be logical in the sense of self-consistent.*

---

* This has nothing to do with their real applicability; though it may well be that the more self-consistent the less applicable: Utopias, by semantic definition are likely to be much less descriptive than Cacotopias which often refer closely to existing societies — e.g. George Orwell's.

The inconsistency and effectual circularity of Mr Rawls's state of conceptual innocence are more strikingly obvious in the case of the second proviso. Equality cannot, as we see, be really conceived as *tabula rasa*, and neither can justice itself whose principle is the theme: for the second postulate, or assumption to be agreed, already prescribes something essential, some *sine qua non* of the way in which 'social and economic equalities' are to be justly arranged – these innocents are already supplying to the idea of justice an unpredictably positive content. It all sounds as if we were being asked to accept at least the project for an economic social and moral edifice and being bidden, at the same time, to assume that it is not yet possible, and perhaps may never be, to lay our hands on any materials or dig any foundations – since we have foresworn the know-how; we are asked to conceive some premises but no bricks.

This reveals the special significance of Mr Rawls's explanatory subtitle. His theme is 'A Theory of Justice as Fairness'; that must mean, among other things, a theory of justice, not only as social justice – justice between individuals and competitive groups – but also economic and distributive justice. A state of 'justice' would in practice imply that people are getting fair shares. But this is not something which can be conceived abstractly or in advance; 'justice as fairness' can have meaning only in actual social relations – where there is something, or are some things, to be distributed, fairly or not: that further implies that Mr Rawls's 'Difference Principle' (as the second proviso becomes known during and throughout the development of the book is something which the willing or consenting participants in a democracy adopt as their clearly visible and practicable principle of justice; it would be seen by a sufficient number of citizens as the way to make their democratic society work. But this is to assume not only (again in advance of, or we might in this case say in contradiction of, experience) that a sufficient number of the citizens concerned in any distribution of social values – immediate goods and benefits, resources, time, capacitations like education and so on – will be able to see the most highly advantageous arrangement for everyone, either including or apart from themselves, but that those who have this clearest vision will love it when they see it. It is moreover to assume that those who lack the vision (again in advance, their eyes being, if not blind, shut) will accept it from those who have it;

still more importantly that on the strength of this superior vision, whether they share it or not, those to whom it apportions a lower standard in the distribution will dutifully accept it as fair and do their prescribed share in making the distribution work. In short, among the things that Mr Rawls's contractualists sign away in advance is a principle of individual equality (it is not important to consider here whether this is anyway chimerical, only to note that they forswear it): and at the same time they consent in advance to a principle of hierarchy (probably in the form of a meritocracy). Mr Rawls in theory is not trying to give even a working blueprint of justice or actual 'fairness' in a democratic society. In defining what is to be believed or accepted about 'justice as fairness' in his ethical democracy, he ignores or sets aside the experienced probability that the practical definers will still be the top classes (those who through greater strength of wits or financial resources have got to the top). They will be, as now, judge and jury — also on behalf of the bottom classes — to decide what is distributive justice; or fairness.

We have come, it appears, to the real disjunction between liberal and socialistic theories of both political and social justice; socialistic democratic theory is in intention at least strictly egalitarian, in the statistical or individual-atomic sense; it is on that basis that justice is conceived as fair shares and, even if it is fictitious and understood to be so, it provides the guiding socialist ideal: understandably, because throughout their history socialists have been professionally committed to dealing with a situation of gross material inequality and justice. Beneath moral parity, it has not needed, to honest and humane eyes, any special or abstract moral definition. Thus, however collective their organization, with whatever hopes or intentions of fraternity, both socialists and communists have at their best not been able to produce any very convincing model of a living and creative community life which their free equal and statistic individual might be able to build on his established fair share: their agenda for the individual only allows for moral adjournment.

I am not for a moment suggesting that liberals in general have been any better at working out an inviting or even a likely futurology for a humane community. Nor, as I have tried to show, have they been particularly successful at the empathic realization and presentation of the human individual or therefore in avoiding the statistical or atomic treatment; in this way they have hardly if at all improved on the socialistic imagination. Nevertheless, however little they have been able to apply it, the belief that 'Man' is potentially a moral being – that includes an imaginative and creative one – is part of their philosophy. Theoretically their agenda of the order of rights is one of release: 'Man' will (in certain conditions) come into his moral own and that is the purpose and goal of equality. One starts with equal rights because rights are right: individual people have an inalienable (or abstract or heaven-sent) right to make the most of themselves spiritually and materially: and these two aims have to be achieved more or less concurrently, otherwise liberalism disappears in the crevasse. Democratic socialists, if not communists, would and do give lip-service at least to this liberal intentionality and to the more rounded conception of human being which it implies (and to which the liberals also give only lip-service). That is, many liberals are philosophically idealists and many socialists are emotionally liberals: the distinction is that socialists believe that moral adjournment is not only possible but necessary: in other words, that the complexity of human needs can be unravelled and dealt with, according to some best logical and temporal order, which can be objectively established. If liberals do not believe this they generally have to behave as if it were true. Liberals therefore are not very happy, or anyway do not achieve very happy results when, at any part of their discussion, they are obliged to consider equality – abstract equality, equal rights, and so on. (On the difficult subject of what are really *human* 'rights' see Maurice Cranston, *What are Human Rights?*.)

As soon at least as they approach consideration of the real conditions of human life in society liberals appear to have been using the wrong map and to be faced with an impossible ravine: equality of rights, which implies an aboriginal and inalienable nature, is on one side: that of theory; and life in any group, society or community, is on the other: that of practice. And the one does not necessarily connect with the other or may indeed be in contradiction with it.

Mr Rawls's two provisos then are in different and incompatible categories. The first derives from the abstract theory of natural rights – that men are naturally free and equal; and it implies that a society would be moral or just in so far as it distributed its dues and benefits according to this definition of equality; the 'fair shares' of whatever it is, would be, at least ideally, equal shares. But Mr Rawls does not appear to admit this implication of his first proviso, which is simply an analytical statement of what could be taken as right if we had rights: something which cannot be assumed *a priori* if we start from either a state of nature or a state of 'ignorance'. Those are more alike than we might at first conceive. In the second proviso (p. 153) Mr Rawls is talking about what would be the social basis for fair or just distribution, while ignoring the natural equality which is his first proviso: he starts in fact from the assumption that the principle of justice which it is his object to research has, in the establishment of social organization, itself also been established. Or that it is not only the intention but the formative principle of democratic societies to order themselves around fair distribution in such a way that all the members of the society (or group) will be satisfied morally as well as materially: they will see that justice has been done in a special optimum sense: no one will be in the situation of 'winner takes all', nor therefore anyone in the situation of total loser: all will be able to confess that their comparative needs and dues have been taken into account.

But by whom? For democratic social justice there must surely be the means of agreed communal assessment of both abilities and needs. It is surely not insignificant that in all the forms, phases, and degrees of democracy, liberal or socialistic, that we have so far witnessed, this has not only not been achieved but hardly seems on the way to achievement.

We see that ordinary egalitarian or statistical 'equality' is irrelevant to Mr Rawls's discussion of justice: and that he is substituting something he calls 'fairness' (which would indeed no doubt result in 'fair shares' even perhaps in the sense that they would generally be regarded as fair). But throughout the book he does not seem to recognize that he is confusing an objective with a subjective category (one referring to *de facto* political and economic organization, the other moral and psychological): there is a confusion between, on the one hand, a *principle* of fairmindedness and, on the other, fair distribution.

To this particular fallacy the liberal mind, no doubt because of its preference for an Idealistic philosophical climate and its faith also in the Original Virtue of the human individual (never quite forsworn) is prone above the average. It is one of the ways in which theoretical political liberalism becomes, to the outsider anyway, indistinguishable from theoretical socialism. In the case under discussion, a thesis which is committed to the discovery of a principle of fairness (justice), Mr Rawls becomes more and more occupied with fair distribution: a question, one might imagine, which we cannot begin to decide until we have been able to show in what fairness consists: and where we can discover and recognize it. That in turn must depend on a predominant fairmindedness (or *preference* for fair play) in the community; and that we have to be shown how to achieve. Here the liberal theorist is no more successful than anyone else, although probably more evasive.

Faced with the appalling difficulties of even imagining, let alone helping to create, what would be in his own terms a genuinely free society, the liberal fideist not infrequently relies upon a miracle. He has recourse to the millennial hope which is represented in the third member of the Liberal trinity—perhaps it is the Holy Ghost: fraternity in some guise or other: the realization of their brotherhood by all men in whom it must have been potentially present in their Original Goodness. (Socialists and communists can employ the full slogan—and still do, very liberally—because they have no commitment to a subjective individual.)

I am not calling Mr Rawls a 'liberal fideist'—one can only guess at the way he would formulate his social views and hopes—I only say that his book illustrates patterns of liberal thinking.

Of course he scrupulously avoids emotions and slogans. But at the back of his impeccably 'philosophical' analysis there is the unavoidable implication that there is no visible solution for the injustices of our society which does not involve a change in the values, purposes and relations of ordinary people from crude self-interest to a more welcoming awareness of the Other. Mr Rawls actually uses the words 'fraternity' several times and in a way that assumes it as essential to human relations when they appear to work at all—e.g. some aspects of fairly typical family life. (This is also true of other democratic analysts, e.g. C. B. MacPherson, later discussed: see p. 251).

Later this Third Person of the liberal Trinity must be considered. But first there is something more to be said about the Second—'Equality'. If we accept—with, in effect, most people of any political complexion—that 'equality' is mainly a statistical notion only applicable in very limited and shallow conditions of *treatment*, like birthday cakes or old age pensions, we may think that it would always have been better to refer to this department, as 'Justice'. This Mr Rawls mainly does: *Justice as fairness* is his theme. But if we interpret this, as in his context we are entitled to do, as 'fair shares' the quantitative conception of 'equality' still remains uncomfortably visible, resisting digestion into the moral notion of Justice.

Justice, most democrats would agree, is not an arbitrary matter, it demands both a principle and an administration which can be universally recognized; and it must be 'seen' to be done – in both senses: we must be able to see that the administrators are doing their honest and intelligent best, both to discover the principle and then apply it and make it work. We may only be able to recognize in social behaviour what is, in the visible condition, just or unjust: but there must also be something which we can discern which shows that fairness is fair and justice just.

Mr Rawls's 'Difference Principle', which develops from Proviso 2 of *A Theory of Justice* formulates distributive justice (or fairness) to the effect that gains or advantages made by some are just if they entail some benefit to those who in the social context are worse situated. While this may well be accepted as a working definition of social and economic justice it is not descriptive of any society we have known; that is to say, we have never known a just society according to this definition; and it entails no motivation to form a different one.*

Even if it were true that enough people could be found who were fired with the idea and intention that they would not benefit themselves or their connections in a way that would leave any other people concerned in the operation worse off, even if they all intended and aimed at leaving the lot of the other parties somewhat improved, they would not know how to succeed; and the history not only of our democracies, but of all socialminded movements – which is also the history of omelettes and eggs – appears to confirm that they would not.

Through natural insensibility, a principle of benevolence –

---

* It works out as a justificatory formula for the laissez-faire of Mandevillian free-enterprise society: that is, if not precisely justifying 'private vices, public benefits', it lends too much status to the striving individual acting as a moral arbiter – he will benefit his own group or family according to his lights: those bits of his society that he can see.

utilitarianism in operation – is inevitably despotic to some people in some of their needs and to some people in all of them.

Recognizing that 'equality' has very little meaning, many liberals now substitute 'equality of opportunity'. So, at first sight perhaps surprisingly, do many thinkers in other fields, not necessarily political – who appear at least covertly anti-democratic.

Even Mr Rawls's 'Difference Principle', leaving the assessment and apportionment of benefit and 'opportunities' for others to those who are better off, in whatever the given situation may be, can be interpreted as paternalistic. It tells us nothing about the fairness of fair shares, it cannot enlighten us about 'equality of opportunity'.

As things are, the liberal can hardly help cherishing this notion as still his most practical hope for social and cultural justice. With it at least he recognizes some of the impracticability of his original axiomatic 'equality' and attempts a transference to the actual world of social compromise. But he still believes in a natural justice based on needs and capabilities of individual people which the formula 'equality of opportunity' best serves: all he has to do is to look for a real and recognizable content for it. But here he can be caught in a circularity. For instance, he can agree with what Mr Rawls implies: that equality of opportunity is a case of distributive fairness; but as we are, and as our societies have worked out, somebody or some people would have both to discriminate and to apportion the 'opportunities'; and that would immediately prevent them being equal. Real opportunities must respond to real preferences of real people; and they can only be *just* (since we have to discard 'equal' as too ambiguous) if they are discovered or created by those people for themselves. Benevolence – if it were available, and even in the intellectual form of Mr Rawls's 'Difference-Principle' that we all understood and saw the necessity of arranging our own benefits always to include the benefit of others – could not, in justice, do more than leave the opportunities lying across their paths: in justice to free men they themselves must be allowed to decide what are 'opportunities'.

Moreover to give the opportunity of these opportunities, with any clear intention of good will, would imply that a majority had already absorbed and adopted the principles of justice and fairness as the working ethos of our society.

Clearly if there is any movement in this direction it is so far only superficial. We may think that what we vaguely lump together as our liberal-democratic-societies — and there are not too many even with those which vaguely profess to emulate our vague principles — more nearly embody the ideals of justice and fairness than any others the world has so far known; and if we are to be described, if vaguely, as liberal-democrats, that is what we have to think. But still the concrete embodiment is elusive: justice remains rough; at its best — its more liberal and democratic — it is a ring held to circumscribe the competition of warring groups as much as possible: perhaps chiefly to define it as acceptable gamesmanship. There is always the root-dilemma: for collectives — in which we all live — justice can only approximate to the abstraction of the legal terms in which it has to be expressed, and refers at its most realistic to generalizations of special and conflicting interests. The liberal still wants to give *each man* his own; he still wants society to start from the individual, embodying certain natural and inalienable claims which appear as its duties, the first charge upon all its resources. If this means anything at all it demands absolute respect for all human personality, which is also the axiom of Christianity; there seems no clear reason why it should be more successful. However anxious and careful one may be to distinguish political and economic liberalism, at its peak in the last century, from the modern liberal spirit — which is homogeneous only sporadically in resisting given and identifiable aspects of authoritarianism — one may more than suspect that the principle of individuality which we retain from our forerunners has a dangerously high concentration of old laissez-faire in its system, which also perhaps we cannot eliminate.

Examining the actual distribution of 'opportunities' one may come to think that it looks at least as fair, and only as fair, as a treasure-hunt; in fact that in Western democracies the treasure hunt is the true inheritance of laissez-faire. The metaphor applies best where competition is still 'free'; that is, unregulated and therefore above a certain level of existing economic success or viability. The treasure-hunt, that is to say, takes place on the upper floors only, or where the treasure is; still a large area covering the worlds of what we call culture, as well as big sideline business, e.g. directorships for peers and ex-statesmen. It is perhaps only the liberal who sees with any hope that if a semblance of democracy is to survive, the treasure-hunt has to be controlled, if not superseded by the rules of what appears to be a more ethical gamesmanship.

At this point he has to be careful not to join a new kind of hypocritical convention, merging with other groups whose thinking is really quite alien to his own but who have this in common, that they have found a practical use for the verbal slogan 'equality of opportunity': not only as cover for their different beliefs and intentions, but as a sop to democracy and as a psychological weapon — often against it. Because they generally look on even the definition of either equality, or equality of opportunity, which a liberal could genuinely accept, as not only impracticable but irrelevant, they do not have to share or even much examine his problems.

That does not mean that 'equality of opportunity' cannot be used as a Trojan Horse. Those, many nowadays, who, on 'scientific' grounds, either biological or psychological, propose what they regard as a better, more natural society, based on 'natural inequality', often stoutly support it, knowing no doubt how difficult it is to pin them down. For the same confusion of category applies here: 'equality of opportunity' cannot be defined with total objectivity; it implies some power of insight, with some imaginative estimation, into real needs, first one's own and then those of others.

8

The Opium of the Omegas

There are various studies and schools of thinking about mankind which converge upon the idea of the Inequality of Man. That is not at all a new idea; in fact equality is the novelty. In many parts of the world the main social distinction has been between master and subordinate (if not slave): the world history of liberty has been of a very partial enfranchisement, sometimes gradual, sometimes explosive (and insecure) of sporadic groups.

The liberal may recognize that our inequalities are real; but he would like to compensate them and make us as equal as nature will allow. Many if not most of the individuals and the schools of thought to which I shall now refer have a different aim — at least as a priority. They are convinced of our inequality — often with a realistic backing of properly controlled and tabulated observation, let alone respectable statistics; but in general they see that many of us are not convinced of it and, moreover, intensely dislike it (which makes for resistance to conviction, anyway). They see also therefore that they must sell us this idea; at the same time that it will be a hard sell, and that many of us will insist on a balance of payments. 'Equality of opportunity' is what we are offered in exchange for our illusion of equality.

The cases I am about to discuss fall into two classes: or perhaps one may be allowed to say, two sects. What links them is the acceptance of the idea of 'equality of opportunity', either overt or implied. The acceptance may be more apparent than real and may indeed be little more than lip-service to a conventional ideal which has become, if not sacrosanct to analysis, a cliché. Admittedly, 'equality of opportunity' is not easy to estimate let alone to realize, and in the cases I shall discuss neither 'sect' seems to manifest any very clear or practical notion of the way the difficulties ought to be tackled.

The parties of the first part are scientists – 'human' scientists; behavioural psychologists, ethologists, or ethological popularizers. By different methodological approaches they all arrive at a similar twofold assertion that men are not only naturally unequal but that societies are (*or ought to be*) to an important extent structured to embody this inequality. I am not (at present) challenging the claim that the methods by which they all reach this dual conclusion are orthodoxly scientific. At the moment I merely comment that the consolation prize which they offer, 'equality of opportunity', may appear like a gratuitous generosity which in the security and confidence of their scientific rectitude they feel able to afford. It doesn't mean that they have given any thought, scientific or otherwise, to the practical, social, emotional or ethical consequences of their human generalization. Some of them, no doubt, take the view that science – 'human' science not less than any other – is morally neutral, a subject already discussed which will be referred to again. (It must be added, in passing, that that subject is still very much alive to argument and does not become less so in the case of the 'human' sciences which, because of their subject-matter, are better able to produce predictions about human behaviour, of a self-fulfilling kind – or 'oedipal' as Karl Popper calls this kind of prophecy in *The Poverty of Historicism*.)

By the technical or engineering methods with which they are inevitably associated they can more or less forcibly or more or less subtly alter the development of what they observe: they can help to induce human beings to conform to the 'human' pattern they claim to have discovered; and do it in the impeccable name of science.

That, it appears, is the real danger, particularly of behavioural science: the scientists' intellectual claims may be demonstrable, a true if partial description of existing 'human' nature – or rather behaviour; the danger is in the fact that they can make them work, *make them come true*.

In the section that follows, the discussion is mainly based on an analysis of H. J. Eysenck's 1973 volume *The Inequality of Man*. Here he refers to and summarizes much of the prominent work that has been more recently done on the genetic study of human intelligence. Most of it supports his own conclusions but he offers some criticisms (e.g. of Herrnstein) where it diverges from them (not very seriously, at least in its social implications).

Much of Eysenck's earlier work was directed not only to intelligence tests but to the testing of personality. For a theoretical discussion of the inequality of Man this can at present be largely left aside. For one reason, Eysenck himself touches on it comparatively lightly, his main concern being with intelligence and its heritability. Another reason is that Eysenck appears, anyway at first sight, to take a more liberal view of the social claims of personal differences than one might have expected from his earlier work on behavioural diagnosis and treatment.

In *The Inequality of Man* he puts forward what appears to be the reasonable belief that we ought to be more scientific in our judgments of human nature and behaviour if we want to improve society and that so far we have fallen lamentably short in this respect. Obviously, one of our worst shortcomings is that our social and educational system still provides no kind of guarantee that the right person will get the right job or status; in other words, there are far too many round pegs in square holes and vice versa. (However, we may think that Eysenck treats the nature of holes lightly, ignoring that they are formed by the self-structuring of an established system.) But Eysenck thinks that a scientific assessment of pegs will go a long way towards improving the fit with the available holes.

We can accept that for certain purposes and certain jobs at least, the tests are as valid as the rule-of-thumb methods of those natural psychologists, experienced managers and army leaders and their like; and almost certainly fairer, in that they are more open to public scrutiny. But there are possibilities of wider applications. They can be used to influence or even decide collective policy towards individuals (who may include not only 'criminals' but other 'deviants'; and *they* may include those who are simply not up to the 'scientifically' accepted standard of mental and social health or — I fear, with no extreme extension — those who are maverick in their views).

In the case of intelligence, Eysenck's strictly hereditarian view implies that nothing, educationally, psychotherapeutically or socially, can be done that will make any considerable alteration in the individual's level. The matter of interest here is that Eysenck does not seem to hold entirely to such an unshakably pessimistic prognosis in the case of personality — in spite of what one would imagine to be its far more complex elements. Eysenck believes that personality can be changed. He means of course where it is unsatisfactory: we must agree that he *also* wishes to mean 'where it is unsatisfactory to the personality immediately concerned' and he appears to be scrupulous about the ethical question involved when an opportunity for change is offered by outside authorities and experts. There is some question whether or not this is a real inconsistency with his behavioural system which, like Skinner's, treats personality as an environmental response and therefore essentially adaptable by physical (often 'aversive') methods: but not by rational persuasion and conviction. (See B. F. Skinner, *Beyond Freedom and Dignity*.)

For example, he gives favourable consideration to what is known as the 'token' treatment of convicted criminals (obviously in need of 'personality' therapy).* This is a system of rewards and remissions for good conduct and co-operation in work tasks and schemes. The 'token' is the quantity of pay or privilege you can earn according to performance. Eysenck is inclined to favour this system as a humane and reasonable approach to the demands both of justice and of rehabilitation. He is careful to add that even the token system, liberal though it may seem, must be introduced to the prisoner by rational persuasion which leaves him 'free' to choose it or not. There must be, we may say, no smell of 'Daddy knows best': and there must be no suggestion that Daddy is going to make his own usual independent decision. But it must be said that this tenderminded concern for freedom of choice – which might look even touchingly old-fashioned – either for the criminal or the 'pathological' class, comes from Professor Eysenck as an agreeable surprise. It is certainly a change from his earlier engineering therapy. In his previous work, which refers to reconditioning social and moral misfits, he has generally been satisfied to accept that the social situation in which the subject finds himself (from prison to social obloquy – the latter may be a response to e.g. 'deviant' sexual habits: see *Fact and Fiction in Psychology*) is sufficient argument for a 'cure' or an adaptation which is in effect imposed by professional psychological authority. It is true that where he deals with the description of methods and the estimate of successes

---

* The quotation marks refer to Eysenck's definition of 'criminality' – it is what society has legally proscribed: this definition is acceptable to strict Machiavellians but not readily to others who think about it: and certainly not to the most moderate liberals.

in such 'cures' or adaptations, Professor Eysenck insists that 'consent' to aversion-therapy or drug treatment for habitual legal offence is and must be obtained. But that hardly eliminates all blackmail from the proceedings. People do not 'consent' to a radical alteration of personality unless they are convinced that that way is the only exit from punishment or from pariahhood.

Now when Eysenck speaks of 'consent' it seems clear that he means consent of a consenting adult—informed consent, therefore, which is genuinely willing and preferential. Nevertheless that does not invalidate the general criticism that 'personality', including 'criminal' personality, is being defined (like intelligence) according to the norms, both statistical and narrowly selected, of a society which has not been evaluated and which may itself be immoral if not criminal.

While we may welcome Eysenck's signs of conversion to suasive methods (and of aversion to 'aversion' therapy or 'treatment'), we may still question that this relieves us from the authoritarian implication.

What the liberal (and I) must still leave open is the question: In what sense are we to accept the behavioural and ethological generalizations about the structure of human behaviour and psychology? Suppose that we come to be convinced of their accuracy, are we necessarily obliged to alter either our concept of society or our social behaviour, to accord with them? The scientific answer of course would be (and is) that to act in any other way is nonsense; when we have at last discovered, or had revealed to us, the real and therefore ineluctable laws of human behaviour dictated by evolutionary biology, we must—for the first time no doubt, but also for the foreseeable future—build our societies around them.

This is still an open question—and must remain so—partly because it comes under the much wider question: Is science to be accorded, at least in principle, not merely intellectual authority (which lasts only so long as it demonstrates itself as intellectually valid) but absolute authority, not only to conduct completely footloose research, but to pursue and even to organize without limit, all the practical consequences of its discoveries?

For a liberal, committed to freedom of thought and inquiry, that wider question is crucial (unless he regards it as no longer a question), but he should bear in mind at least that liberalism has always been an aspiration, a special kind of spirit which takes its spring from desire. Desire may not be totally unrealistic but admittedly it is non-logical; the desire in the case in point is at bottom to be or to achieve something better than we have. And at least we can say that if those who have felt this desire, and gone in for what seemed the corresponding behaviour, had listened to the accounts of human possibility, mostly admonitory, which have predominated throughout history, we should probably have already and finally declined into an antlike civilization acquiescent in exploitation and not precluding organized slavery. Those admonitions, or threats, have come from all, even from opposing, sides. In the past chiefly from orthodox religions; which appealed mostly to our fears. Now we have science — which of course appeals to our reason; having first prescribed and delimited what is reason.

I am aware of the dangers of the kind of scepticism I appear to advocate. My excuse, which I hope to substantiate, is that the 'scientific' psychology that so exactly and with so much moral pessimism plots the limitations of human capacity, is itself limited. That, but only in a descriptive not a theoretical sense, my chief subject, Professor H. J. Eysenck, would admit: and he would add that behavioural science has made only a beginning, but that since it is on the right road (this is an axiom) it will in time arrive at the complete account of our human being. For the moment at least I shall accept that what Eysenck says (I take him as representative because he both summarizes and criticizes the leading allied research upon the subject) is, so far as it goes, a true description of some important human behaviours and capacities.

It is a curious, possibly sad naivety, not uncommon in scientific zealots, that seems now to afflict Professor Eysenck: that in the long term if it is properly put to them people will see what is rational and love it, even when it affronts their own short-term spontaneous and egoistic wishes. In the case under discussion it is assumed that they will accept an account of their own human nature and therefore a prescription of their place in Nature as a whole and in whatever haphazard society they have grown up in, even if it is one to which they are not already predisposed or to which they are by inclination, breeding and habit, opposed. On the contrary if it is properly (that is, by rational demonstration) put to them, it is far more likely that they will be resentful: if, that is, their attention is called to the matter. Thus the question of implementation of social change or acceptance arises: the old alternative of force or fraud. Where rational argument, as here, because it offends a profound and spontaneous prejudice of feeling, must be felt as a form of force, the only alternative is some kind of emotive propaganda which, in the case of something claiming to be scientific demonstration, must smack of insidiously deceptive paternalism. It is quite arguable that intelligent meritocracy ought to run the show; even that it already does so in so far as anything gets run at all; or in other words that our Western 'democracies' would be much worse off if this sort of thing were not in practice going on. But if this either is or could be the case, the meritocratic situation strongly resembles the old-fashioned one of 'feminine' rule — it is done by wiles, and maybe unconscious ones, and not by honestly rational persuasion.

I detect or suspect in Professor Eysenck some of the characteristic weaknesses of the failed theoretical liberal. For, like many another benevolent would-be despot, he has to assume the existent intellectually loose condition of a liberal democracy to be able to put forward his ideas of social order — a better one, of course: a free market, one might say, in the selling of ideas that people do not really want, or would not want if they knew what they were getting. Many of Eysenck's social conclusions might appear, even to a liberal, to be liberal, for he is at pains to show that though the possibilities of individual self-development are unalterably limited, yet education and opportunity, based on understanding acceptance of these inbuilt curbs, would still provide the best chance for individual potential. But whereas the liberal wants vaguely, perhaps even wrongly, to help people to help themselves into becoming themselves, Eysenck and all those, of any discipline, who base themselves on human fixity are inevitably on the 'side' of paternalism, prescribed order and therefore authoritarianism. When Eysenck claims that *all* human behaviour and ability are finally to be assessed by quantitative and statistical methods, he really means *all*: in this book he touches lightly on those human capacities which are commonly lumped together as 'creative' (or original:) elsewhere he has discussed them more widely* and even more tendentiously. What is relevant here is Eysenck's sweeping and

* And so have I. See my *A Soul in the Quad* and *Encounter*, September 1964.

unsupported assertion that intelligence, objectively and comparatively measured as IQ, is still the most significant factor involved
in 'creativity' and not to be sharply distinguished from it. That of
course implies that 'creativity' will also be eventually described
and explained by the same quantitative methods. Obviously there
is something quantitative to be said about everything, even if it is
only that one thing is not another. Indeed Eysenck has already as
he puts it 'made a beginning' towards the exhaustive scientific
description of the creative processes.

In *Sense and Nonsense in Psychology* he sketched a possible quantitative assessment of creative ability. He began with a question-
naire assessing tastes – individual likes, dislikes and preferences,
for example, about colours. And very rapidly and on this ground
he made a notable step forward in aesthetic theorization: it was
very easy to find the average of preference and on this frail discovery we find that he has erected a definition of '*good taste*': it is
simply equated with the majority agreement.

At a later stage of the discussion he compares differential
examination results in student paintings. The examinations of
course were held by *experts* – e.g. professors and teachers of painting – and they reached a surprising degree of agreement in their
judgments: and in doing so, provided Eysenck with another purely
quantitative definition of 'good taste' (it depends here on the majority verdict of a number of 'experts' who are originally invoked as
arbiters of 'good taste' – a circular notion if ever there was one).

Here (and elsewhere) Eysenck seems not to notice that he is
employing two incommensurable standards: the one subjective
and individual and involving evaluation by *personal reference*; the
other objective or what in the context we might reasonably call a
'market' or 'commodity' basis, because the standard, the only one,
admittedly, that *is* measurable, is how well the students did in
their examinations (which surely implies that they were able to
supply the majority demand of that fairly close corporation, the
professors).

Taking this back into the immediate field of discussion we shall
see that it is characteristic. When Eysenck moves back, in *The
Inequality of Man*, into the field of I.Q. measurement, and seeks an
objective standard of quantification for the social effects of different degrees of intelligence, he adopts one which is strictly parallel
to the 'aesthetic' criterion just cited. He admits that it is 'rough

and ready' but proposes it without qualms on the arguable assumption that it is the only one available: Intelligence shows and proves itself in social status and prestige, measured (still more roughly, one would say) by income bracket.

It can be readily seen that this is in the same category as, in the previous example, the 'judgment of accredited experts' which we are required by Eysenck to take as the proper assessment of artistic ability. In that case, too, the experts have got the jobs (professorships, examining roles, etc.) and thus they have proved that they *are* the experts. In the social example just given, a particular minority has got the jobs and the corresponding prestige and income, and thereby shown that they have the intelligence which procures the jobs and the status. It should also be seen, not much less easily, that this is based on a circular argument; a fact which may predispose us to wonder whether Eysenck's whole analysis and that of the other 'testers' is not also circular: I.Q. is the measure of intelligence; and intelligence is what can be measured by Intelligence Testing.

It is interesting that for practical validation of even the existence of the kind of 'intelligence' which is amenable to his methods of measurement, Eysenck has to appeal to the common judgment of the man-in-the-street. *He* does know what he means by intelligence, even if he can neither define nor measure it: it turns out to be what we have said above – success in the world, as measured partly by income but still more by prestige. Here Eysenck seems inconsistent – maybe because income is hard figures while prestige is comparatively nebulous. However, although Eysenck makes a distinction, money is fairly inseparably connected with social prestige – even in the view of many men-in-the-street: large money can even buy it; one is left pondering whether J. Paul Getty had the highest I.Q. in the world with Howard Hughes as runner-up (or vice versa according to the actual figures, not easily available). There is no doubt that we can measure money: social prestige not so easily: the connection between either or both, and intelligence, very much less convincingly.

Nevertheless, let us agree that I.Q. tests as designed by Eysenck and the people on whom he relies – Jensen, Herrnstein and others – do measure intelligence as defined by Eysenck, Herrnstein and others. Let us, if we must, move into these vicious circles and then move out as quickly as possible.

We don't have to agree that the Eysenckian description is after all exhaustive: still less that its social and educational consequences are logically implied or that the opposing environmental point of view is rejected out of hand. And this is so even if we accept that intelligence, as thus defined, *is* mainly genetically conditioned, some 80 per cent according to Eysenck, as opposed to a mere 20 per cent for environmental effects.

We must remember that these designs are by no means universally accepted by other social scientists. There are, for instance, the tests devised by Liam Hudson which distinguish two types of *mind*: thus, among other things, rejecting the definition (and the notion) of intelligence as a special faculty sharply delimited and at the same time transferable to all the apparent varieties of an individual's perceptual and psychological behaviour. (See Hudson, *Contrary Imaginations* and *Frames of Mind*.)

The concept of intelligence as an innate general and therefore transferable ability is, however, fundamental to Eysenck's case. It is not an original idea. It is in line with the dominant academic psychology of the century and derives from Spearman's 'g' — a shorthand which can be used to refer to the agreement among leading psychologists such as Burt and Binet that intelligence is 'innate, general and cognitive' (roughly, that it is a capacity one is born with, to apprehend the world, and thence to make and develop logical deductions; and that this capacity is applicable in all fields).

The critics do not and have not agreed, anyway, that 'intelligence' is 'general'. But on social and educational grounds, the limitations of the definition contained in 'innate' and 'cognitive' are even more important. Before the Eysenck era, Brian Simon (identified with the view that intelligence tests are class-conditioned, which Eysenck rejects, claiming that the contrary is true) proposed that 'intelligence', if it could be isolated as a general faculty at all, was much more like a general *nous* in dealing with the real (and unpredictable) situations of life; maintaining that tests (some of which are comparable with 'Outward Bound' or learner-paratrooper survival tests) should be devised for this kind of assessment; and that children of relatively deprived environments could and did do as well as or better than the products of more sophisticated and specialized training, who probably anyway had been already slanted towards this inherently competitive concept of mental activity, in homes where there was enough money and leisure both to detect and pursue a more abstract understanding of 'reality' and to appreciate its social and cultural advantages.

Eysenck admittedly allows for the existence and the value of what he calls 'associative learning'. This part is considerably based on Arthur Jensen's *Educability and Group Differences* — a recent target for anti-genetic publicity and indeed for strong-arm methods, regrettable both as morals and tactics.

The children, a majority it appears, who have little or no capacity for conceptualization, may very well be quick at facts, quicker indeed than their schoolmates who are more gifted with the power of abstraction. They may, for example:

> coming into a new class ... learn the names of 20 or 30 children in a few days, will quickly pick up the rules and the know-how of various games on the playground ...

It is important to note that Jensen is talking about 'lower-class' children (or 'disadvantaged'—he uses this one of our more nauseating euphemistic clichés) with low I.Q.s.

> Many of these children [says Jensen] seem much brighter than their I.Q.s would lead one to expect ... even though their scholastic performance is usually as poor as that of middle-class children of similar I.Q., the disadvantaged children appear much brighter in non-scholastic ways than do their middle-class counterparts in I.Q.

What Jensen is here concerned with is the question of the 'fairness' or 'unfairness' of the tests for 'disadvantaged' children. He concludes that if they are unfair that is because they do not reveal the ability for associative learning (as above) in which the poor child may be rich. It may strike an outsider that they indeed do not, and that, for that very reason, however 'fair' the tests may be in testing what they set out to test — conceptual or cognitive ability — they must have been conceived in what we can fairly call an 'unfair' attitude of mind: for it is a desertion of scientific principle, and therefore unfair, not to take into account all the possible factors and variants that are under one's nose. It might reasonably be concluded that intelligence, if it is indeed a distinct ability, operates selectively (and not 'generally') in the field of possibility: what material is there presented to it; what appeal as the immediate realities to be grappled with and mastered; what therefore has predominant *interest*. Environment, including class and culture, never presents anyone with a vacuum:

> Nevertheless, to explain these facts [says Eysenck] Jensen proposes the existence of two genetically distinct basic processes underlying the continuum from simple associative learning to complex cognitive or conceptual learning. Ability thus appears at two distinct levels ...

These distinct levels, we are to understand, have a neurological basis. The distinction therefore differentiates two types of mentality which may overlap in part but which in the main are unalterably distinct. Quite reasonably in these terms, Jensen proposes that we should fit our educational system (or systems) to this dichotomy, and thus cease to 'disadvantage' the 'many children whose mode of learning is predominantly associative'.

That is the line that Eysenck chiefly pursues: and he proceeds to give us an admonitory exhortation on our deficient appreciation of factual learning:

> Facts, and the knowledge of facts, are looked down upon as fit only for peasants, and other people lacking in 'originality' and 'creativity' and we have come to believe, it seems, 'that you do not need to know facts as long as you know where to look them up'.

Now of course this is sensible if it can be taken as an unslanted statement; although it must be added that 'knowing where to look them up' implies that one knows *a priori* what facts are relevant to one's concerns; while that further implies that one can see facts as part of a coherence; and that again means that one knows how not to waste one's mental energies: one knows how to use the available resources of retrieval, including encyclopedias. Finally, and also much more importantly, one knows how to recognize a fact — we must, I think, accept the fairly well agreed philosophical conclusion that 'facts' are related dispositions, of variable interpretation, rather than distinct unalterable entities.

It happened that while I was meditating on *The Inequality of Man* I refreshed my mind with Dickens's *Hard Times*, which Mr Gradgrind opens as follows:

Now what I want is Facts. Teach these boys and girls nothing but facts. Facts alone are wanted in life. Plant nothing else and root out everything else. You can only form the minds of reasoning animals upon Facts: nothing else will be of any service to them. This is the principle on which I bring up these children. Stick to facts, Sir.

'It might be thought', says Eysenck (dealing with the 'associative mind'), 'that what is being recommended is a sort of second-best education for some children, as compared with a superior education for others'.

And so it might. No need to deny that we ought to do more, much more, about adapting education to need, and to kinds of mind. Eysenck sounds affable, rational and impeccable:

What Jensen is suggesting is simply that ... If a child of low I.Q. can learn to write, spell, do arithmetic, speak grammatically and generally acquire the basic skills which are needed by him or her to earn a reasonable living and lead a full and happy life, through the use of his associative abilities, it does not seem an act of kindness to force him to try to learn these skills through the use of conceptual abilities which he does not possess in adequate measure, and fail in the attempt. But that is what our schools are doing at the moment, in the name of equality!

But still more, if not in the name, in the hidden tradition, of an older and worse kind of inequality. Our educational systems, so far, have never founded themselves on the psychological and moral unity of humanity—on, that is, the equality of *moral* opportunity; but much rather on a secondhand and compromise intellectualism. That is not to agree with Eysenck's diagnosis or deductions: the emphasis is on 'secondhand' (and reach-me-down); and therefore on deception. Our education still filters down from the kind that was adapted to keeping the top classes in position and which therefore has appeared to promise the bottom classes something it cannot fulfil. It is disingenuous even to suggest that our present system of education could be adapted to a universally satisfactory human fulfilment. In our kind of society there not only is, there will continue to be, a two-tier education.

I use that expression deliberately to evoke echoes of Sir William

Ryland introducing the two-tier post in Britain. That was a euphemism unsuccessful in the way that euphemisms often are: when you use them often enough they become identified with what they were meant to deodorize or make palatable. In the case of the mails, 'two-tier' first barred, and then opened, the way to 'inferior': and now we can observe that a second class stamp on a private letter is widely construed as derogatory.

The analogy may seem slight but it is not inapt: the environmental elements which Eysenck rates so low in comparison with genetic determinants are often neglected, rather than scientifically rejected: and the reason is that they *are* slight and difficult or impossible to measure, although their cumulative effect and their real relational complexity may be, beyond measure, significant. How do you measure the subtleties of unreflected human motivation which may well not appear either in behaviour or in individual consciousness? About these there are, however good and discriminative your measuring instruments may be, only two certain facts: (1) you don't know that they are there; (2) you don't know that they aren't. Agnosticism is the only attitude to these potentials.

How do you measure the muddled, distorted and possibly quite deluded reactions of a child's neighbours—juvenile and adult? It may be of lesser importance if they tell Johnny crudely or brutally that he is soppy or potty. What matters much more is that he may pick up silently from his parents (who will certainly have picked it up from the testers via the school) something that he also silently accepts as *fact*, not with resignation perhaps but without hope, and probably with resentment: that he hasn't made the grade, and that the grade is *something better* which he ought to have and that others have got.

I do not see how you can measure vanity and competitiveness even when you can detect them. They appear only in immediate relations, not in standard and abstract groups. I cannot see how a dual system of education can be devised which is fruitful and just and which does not take into account these omnipresent and often overriding human characteristics; nor how it can fail to be divisive, the more dangerously because it is based on an early and ineluctable assessment of ability and quality—at an age when the resentments are hard to define or even to identify, and so are likely to accumulate all the more densely. We must not forget that while claiming that the adaptive education he proposes is really fairer to the individual, Eysenck also finds in it a support and justification of 'meritocracy', so that the I.Q. test, whatever opportunities it may leave open for the 'associational' kind of mind, does indeed establish the upper of the two tiers.

So what has happened to 'equality of opportunity', or, in other words, to the just society in which Eysenck too claims that he believes? What in fact happens to democracy, imperfect though that may be in all its known forms? The term itself becomes meaningless, for the one genuine essential of democracy is the belief that we can somehow learn to make a just society which must be founded on genuine equality of opportunity. We haven't got it now, we don't really educate for it and it seems that we don't yet know how to do so. But certainly we shall not learn from Eysenck and other Behaviourists.

Nevertheless, if intelligence and one's fixed share of it are innate, there is nothing much to be done about it. A meritocracy of intelligence will be genetically confirmed in advance. As Eysenck defines both intelligence and merit, that is not very different from what we have got – a society in which those who have the quickest eye for the seizure of opportunities will get to the top.

But according to Eysenck, social mobility makes it all fair: it isn't always the same people, still less their heirs and descendants, who get to the top. It all depends on the gene pool, and that prescribes what he calls a regression to the mean: the scales of justice work so that while my family is coming up yours is going down.

All the same, that still leaves us with a two-tier education and therefore a two-tier society – the sharp-witted abstractors versus the rest.

The hereditarian-environmental argument, in various forms and disguises, is not new; and can be detected as part of the underlying morphology of all contemporary intellectual oppositions: Eysenck only claims to be putting the hereditarian argument on a scientific – that is, a statistical – basis. His main source of evidence is the statistical study of identical twins (monozygotic, or MZ). It is already accepted by the vulgar – possibly with a mythological exaggeration – that identical twins are in many respects synchronized: that, far apart, both in time and space, they do the same things and suffer the same disorders often enough to suggest paranormal cognition.

Eysenck, admitting the parallels, would put down these more mysterious coincidences also to a shared genetic inheritance. If I.Q. really depends mainly on heredity we should expect to find that MZ twins not only have near-identical I.Q.s but that the level of ability that this represents is detectable in circumstances of up-bringing and education that considerably differ. Through his representative 'testers' that is what Eysenck finds.

What we are concerned with here is the principle, the implications and the social-educational effects, if we accept the validity of the I.Q. tests and the genetic assumption. That confers a dialec-tic head-start on Eysenck and those he represents: but it has also the advantage of making for a clearer (if more threatening) social prognostication. Moreover, we must remember that, whether their principle is valid or not and whether it is even moral, the tests go on and have gone on long enough to have already affected our social and educational environment: the one that educational environ-mentalists have to work in is already partly engineered or artificial.

For the validity of I.Q. testing — and that, it was said, has to imply also the validity of a fundamental and at present predomin-ant definition of intelligence itself — Eysenck relies in *The Inequality of Man* on a formidable list of authorities, ranging from Haldane, Binet, Burt and Spearman to Herrnstein and Jensen. Since it bears on the definition of intelligence, the fact should be mentioned here that the concept of I.Q. refers more significantly to groups, even nationwide groups, than to individuals: whether or not in-telligence is a general innate faculty, its measurement depends on a statistical comparison: this is important when we come to con-sider its long-term selective and social effects.*

Eysenck's authorities all tally in their figures and therefore subscribe not only to the genetic principle but also to the innate inequality of mankind. There is some slight variation in the age chosen as marking the end of development. Most favour ten to eleven years: but this appears to be somewhat arbitrary: and to be related to a number of other established calendar dates — the transition from primary to secondary school among them, the Year of the 'Scholarship' or the 11-plus. Clearly this date supplies a mass and captive population for 'ringing' — but not of course for perma-

* Cf. the 'comparative' marking system in our comprehensive schools which, over a given area, levels examination results — thus giving some examinees more marks than they have actually earned, and some less.

nent annual remigration and checking. J. B. S. Haldane, on the other hand (particularly striking, as Eysenck emphasizes, in that his scientific integrity resisted his communist affiliations) has seven years (unfortunately if irrelevantly reminding one of the Jesuits).

The figure, it was noted, that Eysenck gives for the genetic conditioning of intelligence is some 80 per cent – as opposed to about 20 per cent for environmental effects.

It is not that Eysenck and those whom he cites do not do their environmental homework: sometimes with what commonsense and ordinary real experience cannot help finding rather odd results. On the educational side, there is the study of the Milwaukee Project in which the investigators, headed by Professor Richard Heber,

> intervened in the environments of disadvantaged infants [says Eysenck] and the claim has been made that they succeeded in raising their I.Q. levels by over 30 points, that is, from dull normal to superior.

Eysenck does not accept the validity either of the results or of the methods, and to prevent the raising of environmentalist hopes supports his dissatisfaction with a long citation from the 'devastating criticism' by the American Ellis Page.

The study was designed to discover the effects of an enriched life environment on 'Infants in slum environments ... coming from low I.Q. mothers ... selected as likely to develop into low I.Q. adolescents': they were divided into an experimental and a control group (the experimental group being the one intensively farmed). The infants*

> were taken early in the morning from their slum homes, driven to the project site, and spent the whole day in the company of a specially-trained intelligent mother-substitute

---

* While I see no ground for joining Dr Eysenck in denigration of the Milwaukee Project, I am struck by its (perhaps necessary) artificiality: were separation and pendulum – or boomerang – psychological effects on the hapless infants taken into account? They were all very young, one gathers, and unable to express verbally what might have after all been a preference, at least for the time being, for their poverty-stricken but maybe cosier environments at home: that must have upset the calculations for the environment and therefore its ratio of importance to the calculations of I.Q. That is not however Eysenck's ground of disagreement.

who had nothing else to do [sic] but play with the infant and give him the sort of enriched background and environment which he would not have had in his real home.* In addition, the mothers of the experimental children received home help and training advice and treatment. Altogether the project made up as many of the environmental deficiencies under which these families laboured, as was possible.

The cited criticism by Ellis Page has three main heads. First, that as between the experimental and the control groups the choice of subjects to be dealt with by the children and teachers was not sufficiently random. Nor, it appears, was the actual selection of the children themselves. Comparing such variables, at two years old, as height, blood pressure, chest measurements, etc., an observer would have thought that the worst physical specimens had been chosen. That anyway is the only sense I can make out of Eysenck's comment:

> The only alternative to the hypothesis of non-random selection would be one of treatment effects — in the sense that the treatment which the experimental group received had stunted their growth to a degree which makes the claimed I.Q. change appear very small beer.

This, one must assume, means that the I.Q.s were so low to start with that any rise could only bring them to the surface or just above, by comparison with their normal age group. What Eysenck seems to ignore is the possibility, if not the likelihood, that the 'treatment' by their impoverished environment *had* stunted their growth, that of all of their class, so that the investigators were not faced, in the particular field, with any temptation to make a 'selective' selection.

Ellis Page's second objection is what is known as 'teaching the test':

> the items on which the children were explicitly trained overlap markedly with items in the test [making] the claimed I.Q. increment meaningless.

---

* Unscientifically vague: in the terms of the experiment practically all of many diverse backgrounds would have been different and better than his own.

This is a well-established criticism made by those who object to all I.Q. testing, notably Brian Simon (quoted on p. 172). In fact children *are* 'taught the test' and raise their ostensive I.Q.s on subsequent occasions. It is therefore a valid criticism, if not altogether of I.Q. testing – since we will accept Dr Eysenck's implication that purer tests can be, and are, devised and administered – at least of the social uses to which taking these tests is put with its uncritical acceptance of the meritocratic rat-race.

Ellis Page's third objection is that Heber's programme is not described in any detail (nor for that matter in any scientific journal – where among other things, no doubt, it would or should have been purified from the language of the tribe).

Eysenck's comment on the second criticism is interesting:

Clearly we will have to wait until the children are grown up before making any claim for definitive improvement in their I.Q.

Clearly we will: but perhaps in vain: it cannot but strike a laywoman that by that time the evidence will have largely dispersed, while the dilution by years of unassorted environmental effects will be inestimable. Eysenck's objections are not very convincing and are certainly not statistical: it is difficult to dismiss the impression that they are partly emotive and that what is allowed to the environmentalist side is rather faint-hearted.

We are, it appears, to believe that the most intensive efforts to improve our educational machinery, with the most lavish and skilful investment of resources, will produce at best only marginal if not negligible results. Eysenck does not seem to see how easily that conclusion could be used as an argument against any disinterested educational endeavour: the inventive effort that is to 'lead out', to adapt education to the child instead of adapting the child to a society already educationally systematized. He takes, moreover, what I believe to be an almost perverse pleasure in undermining even the educational beliefs which have been accepted – by those who have the pragmatic experience – as progressive, and which have begun, at least as ideas, to win a foothold. For instance, what Eysenck dismisses as the 'myth' about large classes. He says that the figures, contrary to the now largely accepted belief, show that in a small class children learn worse not better. I have never met an experienced teacher who did not firmly hold

G

the contrary view. Some have conceded that, in reading, a fair-sized group may act as a slight stimulus. It must be noted that even Eysenck's figures do not favour an absolute increase in size but indicate an optimum level. But one must insist that the general opinion of working teachers, here and in other matters of educational practice, refers to nothing mythical but, among other things, to the way they and their classes of real and typical children are related to one another and mutually react. A class that the average teacher finds too large means a tired teacher and a neglected child. These 'environmental' effects are in the nature of things to a large extent imponderable.

But even if the school cannot do much for the environmentalist case there is still the home. As further hereditarian support and as evidence of the negligible effects of cultural environment on innate degree of intelligence, Eysenck uses a study by B. S. Burks, of the placing of children in foster homes:*

> The children were of varied I.Q.s and had been placed in the house non-selectively.

I suppose that this means that the homes had not been selected with any sharp intellectual or cultural discrimination; one can hardly believe that adoption and fostering do not entail some effort to match like with like. Eysenck says:

> Burks was very careful in rating the adoptive homes in as detailed and fine-grained a manner as possible, *spending four to eight hours of individual investigation on each home*. She included intelligence measures on the adopting parents *as part of the child's environment*, as well as such things as time spent on helping the children do their homework, amount of time spent reading to the children, number of books in the home, education of both parents, parents' vocabulary, *a culture index* and many others. She calculated a multiple correlation between child's I.Q. and *all the variables, weighted, corrected for unreliability of measurement*, and came up with the figure of eighteen per cent of the total variance being explainable by the environmental factors considered. This agrees well with our model of twenty per cent.

* B. S. Burks, *The Relative Influence o Nature and Nurture upon Mental Development*.

The italics throughout that quotation are mine. There are these points to be made about it: it does not seem very much time; against that we must admit that marginal utility comes into the matter: spending more time might have produced more indefinite results; it may also be true that Miss Burks visited so many homes that she could not spare more time for each; or even that her schedule was by definition so limited that eight hours were ample or more than ample. Or it may even have been that that was all the adoptive parents, willing though they seem to have been, could actually stand. Eysenck is so severely scientific that he rejects or neglects any picturing of real situations. Yet we may think we often get a glimpse of them between the bounces of his rather jaunty prose.

Eysenck continues:

> critics usually suggest that some mysterious and unspecified factors in the environment may have been missed out.

For some of these, or something like what they might be, see p. 176; and we might add to them: the economic conditions of the adoptive and of the original home; the way the parents touch and handle the child; the warmth and affection – or the reverse – conveyed by their attitude to the child; the comfort and ease of its dress; its ability to make friends apart from the adoptive parents. It appears from the activities given that the children inspected are all of age to have their I.Q. taken; which is understandable in the terms of the study, but surely to some extent loads it: Eysenck rejects Freud, often with good reason, but can hardly believe that early or pre-school influences are not part of the environment. None of these is entirely mysterious – anyway to an open-minded and sympathetic observer – although many of them may be less easy to specify – and to measure – than those which Eysenck has selected.

That such 'mysterious and unspecified' environmental factors may have been missed, as Eysenck admits,

> is of course possible but is not a testable hypothesis; unless a factor is specified and shown to be measurable, there is little that can be done with such a view.

By Eysenck and those committed to his quantitative assumptions: except recognize, perhaps, that it is part of general commonsense and *practised* experience. But *of that which we cannot measure, thereof we must remain silent.*

It is obvious that intelligence testing can only measure performances. That may perfectly well represent a wide and even a varied range of intellectual ability which may even include some of the special insights into a medium which we are accustomed to call 'creative'.*

But even if this is so, and even if we were to accept that there were a general and innate factor of intelligence (to be called 'g' or 'x'), we are told nothing about how we can evaluate it, especially as defined by the testers: hence it is far from obvious why it should be a classification of merit and a standard for distributing rewards.

Testing tells you only what has been done and, within the limits of the test-definition, what can be done. One must be concerned nevertheless — particularly those of liberal intention must be concerned — with what has not been seen to be done and with the non-doers who have disappeared into occupations and pre-occupations less highly rated or prognosticated: perhaps anonymous, perhaps routine: perhaps immensely, if unintentionally and unreflectedly, valuable to the living human world: they may have merged irrevocably and may never even return to take another intelligence test.

One must not say that Dr Eysenck does not care about this silent majority. He proclaims that he wants a fairer society; and he says, with reason, that there is an important sense in which the liberal notion of equality is more dangerous than the acceptance of biological inequality:

> It would be extremely dangerous to argue (as some modern theorists do) that people are universally entitled to these equal rights *because* they are genetically equal: if science proved that such genetic equality was a myth, rather than a fact, then the

---

* The point of the distinction is that the innovative, original or creative intelligence is apter at discovering the hidden possibilities of the given: this can apply in science, art or the merely social existent; intelligence never works in a vacuum, but the more passive puzzle-solving gets as near to it as makes no particular human difference. Otherwise why are not the members of *Mensa* running the world? Or *are* they, incognito, and perhaps in heavy protective disguise?

whole case for human equality as a human right would fall to the ground.

That seems fair; but we must still insist that, accepting biological inequality as a fact, it is the social and educational use that we make of this fact that matters; as also what we really ought to understand by the fact: some of us, in another than the Orwellian sense, *are* more equal, not only than others, but than others agree, or know how to admit: some of us may really be intellectually smarter than the rest. But how and where we apply what intelligence we have got may *really* on any humanly acceptable scale of values constitute a demand for redefining 'equality', or for discovering what it really is and striking a just and fruitful balance of qualities; *one*, if you like, to mean one human being capable of maturing in his own terms; and one to count only as one. We are moral as well as intelligent beings, both at varying degrees of development: and if we are not moral, or at least concerned with our own morality, we are not, in the long-term or social sense, very intelligent.

Eysenck is aware of social justice and the 'equality of opportunity' which, in the liberal view, depends on it. That, to his satisfaction (and conceivably also as a sop to liberal preference) is taken care of by 'regression to the mean',* a phenomenon which must now be explained:

Heredity distributes the genes which make for superior achievement, high intelligence and great ability, and makes sure that within a few generations none of the existing boundaries between classes shall remain. If anything it is social structure which makes social divisions permanent ... it is heredity which breaks the mould, making for disruption, chaos and revolution. Where there is anything approaching equality of opportunity, universal education and advancement of merit, there we would expect to find a constant high degree of social mobility, with the children of the middle-class parents regressing to the mean, and moving downwards, and the children of working-class parents regressing to the mean and moving upwards ... If intelligence was indeed determined only by environmental causes, then classes would indeed

* Op. cit.

calcify into castes, and a permanent serfdom of the dull would be established, without hope of redress.

That, not surprisingly, is a purely statistic conception. It takes no account of the possible differential values of individuals, considered not merely as walking I.Q.s, but whole persons.

And whether it is statistically true or not, it has no bearing on 'equality of opportunity': it does not even help us to discern the outlines of a possible society which might practise it: though it may help to disguise that ours does not, and hardly seems to be moving towards it. For not only do those with the kind of intelligence whose behavioural and meritocratic effects Eysenck has been able to study make sure, more often than not, that equality of opportunity is a cipher; but equality of opportunity is, more than most, an environmental contribution: it depends on what a society has made a habit of doing with its intelligent (and less intelligent) members.

'Regression to the mean' then can be no consolation to the liberal concern with individuals: it is a blind and very abstract justice that is satisfied with the up and down movement of scale pans: we would really prefer to know that Tom Jones and Harriet Smith got the chance to make the most of their lives, their powers, their sensibilities. It is not much more consolation to us than it would be to them to know that either their remote ancestors or their remote descendants were members of an elite (often promoted on a very mixed bag of characteristics, some humanly and morally dubious). After all, we are all descended from everybody and can be forebears of all the species as long as it lasts. But we think more often, if not more accurately, and we feel more acutely, about *ourselves* in the world today.

A meritocratic society as adumbrated by the geneticists of I.Q. is inevitably a hierarchic society: and the hierarchy proposed is not in any way one of moral merit and will almost inevitably harden into a caste society. In short a meritocratic society cannot be a just society: Eysenck & Co. are dealing in a contradiction in terms.

All that is even more obvious when we look at my other set of social prophets, the popularizing ethologists. They, too, believe that human beings are to an overwhelming degree bound by their genetic and evolutionary past.

It is fair (and it is also interesting) to add that, while Eysenck with his school accepts the probability of a genetic basis for human personal and temperamental characteristics, as well as for intellectual ability, he seems to dissociate himself from some conclusions which have been based on other genetic findings – those of the popular ethologists who study animal behaviour:

Because baboons and lions live in groups with one male dominating a harem of dependent females, it does not follow that this is natural for human beings. Human beings have developed beyond the ape stage in so many ways that any argument about 'natural' and 'unnatural' is simply irrelevant in so far as it brings in comparison with lower animals [*The Inequality of Man*].

That, undeniably welcome, is surprising: for it is certain that Eysenck accepts some deductions about human psychological behaviour made from rats and some other 'lower' animals. It may be because he accepts observations made in laboratory conditions more readily than those made in direct non-interventionist fieldwork. However that may be, the principle is unaffected.

It is true that the ethologists approach the animal world in a way which is far more attractive to its human inhabitants than the rodent operation of the academic psychologists. They choose in the first place more attractive subjects, and study them without anything more interfering than television cameras, as much as possible in their natural surroundings. Nevertheless human conclusions are being drawn, prematurely, as some of us hope and believe, which claim the same genetic force as Eysenck's intellectual classification.

It is true that some of this is tendentious vulgarization – or reads like it: and probably most practising ethologists are in no haste for human prophecy, or even are not interested in it; while by no means all those who would put our biologically deviant societies back on what they regard as the right genetic and evolutionary path have done their fieldwork. But some of them have – for instance, Konrad Lorenz, who seems to be accepted by his greylag geese as one of themselves [see his book *On Aggression*].

The important contribution, for the immediate purpose, made by Lorenz, and one or two others, on the basis of animal observations, is of the genetic nature of 'aggression' and of its ritual control among animal populations. There seems no doubt that Dr Lorenz has observed what he has observed: that there is an intra-specific aggression, meaning a tendency to fight and to compete intra-specifically and also that many animal species have evolved typical performances to contain this quarrelsome disposition and to stop it short of death or severe injury. It is natural to think – and it is a thought that might occur to anybody – 'What a pity human beings haven't taught themselves to do the same thing; I think I could turn and live with the animals, they are so *aggressive* – and self-contained.' And if they can give us tips about how to transmute our nasty habit of intra-specific murder they will be more than welcome. Lorenz is prepared to take this step into the social arena and, because they are deduced from the scientific discernment of a real pattern in animal behaviour, the tips he gives on behalf of the animals, and their human analogy, must be treated with respect. They are still not very good ones: that is to say, they are hardly new and have been tried and found wanting – smash-rooms, athletics, 'creative' sublimations of various kinds, even 'humour' (it is not clear whether he means self-pacification through cultivating a sense of humour or a Freudian type of deflection through wit: either, just about as easy as adding a cubit to one's stature). Lorenz, nevertheless, makes the sensible if obvious admission that human beings, as contrasted with animals, can produce an exponential proliferation of their armament; and that, being detached from intra-specific recognition, we can slaughter our kind because we can do it too remotely to be reminded that these are beings like ourselves.

Even with us he does not despair of ritualized containment of aggressiveness. However, there seems no logical reason why we should not also be asked to believe that the gift of ritualizing, at least embryonically or potentially, is also part of our unconscious animal heritage.

Dr Anthony Storr, author of *Human Aggression* and on this subject a follower of Lorenz, appears to believe just that. At a symposium subsequently published as *The Natural History of Aggression* by the British Institute of Biology, he suggested that the U.S.–U.S.S.R. space race is just such a way of containing and deflecting an instinctive rivalry that would otherwise become lethal.

We may not think much of that piece of speculation. It ignores among other things the machinelike and reflexive operation upon individuals of the political and economic system in which they live, a fault which at least Lorenz does not commit; there is no doubt that the stockpiling of megalethal weapons and the possibility, approaching probability, of using them gives 'aggression' an entirely new meaning.

What the popularizing ethologists do mean by it needs examination.

What we are supposed to accept is not only that we are a naturally aggressive species – warlike, competitive and bloodyminded, clearly an observation one cannot lightly dismiss – but that this is in our genes; a matter of biological necessity. And moreover – no doubt this is meant partly as consolation – looked at properly this is a Good Thing.

It is at this point that we should all take a strong dose of semantics to clear the conceptual brain. Dr Anthony Storr has admitted that 'Aggression is a portmanteau word bursting at the seams'.

And in the popular ethologists' usage, so it is. In the language of Lorenz, Storr, Robert Ardrey and sometimes even Koestler, aggression implies many meanings, some of which we have at least been accustomed to regard as contradictory. They can use it to mean drive, vitality, self-assertion; or, equally, defensiveness and also provocativeness or violence: on the other hand, they can mean by it intellectual curiosity or creativity; and of course *masculinity*, with an honorary assumption of the whole lot; but especially, in that case, creativity or intellectual drive. Lionel Tiger, one of my other subjects, says categorically in his article in *Encounter* in 1969 that 'Aggression is not a human problem but a male problem'.

That might seem to suggest that 'aggression' is something we can and even ought to do something about. But I think that is not what Mr Tiger meant; the word 'problem', too, is being loosely used. What he means is that 'aggression' is predominantly and specifically male.

He also sees this aggression as part of a general amity-enmity pattern (as Ardrey calls it), a general genetic hating-together; inter-specifically, but ritualized and sublimated by 'male bonding'.

'Bonding', according to Tiger – forming organized social groups, teams, societies, school houses, regiments, etc. – is primarily a male habit of genetic and evolutionary origin and, even though it may not nowadays be exclusively male, he offers a strong presumption that if Nature had her way it still would be: and that everything would be much better so. (Of course if Mr Tiger *really* thinks that 'aggression', ritualized or not, *is*, except insignificantly, a *male* problem, among human beings, he is being absurd and, however scientific his observations may be, they do not include what can be found under his own nose. Has he never observed the matriarchs of families in operation, perhaps even in his own?)

The chief point for *us* here is that contained violence is the basis of all social organization. Or in other words liberalism and the hope of moral progress is out: while authoritarian hierarchy plus therapeutic conflict are back in. The only purely social virtue will be playing for one's side. And war. For though e.g. Lorenz and Storr believe in ritualization or sublimation of war, war itself can also be regarded (e.g. by Ardrey) really, if not too explicitly, as a kind of ritualization of our aggressive urges.

Tiger, it is true, recognizes that 'aggression' even if instinctive and genetically conditioned is not like a secretion. He inclines to the view that the social apes are our paradigm, and stresses our social methods of containment as the important part of our genetic inheritance. But of course a lot depends on what you mean by 'social' or 'society'.

A social critic of liberal or even impartial disposition, not necessarily a rabid supporter of Women's Lib, might still think that 'male chauvinism' is descriptive as well as abusive. She (or he) might well agree at least that men are indeed much more inclined than women to get together in a group, a team, a club or a huddle, and even that many results and products which are socially beneficial, and even soundly economical in relation to wastage of effort, have thus been achieved. But team-work is not in itself moral and has not always been desirable. One of the most shining recent examples was the Great Train Robbery. And 'togetherness', organized or informal, not least if it is male, may sometimes be seen by more sober outsiders, of either sex, as one of the surest ways of making an ass of oneself.

It may be true, as the ethological popularizers say, that many animal societies are more peaceful and stable than our own. But it must be pointed out that human societies are in many ways irreversibly different from them and that the price the animal societies unwittingly pay is a much more rigid kind of automatism plus an inflexible structure of domination and subjection. These societies are of course hierarchic; and at the top of the hierarchies are – to use Robert Ardrey's expression – 'the alpha-types', those conditioned by their genes to leadership and rule.

In human societies we, too, have our alpha-types who also get to the top of the tree (or whatever is the best commanding height for *Homo sapiens*) – not an unsuitable location if we conflate this doctrine with that of Eysenck's meritocratic I.Q. Eysenck's 'merit' as we saw, is not very different from a very sharp eye for the main chance: and it is difficult to see, not only on ethological evidence, but from common observation, what 'alpha-types' have necessarily to recommend them in the way of social merit or even social awareness. In human societies, we usually recognize them just because they *have* got to the top of whatever tree it is: they all have 'charisma' of lesser or greater range; and perhaps more often than not it is evil or harmful – Hitler had enormous 'charisma'.

Whether we call it bad or not – and the word is too nebulous – we can see that 'alpha-types' are always primarily concerned with their own power; often in a naively innocent way; for with the most successful it does not readily occur to them that what they want and go for is not also supremely important and actually valuable to all the beta and sub-beta types, or that those do not naturally or even in fact want to submit and follow.

What we can even now foresee is that such a society if it could come into being would be static, hierarchic and goalless (rather more than our present societies) and if, as a Utopian would imagine it, it maintained internal peace, that would be at the price of turning the war outwards – *inter*-specific aggression. Indeed Ardrey for one would willingly pay that price on our behalf if only it were not for the threat of nuclear obliteration, for war is our genetic (male) business.

What he and his like have to offer us is nothing but a *Führer-Prinzip*. We must still ask: where is the Leader going to lead? On this piece of essential homework many of the alpha-types seem to merit beta-minus.

Nevertheless, here too as usual we are offered the sop of 'equality of opportunity' and a 'just society'. One may reasonably ask who is going to dispense the justice and the equal opportunities. As we saw, it is hardly likely that either meritocrats or alpha-types who have made it — still less if they are on the way up — will be much interested in either the understanding or the practical implementation of these concepts. If your goal is domination why on earth should you dispense the equality of opportunities which will surely cramp your style?

Robert Ardrey's definition of society in *The Social Contract*, borrowed from Wynne Edwards's *Animal Dispersion*, includes for us his conception of both equality of opportunity and social justice:

> A society can be defined as a group of individuals competing for conventional prizes by conventional means.

'Conventional means' must imply any degree of force that will be submitted to as the local rules of the game. The handicaps in this competition however are not thus agreed upon or contracted to: they are submitted to as our in-built 'biological inequality'.

While we remain at our present stage of political history, where the labels — or the fiction — of democracy seem indispensable, 'equality of opportunity' is a key-concept. Like democracy itself, the phrase can mean as little or as much as you please. One detects the common authoritarian-liberal dichotomy. For the authoritarians it is at least partly akin to T. S. Eliot's 'piece of meat to distract the dog while the burglar gets on with the job' (he was referring to poetic meaning).

For authoritarians, as political conservationists — who are more impressed with the need for order than for creative flexibility (or 'freedom') — ethological geneticism, with its animal analogies of ritualized hierarchy, provides a satisfactory (if Orwellian) definition of 'equality of opportunity' which they are happy, whether they realize it or not, in not having to examine further.

The liberal-minded are, on the contrary, faced, as so often with a real dilemma which arises from a genuinely dualistic appreciation of the human situation — the human being is a social animal who needs agreed order to sustain his freedom, and if possible to develop it: the state ought to exist to establish justice between individual men and women. It is partly because, nowadays, he has surrendered the ideal and even the idea of 'equality' that the liberal is morally obliged to go as deeply and widely as he can into 'equality of opportunity', because he cannot and ought not to relinquish 'justice' (the better substitute for 'equality' as the second partner of the Trinity). And at some time in his attempt at realization he has to get down both to the contemporary field and the history of the 'opportunities': that is, into the real history of justice (mostly, and inextricably, of injustices) — and by this route to its possibilities.

9

Latter-Day Thoreau

To give any warrant to a liberal hope, the 'opportunities' provided by a society that is both just and open must be moral as well as material: or, rather, the material opportunities must facilitate instead of impeding the moral. They must provide, as it were, an open market in which individual choices can discover not only occasions, but also their maximum meaning.

Here the environmentalists among the Behaviourists are no more helpful than the hereditarians: certainly, if we are to take B. F. Skinner – the American Behavioural psychologist, and extreme proponent of the stimulus-response account of human life – as their representative.

We might think that Skinner's attitude towards the individual is more humanitarian than that of the pure geneticists; and in a sense more egalitarian: for since he regards the idea of individuality, and therefore of freedom, responsibility and moral choice, as meaningless, we are all, one might say, equally corrigible or incorrigible.

That of course is not how he puts it, or not as a primary statement: instead, that we are and always have been throughout our lives, totally conditioned by our environment; in short, that what we feel to be our moral individuality is nothing but an expression of that conditioning world. If then we are to try to improve society and create happier conditions for everybody, we must try to alter the environment, not man.

As with the geneticists of all kinds, this obviously leads to the 'expert' or engineered (or authoritarian) society. Indeed Skinner is one of the most open and uncompromising advocates of direct social and psychological interventionism. We see this, as a sort of blueprint, in his curious novel *Walden II*, a fantasy about a Utopian community run by a paternalistic (and omniscient) latter-day

Thoreau who acts as a mouthpiece (and mask) for the professor of psychology who is the narrator.

From that book by itself we might infer some inconsistency in Skinner's environmentalism, for here it seems obvious that by various means (and even, possibly, tricks) the 'individual' is being adapted to his environment and not the other way round.

The question is simplified and – perhaps at least to Skinner's satisfaction – the inconsistency removed, by the fact that Skinner does not believe in the reality of the moral individual. What troubles men, he holds, and society, are illusions about freedom and dignity (see his *Beyond Freedom and Dignity*). These, we must note, have mostly been stirred up by liberal theorists and idealists. Thus he wipes away the ethical foundation for liberalism and its 'literature' (which really comprises literature in all its senses – a subject still to be touched on. There is no doubt that the origins of liberalism are idealistic and literary). What has to be realized, according to Skinner (and here obviously we have the educational aim of reconditioning), is that these 'values' – and all the others, including the ideal of justice, I suppose – are simply a chimaerical superstructure which misinterprets for us our automatic behaviour. (It might then appear that ceasing to bother about 'justice' is one sure and essential step towards getting a just society.)

Skinner's crucial topic is free will and the meaninglessness of real individual choice: and he comes out on the side of the most rigid determinism – the classic materialistic hardline which philosophically is often now regarded as old-fashioned.

I have said very little on the perennial topic of the freedom or otherwise of the will, because from the point of view of this book it is somewhat abstract. It is not likely on purely theoretical grounds to be permanently settled; and indeed on those grounds the determinists have an air of winning. It is difficult, anyway, to show that there is any such phenomenon as an unconditioned or absolute spontaneity: and although it may be said that that spontaneity is precisely an essential characteristic both of biological mutations and of the movements of particles, those appear throughout evolutionary history not to have been accompanied by individual consciousness and self-awareness or by purposiveness or even evolutionary direction – all of which would seem to be part of the definition of free will as human beings recognize it.

On the other hand, a large number of people – perhaps the

majority of those who appear to think about the subject and who constitute no doubt a comparatively recent phenomenon — have a strong feeling that they are themselves responsible for their preferences and choices, at least within the limits of the actual alternatives offered them by events and circumstances; that choice appears to them to be real if narrow. To the strength and authenticity of this feeling in itself, it makes surprisingly little difference whether or not they achieve some or any of their wishes and intentions. One may say too that 'liberalism' itself is psychologically just this movement towards detecting the preferred possibilities in any situation. *Beyond Freedom and Dignity* is a fundamental if not very original, or newly informative, attack on the freedom of the will and on evaluative morality. It is significant precisely because Skinner thinks that free will and human values are important enough to be not merely dismissed but dismembered; the book is an admission that they are among the most profound and formative of human convictions about our own humanity.

We may be wrong but our erroneous belief produces effects which would come more naturally and accountably if it was correct: for instance, people who know what they think they are aiming at — particularly in a detailed and coherent way; that is, with a skilled and critical cognizance of their environment — more often achieve what appears, and what they tell themselves to be, their goal, than those who drift with the tide.

Skinner and his adherents in effect tell us that this conscious relation both to our environment and to our memory and judgment of our own past is a delusion, and without logical connection with our immediate activities and performances or those of others.

According to Skinner, when we think we are preferring and choosing, *thinking and acting freely*, we are in reality being wholly governed by a convergence of what he calls 'inconspicuous contingencies'. The world, the environment, is a flux of physical events by which we are absolutely conditioned and from which our individual existence has no real independence. Our feeling of freedom, even our judgment of assent, arise merely from the fact of our ignorance: the totally determining effect of this flux of events or contingencies is 'inconspicuous' to us; as a general rule it is too microscopic and too densely integrated for us to detect it.

This is the Darwinian and neo-Darwinian description of our human status as it depends on our physical and biological evolution. As Skinner uses it it looks very like the old billiard-ball account of causation—one is a shoved shover: but on the other hand more up-to-date variants on the theme of causality, for example the Heisenberg principle of indeterminacy,* do not do anything for our human sense of freedom. By the time we reach the human scale, the idiosyncrasies of particles are not relevant. Nevertheless, Skinner, whose argument ties him to the microscopic or 'inconspicuous', gives most of his examples on the human or macroscopic scale; that is, he describes some of our psychological habits, especially those that appear to us to register volition or value and which are, as I have no wish to deny, certainly part of our unprovable feeling of freedom—tacking on to the description (which may in some or many cases be valid) an interpretation of his own, not only assumptive but question-begging. It is question-begging because the interpretation given by Skinner assumes that our positive feelings always depend upon ignorance of our real circumstances. Take his example of admiration (op. cit.) and what and why we admire (or surely in correct Behaviourese, what we deludedly believe that we admire?). (Or deplore.) It is true that we clap or boo performances and skills and that (particularly in the case of magic) our wonder depends to some large extent on not knowing how it is done and on not being able to do it ourselves: and (*mutatis mutandis*) our contempt. But it is obvious that we are also susceptible, or a good many of us are, to *moral* admiration and contempt and that these largely depend on what we can divine or discern of deliberate intention: and moreover that in this our uncertain judgments have often enough the confirmation and support of legal justice. It is that intentionality which we experience and discern that I believe Skinner wishes to undermine; hence his extraordinary account of our motives for admiration and for our habits of reward and punishment.

'The behaviour we admire is the behaviour we cannot yet explain.' Or, 'Credit is in inverse proportion to the conspicuousness of the causes of behaviour'. Those are the crucial generaliza-

---

* Heisenberg's principle of indeterminacy states that it is impossible to determine both the position and the velocity of a sub-atomic particle at one and the same time. This indeterminacy is entailed as a scientific method of investigation. In other words, the technique of inquiry has inherent limitations.

tions. They lead to some remarkable statements and conclusions. We admire, it appears, someone who has learned to 'operate his equipment' (manipulate his environment, do a skilled job, learn or understand something, make a scientific discovery, etc., etc.) off his own bat, without help or instruction: and not by copying or even by following verbal or written instructions. But of course, according to Skinner, the appearance of originality and initiative and immediate skilful judgment would disappear if we could observe that the operator's 'behaviour has been shaped wholly by the relatively "inconspicuous contingencies" arranged by his equipment [environment, perhaps, rather], and these are now past history.'

Similarly: 'We commend a prompt child more than one who must be reminded of his appointments because the reminder is a particularly visible feature of temporal contingencies.'

That appears to be behaviouristic gymnastics of a peculiarly athletic if not tortuous kind. I assume that what Skinner means is that the child would or would not keep his appointment, entirely according to his past conditioning by 'contingencies' of which neither he or his mentors took note at the time nor could take note because they were 'inconspicuous'; and that now in the particular circumstances of being on the dot, we are pleased to be able to persuade ourselves that our educational methods have after all been effectual and indeed causative; thus we express our pleasure in commending him (and by implication ourselves). In fact we might have saved ourselves the trouble: and indeed so might his pastors and masters, because there is no knowing how, if at all, their conspicuous attempts at intervention could possibly have competed with the 'inconspicuous' flux of his environmental conditioning. If Skinner does not mean all that, I admit I don't know what he means — except to prove his case at all costs. And I think it does not matter too much: since I also think it is obvious that, *among other reasons*, we *commend* (or reprove) because the beneficent or maleficent *results* of punctuality are immediate and continuous — much more visible than any other temporal contingencies. But to go so far is to give at least the appearance of accepting another of Skinner's more staggering assumptions about motivation.

It appears that Skinner does not understand or anyway has not observed that people can act from other motives than the one of obtaining credit. No doubt it is true that with many people that is the motive most commonly met with, and conceivably with some people it is the sole motive apart from necessity. But the rest of us can often observe that there are some people who, although they may have no objection to approval or applause, and may by no means try to avoid them, perform or act at least with the accompaniment of a great variety of motives which we can call disinterested or even positively benevolent.

Even of scientific curiosity or interest, Skinner seems to claim that the 'credit' is part of the *determination* (the determining cause) for doing one kind of work rather than another.

That may be more often true when science, as with ourselves, has moved into the stage of epigones: when we are, as it seems, beyond the age of original and individual discovery and creation, and into auxiliary elaboration and technical teamwork or research, geared to the funds available, and the projects not yet earmarked.

'Credit' says Dr Skinner, 'is in inverse proportion to the conspicuousness of the causes of behaviour.' He means that we only admire or approve behaviour of whose causes we are ignorant or which mystify us. We earn and receive maximum credit for what we have achieved without help (i.e. owing nothing to any instruction at any time; or, as *we* might say, with originality) since our behaviour *'has been shaped wholly by the relatively inconspicuous contingencies arranged by [our] equipment'*. (The word 'equipment' probably in Skinner's usage includes 'environmental causes': but it also has the purpose of avoiding any reference, however natural and convenient, to personal individuality or consciousness.)

And those 'contingencies', Skinner continues, 'are now past history'. It would appear, then, that a remote and impersonal past of now inconspicuous events wholly accounts for the particularity of any of our present concerns and occupations.*

Common sense replies that present motivation (or what appears to be so) is not in the same category of experience as past determination or conditioning: for motivation is felt as experience whereas determination according to Skinner is *not* experienced. And it does

* The suggestion parallels Freud's argument that infantile experiences precisely condition the later events of adult personal life. But that my Aunt Jane kicked me in the teeth *aet.* 3 does not cause me to kick my sister Muriel in the teeth *aet.* 18. I may just as well box her ears; or even leave her alone.

not seem possible to allow that immediate (and conspicuous) causes, where they are determinant, are so in the same sense as the past inconspicuous ones (whose existence and power we do not deny). For at least the immediate and conspicuous causes are what we *think* we choose; and for what we believe to be reasonable reasons: we see 'why' and if we did not have this convincing insight we would refrain.

To be consistent with his own claims for environmental sovereignty Skinner would have to maintain that where we consent to it, as we do whenever we fancy we 'select' the most realistic and logical alternatives that it appears to offer, we are automatically wrong:* that is, that our going along with the environment does not mean what it says or preferably is meaningless. For the environment, whatever it may be, in being causative, is immediate and present, and so *conspicuous*. Are we to suppose that we *necessarily* choose from it the wrong or irrelevant motivation and cause? Or, conversely, that the inconspicuous past does not allow itself to be usefully or even validly interpreted into present conscious and deliberate selection? (It may be noted that the distinction between voluntary and involuntary movement is a real one; I move my arm or hand, or refrain from moving them, according to present circumstances, on which I make an immediate judgment or decision. What has happened to my limb in the past through past contingencies is not here decisive or even necessarily relevant.)

Skinner's view of 'inconspicuous determinism' does not allow itself a scientific formulation acceptable by his own standards. For, like other statements of determinism, it would entail the possibility of precise prediction. I have always anyway regarded this entailment as a weakness of determinism, at least in its 'strong' form. Its predictability can never be thoroughly tested. If we knew all causes we should know all effects; that is, all particular and infinitesimal and finite effects. But for that to be tested and scientifically certified, an All-Knower (who of course would also be an All-Foreknower) is entailed. Thus Skinner's determinism, in the final analysis, like everybody else's, parallels the theistic: and is unprovable. Moreover the argument from our invincible ignorance works backwards as well as forwards. Our history of self-causation is 'inconspicuous', or unknowable not only to ourselves

---

* Ironically this also parallels a chief assumption of psychoanalysis.

but to others, with however much superior knowledge they may be able to observe us: thus no one will be able to say by what particular remote causes the particular events of our present behaviour and perhaps illusory choices are being precisely conditioned. What is interesting on the other hand, and important, is that there are no logical or realistic grounds for saying that we may not sometimes get better at digging up some of these remote 'inconspicuosities'. Proffered contingencies may become more and more conspicuous: or, in other words, we may attain a fuller and fuller degree of consciousness. Hence we may increasingly have more and better reasons for matching our tastes and approval to one alternative rather than another and thus behaving, however infinitesimally, less like automata: more distinguishable to ourselves and others; consenting to all valid laws, both human and natural; and only to those we think we see as valid. It may not seem very much: but it is a mark that differentiates the human.

That is no more than to say that, however rarely realized, freedom and dignity – the values of the self – *are* human possibilities: and make liberalism a philosophy for human beings. And it must be that philosophy which inspires the unpolitical and purely moral resistance which we have recently seen in the highly discouraging circumstances of Soviet conditioning (which must surely owe something to Pavlov?).

But Skinner concludes: 'Our task is not to encourage moral struggle or to build or demonstrate inner virtues. It is to make life less punishing and in doing so release for more reinforcing activities the time and energy consumed in the avoidance of punishment.' We have to 'accept the fact that all control is exerted by the environment [he means via the 'inconspicuous contingencies'] and proceed to the design of better environments rather than of better men'.

Who then is in the first place to decide what is a 'better' environment? And by what standards? And by what process of enlightened consent – or of prescription? And how then do you distinguish standards from values – including the values of free choice and justice? How then do you have *better* environments without *better* men?

There is little doubt that in the enormous environmental change we have just alluded to, the Soviet leaders, anyway in the early stages, were firmly and perhaps even reasonably convinced that it was all for the better, and perhaps even that in initiating the revolution they and their colleagues were rather better men than average. In fact they identified their 'environmental' revolution *with* morality (and actually with the release to creative power of repressed freedom and dignity). Not for the first time in human history the end was thought to justify the means: and, as a corollary, force, in pursuance of what was seen as a wholly justifiable goal, was also seen to be, as it is, more efficient than rational persuasion. In terms of their own morality the Bolsheviks were consistent: just in the way that Inquisitors have been consistent: if we are on God's business of saving souls we have no business to waste His or humanity's time about it: not only the shortest way but the most remedial way with heretics may indeed be to send them to hell.

Behaviourists and 'ethologists' who think they know the shortest way to save us from ourselves: who in fact know that they know that the only method is some sort of psychological and social 'engineering', may still delude themselves if they believe, as no doubt many of them do, that this can be carried out by rational, suasive or educational means. But I do not know of any who would admit the only alternative – of force: and yet psychological and sociological 'expertise', especially in a chartered form, is nothing else. Quite apart from directly 'aversive' techniques, there is no way, once psychiatric and social welfare schools are medically and socially recognized and given a chartered status, for a lay patient or client to know what kind of intervention he is getting.

Behaviourist treatments or 'therapies', as we have seen with Skinner, have no theoretical or ethical difficulties of the kind that a liberal or humanist (or a Christian) would be obliged to recognize. They do not have to trouble themselves about liberty and free choice of the individual because they look on individuality and freedom as illusions: and this though it is still part of their democratic etiquette to receive the postulant for alleviation as though he could understand what he was in for. Therefore the political and social philosophy implied or assumed by such methods of adaptation has to be to some degree misleading if not actually fraudulent.

Behaviouristic intervention, in short, takes advantage of the accepted moral eminence and Hippocratean integrity of the healer which prescribed that benevolence towards the patient has over-

whelming priority while novelty or experiment can only be sub-
sumed under that intention.

As factual effect, and after the event, Skinner, in any given case,
might demonstrate that freedom and dignity are illusions. But
that we have *values* is not an illusion: and in the case of most
human individuals at however low a level of consciousness and
knowledge the attempt to persuade them otherwise will most likely
fail: at least if it were honestly made. Most human beings that one
meets or observes, however oppressive their conditions, will not
be any man's thing, if they can help it and provided that they can
see, however dimly, that that is what is being done to them. If we
are to be engineered into being a different species on better terms
with our better environment, we shall first have to be reconditioned
out of our queer liking for 'Freedom and Dignity': the prejudice
of at least some of us for morality will have to be overcome.
Skinner's confidence in improving the environment and therefore
in an improved society with greater happiness and satisfaction for
its individual members, which some of us foresee as Cacotopia, is
obviously based on a certainty about human nature and its possibilities of conditioning and deconditioning, which he regards as
scientific: the characteristics we have just referred to as human
potentials he would not accept as either universally or realistically
so. Freedom, dignity and general moral concern are not only
illusions but essentially *liberal* illusions. In his conclusions he goes
very far in attributing all the most important psychological blame
for our continuing and age-old predicament to the liberal heritage.
To recapitulate part of our quotation 'Our task ... is to make life
less *punishing* and in doing so to release for more reinforcing*
activities the time and energy consumed in the avoidance of
punishment.' (My italics.) Skinner continues:

> Up to a point the literature of freedom and dignity have [*sic*]
> played a part in the slow and erratic alleviation of aversive
> features of the human environment—including the aversive
> features used in intentional control.

That paragraph like much of behaviouristic literature needs a

---

* *Reinforcement*. Semantically interesting. An ambiguous term which can be
used positively or negatively: a reward is a positive reinforcement; a punishment a negative one. Very reinforcing to the jargonist's need to control by
mystification.

glossary—apart from what will be expounded below. The most important relevant point is that by 'literature' Skinner means not only 'written material' but Literature. Obviously the political pamphleteers, the political theoreticians and the philosophers have not been the only ones, not probably even the majority of those who have striven to exercise a liberal influence on human life and society. With no doubt a myriad different, even opposing, assumptions and implications, the *problems* which have engaged and unfortunately, more often than not, defeated the liberal, have been the central preoccupations of imaginative literature: freedom, dignity, the nature and difficulties of any morality, and the overriding necessity to have one of some kind or another. So that we can at least say that 'Literature' in a broad sense has been about the possibility or not of being a liberal: and there is no need to deny that a great deal of it, by no means the worst, has decided for impossibility (Shakespeare, I should say) and some or much has discarded any earlier liberalism as immature romanticism. (Wordsworth, I should say.)

All I have just said, or at least implied, is that liberalism essentially is what ventilates these problems, where an original authoritarianism can only stifle or dismiss them. It is the natural and valuable contribution of the sound, if still youthful, spirit of *authentic* romanticism: what spontaneously concerns itself with the realization of problems, moral ones of course, that come to all of us in our condition of being human (although they may depart from us very lightly). The minimal realization is that the problems must be detected, recognized and stated, generally in the most dramatic form available to the maker, because that dialogue and balance is the natural exposition of justice. It is because all 'Literature' that has much impressed itself upon human beings has had to make up its own mind about these fundamental moral demands that it has never appeared stupid to identify it with a liberal spirit (and the only excuse for Skinner in doing so): that it has always had to find its own voice and open its mouth—still and small, or a shout—and in its own essential interest demand, indeed begin by demanding, freedom of thought, speech and expression. And the greatest of these is freedom of thought. Without it the other freedoms are morally useless. It may be said, it often is said, that nobody can stop you thinking your own thoughts; and that the important freedoms are the rights to utter and act upon them. But it should, on the contrary, be obvious that freedom of thought is what is often stifled at source: and that what we call democracy, even with the most favourable connotations, has done little to encourage us to understand ourselves in our world: to educate us in the skills of open and honest inquiry into things and thus to learn to see them as they really are: while in its false liberalism of an open market for insidious interest and bias it has even helped to discourage the great majority, thereby undermining its own prospects of survival.

Justice is the important principle of liberalism: and morally democracy is valuable only as a tool for its pursuit and discovery: the 'freedom' in freedom of thought is no more than the power to learn to use that tool through understanding and inquiry: certainly secondary adjuncts are entailed; but primarily, if liberalism is to be a genuine humanism, justice must be seen as a principle of recognition of human needs and powers, including one's own.

That is not egalitarian: on the other hand, whatever we concede to biology, it is no assumption of inequality. All it says is that the liberal's primary, essential and defining interest is justice, that it must be his supreme value; that he believes its nature can be discovered and that he hopes that one day the discovery will be recognized and the principle established. But he does not or should not deny the strength of the forces that are ranged against it: nor fail to see that we must learn to know it only in concrete immediacies, chiefly in the recognition of injustices private and public, and resistance to them within our means and powers. Here is the importance of Literature—in the imaginative sense: which is built on the reactions of moral individuals to these felt immediacies. That is not at all to deny that the individuals concerned can and often are also 'immoral', at least by the social definition, nor that their reactions (or 'responses') are not often conflicting.

However, if there is no possibility of a universally recognizable principle of justice, it is nonsense to talk of a 'just society' as our genetic authoritarians insist on doing. That is so even if it is never wholly recognized in any actual society and if no society then can ever be wholly just: and even if what justice we know is a conception no more 'universal' than the agreed convention of a group. In fact, we do judge societies comparatively; for their comparative justice too, and not merely according to their internal standards: that is according to a principle claiming to be universal.

Because he wishes to eliminate moral evaluation from the human description, Skinner hardly finds it necessary to refer to justice: yet, since he believes that his environmental yoke and burden is much easier and lighter than anything we have so far been provided with, even by liberal democrats, we are warranted in assuming that he also thinks that the result would be a juster, even a just, society: and that he is implying that liberalism is what stands in the way of this more benevolent justice.

Skinner's 'Character of a Liberal' has elements both of the true and the bizarre: but does not wholly emerge from obscurity; while what can be deduced is not very easy to recognize.

'The literature of freedom and dignity' (Liberal literature, plus 'Literature' itself) according to Skinner, has served the intention of *preserving punishment*. (Those liberals have not wanted to part with punishment because without punishment we have only 'automatic goodness'.) 'Under punitive contingencies' says Skinner, 'a person appears to be free to behave well and to deserve credit when he does so.' The liberal, it appears, wants free choice and responsibility and *therefore* wants to reserve the right to blame. Skinner does not want free choice and is willing to trade in credit. There is no question of merit or demerit under the auspices of a well-run environment. (It is doubtful whether for a liberal 'goodness' *can* be 'automatic'. But in any case, there is no reason why 'automata' left without free choice or moral discrimination, should be described as either 'good' or 'bad'.)

Now in reality liberals come in all sorts. Some are indeed moralizers; not necessarily even so all of one category; many have a bias towards a Christianized and sometimes rationalized ethicity: and for some of all kinds that means reserving the right at some point to punish (or reward). But all those who can fairly call themselves liberals have at least this in common: they believe that punishment (or reward) should be deserved and relevant, as well as effective. Liberal character, if it is to be realistically described as well as if it is to preserve connection with a changing reality, must and should be capable of change and development: liberals may have been excessively preoccupied with the ideology of freedom and dignity: a liberal philosophy now can reasonably be expected to see those values in terms of real justice.

And many liberals have noticed — what Skinner also has apparently observed — that the environment itself (or 'Nature') can be punishing (or rewarding). That means only that environments, which must surely include human parents, can sometimes be *educational*. And certainly they can appear to reward or punish. The price of error is often pain: yet unless we have remained primitive animists, we do not attribute this effect to a punitive spirit. If environmental forces reward or punish, they work through 'educability' — 'learning' (to Skinner). This is how animals, quite apart from rats or humans, select and adapt to their environment — find out, in short, what *is* their best environment. Environmental 'contingencies' accidentally appeal to realism; to appreciate which there must be, or be developed, some sense of reality. That is what the educator, liberal or not — the human parent or the cat that cuffs its kittens — is in practice inculcating. It is a question of what language can be understood.

One might think that Skinner can only understand the permissive or Spockian liberal, and takes that as the representative. Clearly what Skinner doesn't approve of, or admit, is the reasonable realistic liberal. Thus he himself is the antagonist of that 'freedom of thought' which insists on seeing things for itself and resists all dogma, even that of experts.

Skinner wants us, it is clear, to give up moral education: not only, it seems, of a traditional, but also of an individualistic experimental kind: or for that matter, one would imagine, any kind that depended on the direct influence of an older upon a younger person — which would cover many parental attempts. The behaviouristic intention is directed first towards environments not people. We, liberals and all, who have already wondered how you recognize a better environment when you see it — except in so far as it has produced better men and women — must now note that something you can call people (including teachers and parents) is an unavoidable part of the environment.

Whatever in the context you come to accept as better, happier, wiser, more productive, more creative, both kinder in co-operative or immediate relations and more able to receive stimulation from them, thus furthering general human productivity (we could afford to allow a long and varied list) — not much of it can be defined in advance. If the environment is in the long run to do all the important work, you must learn from it rather than prescribe: that part of the environment at least which is real nature, whether genetic or physical, before you have discovered enough to intervene, must be given a chance. Then if you wait till the environment has had a fair run and, with proper scientific empiricism, leave it to teach you how it has made things better, your only sufficient test will be after all that it has made people feel and behave better (in one or more of the senses given above, or as many more as you like). That would be a natural environmentalism: but of course Skinner means something different: an artificial environment engineered by Procrustean experts.

If you have precluded the desire for freedom and dignity (which must include at least also the desire to have worthwhile and respectable opinions — to be able to judge and to choose what one prefers) there will not be any people, not ones certainly that you will recognize, who will be able convincingly to inform you how the environment works, and is better, for *them*; still less how the particular one, by comparison either with historical or common-sense standards, can be objectively described as better. Most people will not know anything about history in the sense of the way that the now discarded tradition did or did not work for their forebears, even the most recent: and commonsense will also have been ruled out if you have left nothing common in human feeling and value to appeal to: there will be nothing left except resignation to a purely social fate; except, no doubt, a sporadic will to destruction.

The permissive or laissez-faire liberal might find a sense in which he could be said to leave education, moral or otherwise, to the environment: but only because he was of the type that subscribed to the Pelagian article of faith in Original Virtue — people will find the way to their best life if you leave them alone enough. But no honest liberals have ever made this total non-intervention work: they always find that the environment, whatever or wherever it is, begins as a jungle that demands rational clearance and moral colonization.

On the other hand Skinner and his followers or kind certainly do not believe in moral and psychological laissez-faire. They do not propose to leave the environment or its individual inhabitants alone for five minutes; but to manipulate the one and thereby 'improve' the others. We have seen that they cannot know what they mean by this intention and therefore we must also ask who is to try and carry out a probably meaningless and certainly hypothetical aim by techniques which cannot help being dangerously experimental.

The answer, no doubt is – They Themselves, or the representatives they have succeeded in indoctrinating – a highly specialized elite which would establish itself by the most benevolently despotic brainwashing: and thus, as we may reasonably conceive, could never be overthrown; since its infiltration of human aspiration and self-cognizance would progress towards the irreversible.

Even in so admirable a book as Karl Popper's *The Open Society*,* which goes as far towards tackling the liberal-democratic problems, political, psychological and moral, as any I know and which proposes so much that keeps the liberal spirit attractive and also appears to make it commonsensical, we see that very good liberals and thinkers can be far from averse to social engineering. Popper stresses that his preferred kind of engineering would be 'piecemeal' (and not, therefore, authoritarian). But he does not solve, or even much go into, the problem of the 'engineering expert' nor hence convince us that engineering, piecemeal or wholesale, can be accepted with gratitude and without unease.

Popper pins his democratic faith to our institutions and our willingness to preserve them (which of course already depends on the extent and degree of our civic enlightenment). But as basic and practical politics he does not tell us much about what these irreplaceable institutions are, or how they can be preserved in function. The most important of them – at least the one that is so obvious that it can hardly help naming itself – is our right and ability to give our rulers the sack every so often.

That is no doubt a splendid and perhaps the best democratic invention. But to be securely useful it must surely allow us to assume that our rulers recognize for themselves the obligation to go: moreover, that we can sack a whole class or type of rulers, who will not be able to leave behind them an indistinguishable set of seat-warmers.

It is in some ways analogous to that other invention which we are often told is the most splendid of all: the T.V. switch. And it is alike in its characteristic weakness: it is negative and therefore obscures reality; we think we have done something and that encourages us to withdraw from finding out what is really being done. Getting rid of the government wipes the slate clean for its

---

* See p. 256 for further discussion.

members—it is a five-year statute of limitations on their offences; which applies to but few other crimes.

What is troubling about Popper's institutionalism is that it is political and social only—in the narrow sense of the terms. Our political and administrative institutions no doubt represent fairly respectable compromises; our social institutions more often than not are *respected*, or at least for the time accepted, conventions which represent the more successful of a number of partisan prejudices. It would be surely impossible to spread this institutionalism to the social engineering on which Popper bases his hopes of a better world; even if it *were* 'piecemeal' and so without any generalized authority, even abjuring it: the more so indeed if it were 'piecemeal': because no piecemeal 'engineer' can with justice deliberately try to institutionalize his expertise, however intelligent and well-intentioned, beyond its self-prescribed field.

That is, nevertheless, what experts and engineers (political of course, but also social) are inclined or tempted to do. It needs small acquaintanceship with human affairs and behaviour to recognize that as a rule specialists, either as particular individuals or as members of groups, want to become authorities and to extend their empire: and that within their professional groups they also mostly want to lead, or become the local 'alphas'. Moreover, although their professional work may remain geared to the concrete and practical, experts, not less than other human beings, fall readily into inflated ideology of one kind or another. If this remains within the area of professional competence it may well receive automatic correction from colleagues. Or it may be only of a negative or exclusive sort, inflating perhaps the professional status or mystique and keeping outsiders (potential critics and common realists) outside. This has already been discussed in relation to some of the so-called 'human' sciences, both in the social and the psychological areas, where there is often a concealed and exclusive definition of what may be called 'science' which includes some preselection of what in the circumstances may be treated as 'human'—and which is therefore circular.

That situation of the 'human' sciences seems to me to provide a liberal argument against social engineering even of the modest 'piecemeal' type. There are no obvious built-in safeguards to inhibit the 'engineer'—social worker, therapist or administrator—from preferring his own speciality and therefore from seeking to generalize it. Or from preferring next his own clan: or even from turning it into a mystical club and blackballing the would-be novice. Or from helping to discourage charters for competing clubs. In some clubs the rules are relatively simple and cut-and-dried and can hardly avoid publicity. (I am not of course referring to the rules of examination for admission to many professional bodies, which are necessarily public: more, rather, to the 'form' in the Guards or Etonian sense.) In those professions which have very strictly prescribed techniques (but which also are safe only with the inanimate or at least the non-human) a similar public vigilance is possible. But medicine, with the psychotherapies, for one example, is at least a borderline case. Certainly many of its techniques are indeed strictly prescribed and others strictly limited. But one would be hard put to it to deny that the profession has many aspects of the mystical Club and the mystique. That implies that many of the practices of its individual practitioners derive their authority from an inflated ideology, from assumptions about privilege and exclusive status, which have no logical or empirical warrant and which are self-generated by the traditional group.

I do not see why 'social engineers' should be in less danger of *hubris*: and this whether they adhere to some political or social establishment, or on the other hand are ideologically reformist or revolutionary. They, too, like priests and doctors, are at both their most admirable and their most useful as 'amateurs' (never when correctly used a term of derogation, but meaning rather one who follows with spontaneous human concern a loved vocation).

One must admit that human beings do not seem to be able to do very much for large numbers of other human beings (who must most of the time be in actual need of having something or the other to be done for them) without large-scale and complex organization. But perhaps more than ever when we can do such a lot of things, many of which many human beings at any given time must find desirable or even necessary, we need to be meticulously careful as to what we are actually doing, and by whom and to whom; and also to *know* in advance as far as possible what it is and how it is likely to turn out and be metamorphosed in the activity. One of the universal initial problems here is that the unity of theory and practice is mostly so poorly grasped and so misleadingly interpreted. Social action as such has great prestige – 'producing results' *tout court* is accepted as a laudable noise: whereas action, whatever it is, is even if harmless, meaningless, unless it is informed; while results unless they have been *reasonably* predicted, are not even *results*. Social 'experts' often not only treat the rest of us (often unreflectingly or even with the 'best' intentions; that is, often no intentions) as guinea-pigs but also share and take a large share in our general human feeling that it is practically always better to do something than nothing.

That is a natural emotional response to our private and public disorders which look to us as if they are always rushing to the brink of disaster — of these we have enough. And we always have had. And no doubt many people have always said: Will somebody please *do something*? (in the past to God or to the local magician, whose excuses were supernatural and therefore infinite). The moral danger we have to face and to evaluate springs from the fact that we can now do so much that the inhibiting and judicial safeguards can hardly operate. The political and social danger lies in the assumed rule that *What you can do, that you may*. And one suspects that sociological experts, often remaining academic even in their statistical investigations, are not always above a theoretical invention of new emergencies.

It will be seen, I hope, that I am talking about the likely human situation of our labours of amelioration and social progress, to which the liberal is naturally and inevitably attracted while he recognizes that this must have machinery and that somebody must administer it. He may, and should, also recognize that he and his kind are not specially good at taking a hand in them: and perhaps for the very reason that he really wants to be better, and flatters himself sometimes that he is better, at dealing with immediate personal relations, his friends and family and those who have any reason to depend upon him. What he less often grasps is that there is a genuine hiatus between the two envisagements of human problems and relations and that those who are good at the immediate may be less good, or even bad, at dealing with the objective and ramified. It might still be true that you can organize human beings, even for their own genuine if partial good, if you can handle them, or be schooled to handle them as objects or things. That ability, in special and genuine emergency situations, makes a good doctor. But he is not the only kind of good doctor, and we don't want him exclusively or all the time.

It appears nevertheless that, for the foreseeable future anyway, all 'engineering' of society will require some kind of 'elite' or control by experts whose function will be at least covertly paternalistic. Admittedly this is not new: most societies that we know of have been run by a minority, even an oligarchy, of 'experts' or authorities; but until the age of universal franchise and parliamentary democracy it has been in practice accepted tacitly if not openly that these authorities were chiefly experts in their own interest — with which one could — or could not — identify: often, if one was honest, admitting that in their place one would do the same and hope to be regarded as equally or more 'expert'. Formerly the authority, however much more expert than the average at whatever had to be performed or carried out, did not have to be specialized so hopelessly far beyond the average comprehension, at least as the average needed and could make use of it.

As a corollary to this, we might add that by now there is some excuse for thinking that that democratic necessity, freedom of discussion, which surely ought not to preclude the ability to identify and criticize one's automatic or reflex responses and one's merely received opinions, is made harder instead of easier by technology. One can put it another way by saying that the media of so-called communication can further split genuine communication between the 'expert' (temporary or professional, airing opinion or knowledge) and the common man or woman. The expert's 'authority', even where it might be potentially beneficial, must be too little and brief to effect any coherent change in understanding and outlook. The Message of the Media is likely to be *Only disconnect* (in more senses than one).

H

10

Surely I Have a Right to My Opinion?
(A Note on Democratic Discussion)

There is a legal fiction that everyone over a certain tender age is understood to understand the law. Our democracy has erected itself upon a comparable fiction: that everyone can understand or may be safely assumed to understand everything, since everything may at some time concern his life and welfare. There is a Common Man (another fiction) who is capable of total information, maximum and unimpeded enlightenment. Technology, too, in the form of television, has even made him/her visible so that we think we recognize and can identify what in him/her is both Common and individual. That makes it only more obvious that more of us are more than ever run by an elite of 'experts'. It is true that the 'elite', often because it has to rely on the skill of technological teams, is far more diffuse than has been known before: and that therefore a hierarchical structure in our societies is less prominent and that, where it exists, it is largely embedded in the mechanics and routine of administration. What has already been implied may also be true – that many of the 'experts' are really only experts of opinion: adept, that is, in presenting opinions which may or may not have any bearing on realistic meaning. That fact might appear democratically hopeful but is actually democratically misleading. For example, members of the public may be and often are invited to give their own opinions in the public eye of box-watchers: free and open discussion with admitted 'experts' (of opinion, as above): and *their* opinions will certainly be listened to or at least monitored, further up the scale. But there in effect the listening ear will be listening to, and recording, not much of the intrinsic value of these opinions: but rather trying to gauge how much influence they really represent: and the ears will be those, in this case, of other 'experts' in all sorts of fields which to the lay eye may seem only remotely related, if at all. The expert eye, on the other hand, will be fixed on the way its speciality is faring.

All that implies that the elite is by no means homogeneous; not sufficiently, so many would say, to form an elite. But even if all they share is 'expertise' in something or other that the community has been persuaded to believe it wants, the classification can still hold. Indeed we may not be strictly hierarchic; but as Ralf Dahrendorf puts it in *Society and Democracy in Germany* there is still an Above and a Below. It may be held that the 'experts' are so many and so diverse, as well as so widely ramified, that though their specialities may often be linked more or less closely, more or less remotely, they are necessarily, in any conjunction, conflicting: and what then could be a better illustration of liberal democracy in function — free discussion? free-for-all argument? And after the very heart of J. S. Mill.

But in practice there can be few ways in which we show ourselves as more enslaved than we are in our conception and habits of discussion. The common (and vulgar) discussion about the 'irrationality of Man' is highly objectionable, but it can here be taken as an illustration: Man is an irrational being; Man is Rational. Apart from exhibiting the usual logical error, the Either-Or already complained of, this leads away from a useful and observable meaning: that human beings only sometimes arrive at their conclusions by reasoning. The rest of the time they act according to habit, convention, prejudice, and sometimes passion; in other words, *non*-rationally.

It is a typically liberal-democratic hope that medial communication might in this matter improve us; that by giving us, or some of us, a chance to bring our bad habit into the daylight, we might even raise the level of *reasonableness*, or at least learn that it is desirable to do so! (*Reasonableness* — not 'Rationality' or 'Rationalism'.)

But the inevitable show-biz competitiveness of medial discussion makes this less than likely, because it wonderfully concentrates the mind on one's common-denominational passions.

Nevertheless, by 'reasonableness' I generalize (and so does Popper in *The Open Society*) a quality which some human beings display and which is in all at least theoretically potential. I mean by this a willingness to discover for oneself, or to listen to, an argument or proposition, to examine with as much honest disinterestedness as one can muster in order to see whether or not it is an accurate and honest deduction from premisses rooted in real observation: and if it passes these tests to be persuaded, or even converted, by it. Of this kind is the only genuine free discussion. It has, moreover, a great deal to do with freedom itself, as a value and as a fact: it entails respect for the freedom of others to find their way unhindered. And it is the essential though not the sufficient instrument for arriving at conclusions that are true, valuable and humane; that means also for initiating valid changes that are morally necessary and for making correctly the step — which is also necessary — from theory to practice.

It is something that as a species we need and have always needed — quite urgently — and something which we have not yet achieved; a need which we have hardly begun to realize.

Free discussion in the sense I have given, is almost entirely lacking from our exchanges of argument, public or private. The apparatus of democratic control — chairman, rules of procedure, accepted manners of debate — affect only overt behaviour and do next to nothing to educate attitudes: if the apparatus were effective, we should hardly need it, for the attitude and habit of disinterestedness imposes its own much stricter rules. The habit is moral rather than intellectual: at least it begins in the humility that teaches impersonality.

It must be expected that a great deal of discussion, both private and public, will be ignorant: in which case one may be justified in regarding it as useless and in preferring the search for information instead. That brings us to one aspect of one of the liberal's most hazardous problems. It is only one, but since it is relevant I shall mention it here briefly and apart from its wider political aspect. That may indeed be wider but this is perhaps deeper: it belongs to the real 'infrastructure' of all our cultural moral and educational habits; for that reason its significance is obscure and often disregarded. The problem is not only that of Free Speech and Free Thought, in general in the abstract, but of what this actually entails in civilized and moral behaviour towards one's fellow-beings. What does the demand for 'Free Speech and Free Thought' require of us as both correct manners and correct morals? One of the commoner human plaints is *'Surely I have the right to my opinion'*. And — more often in public than in private — we are constrained to behave as if we admitted or conceded this right to others as well as to ourselves. But in fact we do not, as the structure of our arguments will reveal to not much more than a cursory glance—*argumentum ad hominem, ignoratio elenchi*, the whole range of veneered abuse of faculties and personalities. How shall we escape both from competitiveness and hypocrisy, how shall we maintain—or rather develop and improve—our respect for other individual human beings unless we first recognize and admit, for ourselves as well as for them, that: '*No, you haven't a right to your opinion until you have done your homework on it: until you have done all you are able, to make sure that it makes both conceptual and moral sense; that it is both honest, and as accurate as you can make it: that it is not only worth listening to but that it is indeed your own opinion—not merely prejudiced hearsay.*'

That opinion ought to be individually informed (and as an entailment invariably modest, if not always tentative) could not adversely affect any desirable and essential role of the expert, even if it were generally accepted. All day and every day we rely on special skills, from bus-drivers to surgeons; and we are not only on the whole justifiably grateful to them, and willing to depend upon them, but also seek them out and resent it if their specialized services are not available when wanted. Further, we often do not know how to discriminate among them, nor what kind of expert our actual case demands. It may be that we sometimes need a superior order of expert, an expert in expertise, to tell us this. Politicians, too, those who run the main machinery of a society, have for a shorter or longer period to adopt the expert's role. That the democratic electoral procedure makes it at present feasible to keep the period short does not mean that we can sack the concept of expert: we simply have to find another expert who will play the role, with more or less persuasive cogency (or more or less meretriciously), and thus again for a longer or shorter period. The old problem remains: *Who are to be the experts of experts?* For they would need to be disinterested to a point of detachment which would be unacceptably dangerous in a democratic society: and this elite would be unelected.

I know this is only the old problem, too, of the Guardians and that this notion or fantasy is also a problem of what the logicians call Infinite Regress. That does not alter the fact that it represents another unavoidable dilemma of would-be liberal democracy. Genuine consent to the procedures and effects of rule demands enlightened participation in decision-making. Every thinker and writer who has had to examine the meaning of democratic freedom under control has had to put up some show of facing this fact and this dilemma.

The 'solution' may often be an abstract one, like Rousseau's General Will which is no man's will — and therefore specious. It will be remembered that in Rousseau's democracy we do not delegate, we are not represented, but the General Will is our own will as individual members of the society, although admittedly revealed to us as such only in the acts of government which we tacitly authorize: and the Will thus being our own, our very own will, it cannot diminish our freedom but only augment it. It might be difficult to see how the participation and consent we are supposed actually to enjoy in our existing democratic societies is so very much less fictional than this; although it must be added in fairness that they are very much less fictional than the 'democratic' rights of, say, Soviet citizens: and even that not all legalistic fictions of the type are necessarily bad or useless, since they may maintain respect for laws which even if very imperfect are not wholly unrespectable.

Part Four
New Consciousness and Old Gnosis: Ludists and Luddites

II

The New Sensibility

If I include my next two subjects on the libertarian side of my Great Divide it is not because I am deluded into thinking that they can be classed under any of the political or economic headings which we still retain for talking (loosely) about liberalism. Nevertheless, both are in the tradition of liberal Romanticism. They are both in fact prophetic or even apocalyptic, and qualify for those descriptions in the traditional ways: among other things they tell us how we (or most of us) are all wrong and, without being very convincing in telling us what we ought to do about it, they are highly admonitory in telling us what will happen if we do or can do nothing.

When I say that they are Romantics I am drawing attention to another dichotomy, either wing of which has an essential association, the one with libertarianism, the other with authoritarianism: they are subjectivists referring to Man the introvert, while the authoritarians tend to be objectivists and extravert. That is not to say, however, that the subjectivists are always or generally much better at giving us a real insight into real people.

Herbert Marcuse's ideas are widely disseminated and no doubt ardently discussed in what is generally if vaguely known as the Third World: which here covers not only the emergent or new nations but the students, the wretched, the Blacks — $n + 1$ Worlds, one might say. As far as his readers go his appeal is certainly more emotive than intellectual or theoretical. That is not to deny that some of his insights are acute or that the psychological and material structures of society which he identifies are often originally and profoundly descriptive. He is not a Liberal- (or Social-) Democrat or any kind of Democrat; and he does not fall in with any of the policies of welfare and social justice which capitalism still feels, here and there anyway, that it must, had better, possibly still can, afford.

To him, liberalism is chiefly capitalism's most valuable instrument of cultural corruption: more indeed like a new limb or organ because, over time, it has been devised by a natural and unconscious cunning to meet a challenge of social mutation.

Affluent liberalism, he holds – the liberalism which capitalism still can, and feels it must, afford – suffocates true liberty; one might almost say it kills us with its emasculative kindness, and with its plethora of apparent choices overwhelms our very power of choosing. Liberalism is the opium of the affluent society. As he says in *One-Dimensional Man*:

> Under the rule of a repressive whole, liberty can be made into a powerful instrument of domination. The range of choice open to the individual is not a decisive factor in determining the degree of human freedom, but *what* can be chosen and what *is* chosen by the individual ... Free election of masters does not abolish the masters or the slaves. Free choice among a wide variety of goods and services does not signify freedom if these goods and services sustain social controls over a life of toil and fear – that is if they sustain alienation ... the ideology is in the process of production itself ... The productive apparatus, and the goods and services which it produces, 'sell' or impose the social system as a whole.

There is no doubt that this is a true insight into the real structure of the inner relations of affluent democracy. We might, nevertheless, ask what precisely 'the free election of masters' means. For we do not in practice elect our masters, in freedom from propaganda and hidden persuasion – they too are sold to us.

In *Five Lectures* Marcuse writes:

> The totalitarian state is only one of the forms ... in which the battle against the historical possibility of liberalism takes place. The other, the democratic form ... is strong and rich enough to preserve and reproduce itself without terror: most individuals are in fact better off in this form. But what determines its historical direction is not this fact but the way it organizes and utilizes the productive forces at its disposal ... It too works against the new forms of freedom that are historically possible ... although ... with more painless and more

comfortable means and methods. But that it does so should not repress the consciousness that in the democratic form freedom is played off against its complete realization, reality against possibility.

Liberal capitalism can in fact, and in short, meet and cap all our budding challenges, cultural and moral; it can not only anticipate our slightest wish in these categories; it can not only go one, or several, better; it can also give us a false consciousness, magically create for us wishes we would otherwise never have known that we owned. If Marcuse did not more unmistakably in later writings (e.g. the *Essay on Liberation*) choose the easier way out, the way of 'creative destruction', of the transvaluation of all values by the disestablishment of all establishment – he would be driven to a sumptuary reorganization of society: and to an almost laughably puritanical austerity (laughable chiefly because in most of his later work he is trying to show the way to undo the puritanical business-ethic of capitalism and release what he believes to be our original virtue of freedom and joy, our Schillerian Play-Man. But to achieve this, Man has to be disentangled from the tentacles of the liberal-capitalistic millepus which can suck in and absorb any of his apparent challenges).*

Again there is descriptive truth in all that: but that the lifting of capitalistic bondage is all that the average individual needs in order to burst into creative living, is a gross assumption which needs examining. The historical evidence rather suggests that the destruction of particular cultures, good or bad, is more often followed by some other party's or authority's sumptuary or selective rule: among other reasons because destructive solutions exaggerate scarcity.

There is something faintly ludicrous, too, in Marcuse's elaborated analysis of the liberal-cultural opium:

Domination has its own aesthetics and democratic domination has its democratic aesthetics. It is good that almost everyone can now have the fine arts at his finger-tips, by just turning a knob on the set, or by just stepping into a drug-store. [For British readers, I suppose, where he can buy gramophone

---

* For example, the commercial exploitation of 'permissiveness'. See *One-Dimensional Man*.

records not 'drugs'.] In this diffusion, however, they become cogs in a culture-machine which *remakes their content* [my italics].

Do 'The 48' and the 'Fifth Symphony' become bad art because everyone now can listen to them: or perhaps, even more significantly, is the Sistine Chapel aesthetically diminished because it can be visited by package tours? although it cannot be reproduced in the home? Reproduction certainly provides in some cases — painting and sculpture, for example — a serious aesthetic question. But that in itself is not what troubles Marcuse: he is not suggesting that present methods of recording won't anyway give us a very acceptable version of the great works of music; his point is that the capitalistic cultural machine, liberal though it may be in all senses, will allow us to hear only what it chooses to reproduce. Now, lacking in proper moral content though the fact may be, it is still a fact that the liberal-capitalistic reproduction machine will allow us to hear almost everything — an infinite *choice* is before us. Nor does the evil lie in the mass availability of, for example, reproduced paintings: the real aesthetic value of the originals is unaffected: either there is a real difference or there is not, and never has been (I am referring only to the best quality of reproductions!): either you can see the difference, if it exists, or you cannot. The real evil lies as usual in exploitation for profit of a real human need or value, and of this the mass availability of works of art, whatever the motive of proliferation, cannot be an example. The restriction of production might, indeed, tend towards that real evil: for the mania to possess the unique original and the insane inflation of price to which that leads is an unmistakable corruption of genuine artistic standards as well as of economic justice to artists living or dead.

Today's novel feature [Marcuse continues, in *Five Lectures*] is the flattening out of the antagonism between culture and social reality through the obliteration of the oppositional alien and transcendental elements in the higher culture by virtue of which it constituted another dimension of reality. This liquidation ... takes place not through the denial and rejection of the cultural values but through their wholesale incorporation into the established order, through their reproduction and display on a massive scale. In fact they serve as instruments of social cohesion ... The fact that they contradict the society which sells them does not count.

He is saying, so it appears to me, that truth and value *have* to be alien to society — if they are accepted they become inherently corrupted. In an important sense this is true and always has been true of any society: one of the reasons, though not the only one, may be that natural and inevitable misinterpretation which, quite apart from evil will or even prejudice, distorts and corrupts not only values but, as we have seen, ideas. We did not have to wait for liberal-capitalism for this. Here Marcuse's theory seems to be a version of that 'conspiracy-theory of society' which by implication gifts the leaders and organizers (and alpha-types) with far too much knowledge of themselves, of their class, and of history, and with far too much intelligent and conscious prescience of the social future.

What Marcuse calls 'high culture' (meaning genuine aesthetic culture) cannot in itself be either granted or withheld by a social Maecenas, however generous, or however disingenuously or corruptly lavish: it will be found and cherished, if at all, as it always has been, by individuals. And for those, their own perceptual growth and maturization in all values, human and cultural, may well be augmented, and can hardly be diminished, by an extravagant provision of opportunities, however basely intended — one cannot see how this treasure can be extended as social blackmail nor where it can be laid up except in heaven.

Marcuse says that 'it is good that almost everyone can have the fine arts almost at his finger-tips', but it is by no means clear or certain that that is what he really believes. If liberal-capitalism provides, for whatever motives, something which in the sense of being life-enhancing and inducing to human spiritual growth for any or some individuals, is good for *them*, then the fact that it would not have been provided in our time and conditions except through the channels of liberal capitalism does not stop it being good. But even if it were good, Marcuse would not like it — and as we have just implied, he would probably like it all the less. Corrupt in intention, there is no health in any of the works of liberal-capitalism: they must all be swept away so that a totally regenerated sensibility or perception can really see (maybe for the first time) *what* is good for the new Man.

As I have just suggested, a total cultural destruction is no kind of evidence that what remains, if anything, *will* be a new and better sensibility or, therefore, a new kind of Man or Woman: Marcuse's implication here is not only a gigantic Either-Or (see p. 75ff): it is a version of the doctrine of 'privileged moral minority' — let us call it 'Schapesheepism' — which vitiates, mostly imperceptibly, many of our social theories, especially those with a futuristic trend — and in fact all the social theories that remain to be considered, for they are all in some sense millenary and miraculous, appealing to a dramatic if not instantaneous change of human personality which we have no obvious grounds for anticipating.

Marcuse's scapesheep are chiefly the wretched and the oppressed (like Fanon's) of the earth, the violent students and the Blacks: it appears, *because* they either cannot or will not sully their sensibility by taking any cultural leaf out of the liberal-capitalist book. If they do not do so — and we may accept that this is often their attitude — it is, however, for a medley of reasons which ought to be disentangled: in particular, whether they 'cannot' should primarily be distinguished from whether they 'do not'. For if they cannot, surely in fairness they should be given the chance of participation, more fully and intensively than they have been, before anyone is qualified to judge whether their deprivation is a virtue and an advantage, or not.

That is in parenthesis. Before we pursue it, we might consider how and why Marcuse arrives at his millenary hope of the refiner's fire.

Like others before him Marcuse has been tempted to try to reconcile Marx and Freud. To him as to these others (often liberal gradualists of about the 1930s) it appears to have been one of those glittering intellectual prizes which appeal to our psychopalaeology; like the Philosopher's Stone, or Squaring the Circle. For my own part, I have always thought that it was in many aspects a work of supererogation. Freud in his own way was just as much a determinist as Marx; and also presented us with Man (psychological) as Marx did with Man (economic) — both implying a merely partial definition of humanity.

Freud, as we know, distinguished between a Pleasure Principle and a Reality Principle: the one characteristic of infancy before educational intervention, the other of maturation; and indicated that though our task in human society is to develop from one to the other, we do not like to and often fail.

Here Freud's semantics are only doubtfully referential and seem to belong rather to his own schematic formalism than to anything we can recognize.

If Pleasure is largely identified with the erotic or its substitutes and sublimations, as in Freud's case it is, we need not be surprised if 'reality' receives an equally partial and selective definition. Freud's sense of history was no better developed than most people's; it is not a widespread human capacity and members of an established and successful class, however critical, are not likely to be better gifted in this respect. For him, his existing society *was* reality: again this is far from uncommon; and while for the majority its relation to 'pleasure', as he understood it, was oppressive, that was a good reason why he was able to look at the more uninhibited activities of the more fortunate, or more affluent, as neurotic.

Marcuse, on the contrary, certainly claims to distinguish between different kinds of social 'reality' and even to look forward to a full and human reality based on a new kind of sensibility and perception which will subsume and supersede all the pre-existing social varieties. His is a doctrine of release while Freud's was one of adaptation. (The analytic technique with its regression to the past is thought of as an instrument of release: but in practice it is a *reculer pour mieux sauter* – in the 'correct' or orthodox direction.) Marcuse's is obviously based on a much wider definition of 'pleasure'. But it is possible to wonder whether he has not, perhaps unconsciously, been too much influenced by the Freudian dichotomy and whether this does not account for an inconsistency in his description of our present liberal-capitalistic society and its relation to its individual members.

It is obvious, and it must be obvious to Marcuse, that our present Western society, though it may maintain a hypocritical façade is far from repressive towards 'pleasure', not least in the narrowly Freudian sense; and that its cultural means increasingly operate through over-stimulation and incitements to what would once have been called libertinism. But it should also be obvious that, if much of this is titillative exploitation, some of it is genuine release from old, irrational and ugly tyrannies.

But Marcuse, aware as he must be that our liberal-capitalistic society, in many ways morally blowsy and even sleazy, has effected

—if only by accident and because it could afford the money—some kind of liberation (even in the availability of the 'higher' pleasures of his wider definition), has all the same, in the interests of his as yet unrealized and unauthenticated 'new sensibility', to dismiss all these results and even put them on the side of conscious hypocrisy.

The principle of 'surplus-repression' which Marcuse thinks he detects in our society is one way of referring to something which actually exists—our stress on work, especially of an executive type, and on the necessity of competing. But Marcuse, as we can see in the term itself, attaches the notion to the Freudian category of repression; and also to something like the old puritanical ethic—the two are in no way mutually exclusive but rather even parallel: work is sanctified because it gets in the way of both leisure and pleasure (of all sorts); it leaves us no time to stand and stare for aesthetic purposes or for mere enjoyment.

There seems to be an inconsistency here. On the one hand Marcuse blames liberal-capitalistic society for its lavishment of cultural sweets and goods (which includes the flattering immoralism of some parts of the entertainment media); it takes up all our time with an excess of opportunities. On the other hand it keeps our nose to the grindstone so that we cannot look around and take our pick or even just enjoy the relaxed deployment of our natural aptitudes.

Now in fact liberal-capitalistic 'society' does nothing so conscious or deliberate. To suggest that it does so is a form of hypostasis which afflicts all notions of any society as a deliberately intervening entity. Marcuse has forgotten that all organized societies are made up of individuals jostling as best they may for whatever they can get from that society in their own interest and that of their inseparable dependents and associates.

It may well be true that the liberal-capitalistic structure of our social relations, with its emphasis on competition and on conformity to that ideal, on keeping up with all the varieties of Jones, is able to sell a renovated, better-cushioned, if still pre-coronary, gospel of work to the economically sharp-witted extraverts or the chronically anxious: and these categories may well constitute a majority. That mainly restates the perennial and unresolved and perhaps irresoluble conflict between the natural and essential liberal and the old authoritarian (much multiplied and more heavily disguised than ever). The sweets of liberty are not possessions in themselves: but they are not less real for being realized.

As always the task remains to detect, and to evaluate them; and at the same time to develop skills in dodging the new authoritarians and their new conformisms.

It may appear that something like that is really what Marcuse means: what is repressed by 'surplus-repression' could be described as our instinct for freedom of awareness and of its expression: our spontaneous enjoyment of ourselves, our lives, our perceptive capacities—and our leisure: our natural preference for working to live in all these senses, rather than the reverse.

Marcuse has been much impressed by Schiller's 'play-man', the theory that all art is play and that it is for that reason that art is our most characteristically human activity. And largely from this theory, if also from a sympathetic observation of hippies and deliberate drop-outs, he draws the conclusion that the lifting of surplus repression, as it has been practised by the puritanical ethic of abstinence-capitalism or by the fraudulent allurements of liberal commodity capitalism, will automatically deliver this 'play-man' from his psychological bonds and release the creative energy of his new sensibility.

We may go as far as agreeing that our present societies—in their educational systems especially, still do little for creative originality and even continue to do much both to distort and to repress it. And we may even admit that, provided 'surplus-repression' in the form described by Marcuse really exists, it is to such an extent a structural characteristic of our typical societies that it cannot be winkled out: nothing but a total and radical change in our dominant social attitudes will suffice to remove it. But it is not certain that it does exist because it is far from certain that, in the sense with which Marcuse is concerned, its victim actually exists: we are not all play-man, any more than we are as a majority mute inglorious Miltons or Cromwells who, given the chance, would have made a better moral job of running the world. Even under liberal capitalism many people find a satisfying outlet for their creative energies which are possibly rather simple, not competitive, and not necessarily in the category of 'high' art or culture. It must be pointed out that 'play' is characteristically a function of young animals by which they learn their necessary skills: it is not characteristic of the mature: nor do footballers and cricketers, especially skilled professionals, commonly turn into the wise old men of the tribe.

Marcuse admits that his prognosis for a liberated society might be construed as Utopian—and goes on to justify Utopianism in some limited form. It is surely simple Scapesheepism. It proclaims a privileged moral minority—consisting of all those who, we can agree, come off worst under liberal-capitalistic conditions: the wretched, the Blacks, the oppressed of our neo-colonialism. But where we have been able to see the violent overthrow of the oppressive regimes, we have not seen liberation either of these individuals or of a 'new sensibility'. We must suspect that the promise of this 'new sensibility' is largely a rationalization of a partial human definition: and we may further suspect only a new authoritarianism—with a new version of puritanism: the material and cultural fruits of liberal-capitalism, whoever manages to enjoy them and employ them creatively, are, because of their origin, inherently evil and must be thoroughly purged.

It may be thought that in my version of the 'Good' and the 'Powerful' I myself am claiming to detect and to preach another 'privileged minority'. In fact I am referring only to possible individuals who prefer life to power and whose sensibilities and judgment therefore exist in a not wholly corrupted condition: and therefore do not necessarily have to be made new. What is needed here is not a new 'consciousness' but rather a principle of recognition which, residing naturally in the intelligence and observation, although it is persistently distorted, could conceivably, at some time, and in favourable and as yet unrealizable conditions, be taught: and which could give them confidence in their own values in so far as these also are natural. I do not say that this new principle of recognition, which I shall later try to explain, either exists or will come into being. Unlike Marcuse, I do not claim to detect it in any special class; or to deny its possibility to any. Nor to be inspired by miracles and prophesying.

If I do not care for futurology, I also do not Praise Times Past—anyway not because they *are* Past. Among those who pin what desperate hopes they have to some miraculous metamorphosis, there is a type of inverse or retrospective prophet who, believing that such a change of human heart or consciousness is possible, believes in it mainly as a reversion. We have been diverted from our true development; once we, or some of us, saw, felt and thought more clearly or truly; in an older and better tradition which some of our forebears really embodied or personified and from which we have reneged or deviated.

The apologists of a revived Christian orthodoxy, Catholic or Anglo-Catholic, which during the 1920s and 1930s flourished on the borderland of literature and social thinking, were undertaking a comparatively simple exercise; and in their own terms they were describing a fact. There *had* been a Christian orthodox tradition (even if its accompanying history was one long fight about what orthodoxy consisted in and how it was to be defined), and there were many remarkable people, in and out of literature, who counted themselves within it. Within their own definitions it was and no doubt still is, logical for its adherents not only to see our salvation in reversion, in changing our hearts and minds back again, but also to assert and to believe – for faith is a virtue both of intellect and heart – that this necessary metamorphosis is possible.

But it is not the same for a contemporary prophet of reversionary metamorphosis. The advantage here of Christianity in any of its recognizable forms, or for that matter of any religion with long-established rules and rituals, is that it is a tradition with a visible history.

It sometimes looks as if the unorthodox or secular 'inverse' prophets have to invent their preferred past – the true tradition from which we are held to have erred: at any rate it is often thin and ideological (just like the 'future' of many liberals and humanists).

Even where they claim to distinguish spiritual and intellectual ancestors who may still seem to have had a better and more imaginative and moral insight into the human condition, they are hard put to it to show that this arose from realistic criticism of contemporary circumstances and behaviours and was thus directed towards practical changes which would bear on human enlightenment, correction and salvation.

Those who, secular or not, have thus believed in a kind of intellectual Fall, and that this supralapsarian condition of mankind or any part of it was historical, have been singularly unsuccessful in bringing us back to the 'right' tradition of thought and feeling: and there has not even been much agreement among them about the way in which it is actually constituted. All that the prophets and the denunciators have ever agreed on (when they have ever agreed) is that things were better in the Past, often *because* things as they may loom at us in today's short perspective often appear to us as if they could not be worse. But on what things and actually when, there has been great divergence.

Here also they believe in miracles — in a super-miracle. For if it is improbable that we shall all be changed just by seeing the light — one moreover reflected from the past — it appears downright impossible that we shall achieve a better consciousness, insight, or sensibility by obliterating all that civilization has painfully scraped up.

Marcuse and his followers do not have to believe that we have fallen: their cleansing destruction is compatible with the belief that we are, given a chance, on the way up.

The secular supralapsarian on the other hand does not have to go in for liquidation. He simply has to call us all to repentance.

In another way, Theodore Roszak (who wrote *The Making of a Counter-Culture*) is also a millenarian of the new sensibility. In a later book, *Where the Wasteland Ends*, he gives, in the first half, a description of our malignant technological proliferation which is at least as good as Marcuse's. Indeed somewhat better, because it is more concrete and the details are less entwined with theory.

The second half is his therapy or prescription for what we ought to do about it. It must be said that even in the first and more satisfactory part of the book the description is acceptable only in so far as it is confined to observable behaviour. His diagnosis, the connection of supposed causes with their effects, is less convincing.

One important reason for this is that Mr Roszak has committed not only an Either-Or, but also a *post hoc propter hoc*. In practice he puts the Devil on one side, and all his works on the other. He denies in effect that he is a Luddite; but in the intellectual sense it is hard to believe that he is anything else: he would like to retain perhaps some of the more comforting and alleviating products of scientific technology while abolishing the theorization and the *Weltanschauung* which led up to them and are their direct progenitors. And he wants to do this retrospectively. Like Blake he wants to wipe the evolutionary slate clean of Newton. This is characteristic of inverse prophets and is part of their wishful thaumaturgy: indeed it is the most extensive of miracles: one which makes what *was, not* to have been, is really more impressive than one which rearranges in advance what otherwise might be about to be: among other effects, it removes or denatures part of the present and hence also of what otherwise might have been the future too. And of course it is nonsense: whatever we may be, we are as we are because what preceded us was as it turned out to be. That is not meant to be a profession of hardline determinism: or a total denial of individual choice in our immediate circumstances as they present themselves to our awareness and understanding. It refers, in the present context, to intellectual and scientific systems and descriptions, e.g. Newton's; they can be proved wrong or modified: and constantly they are. But in their time those which have survived long enough to be criticized were necessarily honest; they were the most comprehensive and evidential accounts of some class of human experience; and they cannot be written out of history. Are we to believe that there are Orwellian angels as well as devils? That it is wicked to tamper with the record of human events and behaviour (which is often faint or false and gives if not an excuse at least an explanation for misinterpretation) while it is proper to doubt or to cast aspersions on the intellectual or scientific record of impersonal events which has been accepted as factual, as part of a logical and public consensus, agreed only as open evidence and demonstration, to later criticism, and to possible demolition and substitution?

According to Roszak the objective mode of consciousness which dominates Western civilization is largely, if not wholly, the *cause* of our unhappiness and alienation. Now in his intention I have some sympathy with Roszak, as I have shown elsewhere (see *A Soul in the Quad* and *Philosophy and Human Nature*). We have shared a common theme, which has two complementary aspects:

(1) that in European thinking there has been a continued and increasing tendency to concentrate upon and to overestimate objective, especially quantifiable, and therefore easily demonstrable, results; a tendency which is particularly misleading and therefore deplorable in the so-called human sciences—for those can quantify themselves out of their real subject-matter, the human personal individual: moreover, that even in the impersonal sciences some subjective ele-

ments—of interest, attention and choice—are and should be present;

(2) the relative social prestige of objective attention and research, particularly of the achievement of exact and demonstrable results, has considerably demoted the subjective contributions of human mind—we don't, for instance, give the *right* kind of hearing to poets, artists and eccentrically wise individuals. This, among others, has a circular effect—we don't know how to encourage them to say what is worth listening to. Finally, this inferior status has been, more than willingly, it seems, accepted by current philosophy, which has also robbed itself of its subject-matter in order to produce 'results': these to be 'objective' have to be purely analytical, hence devoid of human content or, as a philosopher might say—'trivial'.

None of that nevertheless is to say that objective and quantifiable results are not true results; or that they are not achieved by and dependent upon tried and agreed methods of investigation; nor that when they cohere into a systematic picture of the world, or one of its classifiable aspects, it is not, as far as it goes, a true picture of that to which such methods are applicable, which we must accept on rational grounds. Nor indeed is it to deny that the special sciences, since they subscribe to a unified and logically irrefutable method of inquiry, complement one another, and form a coherent body of knowledge which prescribes the way we are obliged in honesty and logic to conceive the universe we live in— to conceive, not necessarily to imagine; as long as we know how to distinguish conception from imagination when it is necessary to do so.

That amounts to saying that I believe that the concepts 'fact, truth, knowledge' are better reserved for the results we achieve when we follow rational and evidential methods of inquiry; but it is certainly no kind of admission that the 'results', whatever they may be, should automatically be put into immediate application (or even circulation). That is a difficult point if we subscribe to freedom of thought and freedom from censorship of any kind: but a scientific or technical capacity, either in research, development or application, entails no moral or prescriptive right nor even any social priority. And it is certainly possible that other intellectual pursuits and other ways of looking at the world may be not only of more general interest, but also of more value, both individual and social.

But the scientific way of looking at the world, within the sphere of its subject-matters and its conceptual limits, is unassailable. It stands for an honest mode of consciousness. A scientific thinker cannot think or conceive other than his observation and experience oblige him to do. Roszak, notwithstanding, challenges both the method of inquiry and the mode of consciousness which qualify scientific thinking: in favour of what he calls 'Old Gnosis'. That it is old, or rather that it is conceived to be old, is one of the most significant things about it: the word, whatever else, stands for that rewriting of intellectual history, already in evidence. Admittedly, Roszak says:

> Yet what is the alternative to humanist resignation? To forbid the quest for knowledge? Return to old superstition? Foster illusions? Deny the truth? Of course we must not grow contemptuous of the truth [as if a great many of us had ever been anything else]. But neither must we grow so contemptuous of our fellow human-beings [as if a great many of those who have governed or led the human race had ever been anything else] as to believe that the truth has been nowhere known or honoured among them except in European society since the scientific revolution.

'Good sentiments' (one might say with Beatrice), 'and well-expressed.'
But Roszak continues:

> To cast aside all the prescriptions and non-scientific realities by which men and women have lived for so long is to settle for a truth that is little more than an operational superficiality, worse, a license for the making of well-informed fools.

Mr Roszak is playing on the word 'truth'. In the first place, does anyone capable of serious reading and understanding believe that true statements were not made, accepted and acted upon before the scientists made their methodological revolution? Or, in the second place, that formerly, as now, a lot of statements were not made which now, if we are capable of any evidential judgment of reality, we must describe as mistaken, nonsensical or lying?

Mr Roszak does not agree: 'What is true to me is what I am persuaded is true.' And he does not mean 'persuaded' by rational argument or by evidence:

> What we are persuaded to call the truth is that which engages us at many and more secret levels until we feel that the whole of our being has been warmed to life ... It is the experience of the truth ... which is universal.

Or:

> Truth to be human truth is what persuades people in their representative humanity—it has to be universal and that means convincing to their common *reason* [my italics].

There *is* an interpretation in which that last makes sense: science, for instance, does have to appeal to a common reason. We reason correctly when, and at whatever level of complication, we make deductions from our experience which we then refer to and test by the way our experience goes on and develops. Scientific thinking proceeds in the same fashion, but of course in a field which is more circumscribed and often also more complex than that of day-to-day experience.

We can say, then, that scientific thinking, if it is acceptably scientific, is a development of 'common sense'. There are, alas, undeniably hideous abuses of the material results and applications of scientific thinking but that does not invalidate it as a development of the correct and natural way of using our minds.

Mr Roszak is claiming that magic, shamanism, and some kinds of mystical thinking, as well as anti-scientific philosophies of various kinds and provenance, must be accepted as having led and still leading to 'truths' which are at least on a par with those discovered by strictly scientific methods: *at least*; for in attacking the actual methods and techniques by which Western sciences pursue their inquiries, he effectually denies that they do make the link with ordinary human reason or 'common sense' or develop logically out of its natural and spontaneous attitude to experience, when that is honest and unimpeded.

I suggest, on the contrary, that magic, shamanism, etc., have done little to encourage common sense and much to baffle it and divert it. 'Old Gnosis' has often been Old Priest (or New, or Old Shaman) writ too large for anyone to see round or over it. Human beings, for the vast majority, have never 'lived' by 'truth' – or by reason or by common sense – because they have seldom lived by individual (and clearly and honestly 'persuaded') understanding, but by authority. And Mr Roszak and those with similar beliefs are mainly, if unreflectingly, trying to impose a new sort of authority: one that, like all the others, can only interfere with or obfuscate this freedom of thought which otherwise is our common and natural *habit* and that of the scientist too. It is the way we receive and deal with our experience *if we are not prevented*; although of course we almost invariably *are* prevented.

The word 'habit' is preferable to 'right' for that last reason, that human beings have to be prevented from thinking 'freely' – that is, correctly – in their given, but limited, fields. Of course no one has the 'right' to stop them or to put obstacles in their way. But in fact they cannot be stopped from thinking freely except by fraudulent or forceful methods, which have so far dictated most of the world's intellectual history. Mr Roszak should at least consider whether advocating a return to irrationality is not in the same category. (Here as usual I am referring to the 'anti-rational'. The 'non-rational' includes imaginative and intuitional thinking. The 'irrational' should not be used to include them.)

The scientist's thinking is in the same natural position of 'freedom': it proceeds as a development of a natural and necessary habit and no one has the right to *impede* it: to try to prevent anyone, scientist or not, from following his thought to its logically honest conclusions and from stating it and them: or to try to pervert it and them by false or tendentious arguments.

I repeat that rational (or reasonable, or commonsensical, or realistic) methods of thinking are natural and are never in themselves harmful. Nevertheless I agree with Mr Roszak, who puts it well, that the practical methods by which some sort of scientific inquiry proceed are open to moral objection and often actual abhorrence. There is indeed, I believe, an indisputable case for control and limitation of scientific research, that many scientists too, young and older, are increasingly aware of and themselves argue. That must imply a limit to the testing of scientific thinking. To guard against ignorant authoritarianism and actual loss of what is communally beneficial in the sciences, I believe that this control would come best from within the scientific community itself (and to be effectual, meaningful, or even possible, it could hardly come from anywhere else). That of course would mean a large change in moral outlook, for many scientists, for many ignorant laymen and for many more exploiters of scientific capacity – something about which we may well feel less than optimistic. Another 'change of heart' or of consciousness: nevertheless not more unlikely and much less remarkable than the one to which Mr Roszak sometimes appears to exhort us.

Let us for the time being give up the words 'truth' and 'knowledge' – and substitute the word 'reality' (with a small 'r', and no cheers at all). That, too, can be used as a 'prestigious', magical or rhetorical word. (It is not so much used by scientists.) But it is also more capable of an acceptable unity of classification: on the simple ground that we *can*, in common usage, mostly distinguish between 'reality' on the one hand, and fantasy and perceptual error and hallucination on the other. (I am not putting the last three in one exclusive category.)

Now common sense and/or reason can make this distinction: and science does not blur it or substitute it; and often helps to sharpen it. 'Old Gnosis', on the contrary, often ignores it.

That by their sense-extensions, microscopes, prisms* or telescopes, spacecraft, bathyscopes, scientific techniques introduce us to levels of experience of which we were hitherto unaware does not make those experiences less 'real'; or even introduce a new philosophic problem about 'reality'.

We have a natural way of comparing our conscious perceptions – what we happen to be temporarily or permanently aware of – with that of others, which is reasonably convincing to all of us. This is indeed so 'natural' that the question of the nature of reality does not usually arise and, if it did, would appear in most circles academic or bizarre: the question for instance whether our new perceptions are real and not hallucinative – ostentation is usually enough – because for one simple reason, we know that they are corrigible. Reality is a world of common faith in which we walk and it exists without support either of intellect, scientific or otherwise, or of Old Gnosis, in the sense Mr Roszak appears to mean. Nevertheless scientific intellection generally confirms it: it is only Old Gnosis, in one form or another, that is likely to start an argument or a doubt and so shake its necessary security.

* Mr Roszak is quoting Goethe in using these examples.

Mr Roszak's account of the 'objective consciousness', which he rejects, seems to underestimate this human capacity to distinguish and, where necessary, to correct perception. But if, as is here claimed, it is essential and fundamental even if it can err (indeed *because* it can err, and be corrected), then consciousness must be regarded, potentially and at least in some or even many people, as a self-unifying process which in a developing mind is always establishing what is real and rejecting what is not.

Mr Roszak claims that there are two kinds of consciousness. His criticism of the scientific kind (as 'objective', here meaning superficial and so limited as to be false to 'reality', compared with intuitive and mystical ways of cognition) borrows support not only from Goethe's dislike of prisms and microscopes, but also from Heisenberg, initiator of the principle of indeterminacy, whom he quotes:

> In natural science, the object of investigation is not nature as such, but nature exposed to man's mode of inquiry.

In short, he believes that scientific methods, and in particular scientific techniques, are illegitimate ways of interfering with 'reality'.

It is surely obvious, if awkward, that scientific description and awareness exist on the same side of perceptual reality as our ordinary unaided sense-consciousness: and that what we see through the microscope is an extended category of that consciousness: while what we see through the prism is the same kind of spectral analysis of which consciousness is capable when the heart leaps up (or not) on beholding a rainbow.

Philosophically, Goethe or Heisenberg tell us nothing more than Kant: that ways of perception, natural or extended, and their communication and interpretation of the world that is not oneself, is a human construction of human sense-organs and human intelligence which we communicate to one another by means of a human language humanly accepted as such. Outside there is nothing, as Wittgenstein, in this case reasonably, might have said, to be *said*, or rather affirmed: what can be said — and often should be, since we are questing, wondering and imaginative beings — is agnostic, speculative; and from time to time hallucinatory.

Mr Roszak simply but illegitimately leaves the door open to a new—but not very new—kind of irrationalism: the fact that not everything which calls itself Rationalism is reasonable does not make Irrationalism as such any more respectable. It has been pointed out more than once that the rationalism-irrationalism dichotomy and opposition not only provide us with one of our leading Either-Ors but actually and historically have participated in a comedy or errors in which they are constantly taken and take one another for each other.

For example, it has been characteristic of theologians, Catholic in particular, to use the 'Rational' and 'Reason' as referring to the completely Universal or abstract Idea (instead of to the actual reasoning processes by which human beings reach logical and demonstrable conclusions based on their experiences: a meaning which is or *should be* characteristic of the opposition when they call themselves Rationalists). The theological 'Rational' becomes identified with some form of philosophic Idealism, which by ignoring the constant intervention of material or contingent existences makes reality consist in universal Ideas. That introduces another semantic confusion—if the Ideal is interchangeable with the Real, both sides—the Idealists and the generally pro-materialist secular Rationalists—can call their philosophy 'Realism' and they do and have done so, thus demonstrating that a rose by the same name can smell semantically just as bad.

Each side in this perennial Either-Or has charged the other with standing Reality on its head—or claimed the credit of having at last stood it on its feet. Incarnation, even in the most secular sense, is unquestionably a great mystery. How do universals arise; how does an experience or a class of experiences of a medium give rise to an idea or a concept, which is able to identify, discriminate, and relate other experiences to the first and thus re-embody itself in the original medium of experience in a shape of change? May we not say that, if we are being both reasonable and realistic—and the two are inseparably related—this natural impulse to the ordering of the complexity of the given results is a unifying and developing process which might even be called a reciprocal education between a person and his environment; the establishment of a kind of osmotic balance felt as a common reality?

It is this process of *realization*, of which human beings are potentially capable, which deserves, if anything does, the name of Realism: and however it is achieved, that is not, as Mr Roszak

believes, by 'Rhapsodic Intellect' on the one side, or by technological interference on the other. We should try to stand 'Reality'
not on its head but on its feet: and no discussion perhaps is more
jejune than the Either-Or between the two philosophic factions
that have dominated alternately our intellectual life since the
time of Plato: the insistence that 'Reality' *is* either the Ideal or
the Material. This is to make a split which the natural human mind
in innocent vision would not make if it were allowed to work
naturally.

But it seldom is, if ever, in our kind of world. And I think that
Mr Roszak, who himself would certainly like to release our natural
mental and psychological powers, is practising a partisan interference—on the 'Idealist' side; and trying to stand what, if he went
in much for philosophical terminology (or jargon) he would call
Materialism, on its head (or feet—it merely depends which you
are standing on yourself at the time).

This causes some inversions which will be found odd, not only
by materialists as well as technocrats, but by common sense. For
example:

> Agriculture was invented by people living within a magical
> world-view and *by virtue* of that world-view. *Most likely* it was
> ... an invention of women, who perceived in the fecundity of
> sea and soil an image of their own sexuality ... The furrows
> in the soil were the female vulva, the digging stick ... is the
> male's phallus [my italics].

Now *more* likely, since my pure guess is as good as Mr Roszak's,
it was an invention of men who wanted to eat and saw that this
was a better way than so far discovered for doing so. Or we'll concede it may have been an invention of women who wanted to do
the same thing and even wanted their children to eat, who also
wanted it. The furrows in the soil were a good idea for planting the
seed, the digging stick also, so that the seed would grow to edible
crops.

That is in no way to deny that *also* 'To see the earth as Mother
Earth is no superstition but a brilliant and beneficial insight' (op.
cit.). Or in other words the earliest agriculturists may well have
lived in the acceptance of an imaginative, even a 'magical' world-
view. But that was not prior or even relevant, or connected to
either their need to eat or their ability to discern and make use of

the natural connections and the practical deductions therefrom which taught them the better way to do so.

What Mr Roszak calls a 'magical' world view (and this would include alchemy and probably astrology in their place in scientific history) may well have helped to direct mankind's attention to real economic as well as cultural benefits: but only in so far as it did not discourage people from learning by experience or positively helped them to do so. Elements of such a world-view can no doubt even persist as a valuable corrective to our abstract and over-collectivized technology in so far as it has lost touch with the living individual human being in his natural given growth both of body and mind. Compost may feed us more healthily and appropriately than fertilizer and D.D.T. Not *because* it is magical, but because compost has shown that it is part of commonsense: and trial and error. But it *won't* feed all of us who are here and therefore want to eat.

It is a great pity to labour the obvious but sometimes it is necessary. Mr Roszak is so relentlessly eager to overturn what he calls the scientific world-view that he will deny what is under either his or any other less prejudiced nose in the attempt to attain a complete reversal of logic and process – including the inevitable and real changes that have been wrought by historical time.

It appears that Mr Roszak would not do away with aeroplanes, though that is not certain; but it would still be logically consistent with his own premises. He appears to allow that to *aspire* to flight has been and still is natural to mankind.

It may be observed that actual flight in flying machines, among all technical endeavours and products, has demanded a long and technical process, a complex factual and material record of experimentation, involving not at first obviously related techniques of invention, discovery, false trails and failures. It has taken place, that is, if we may adapt the title of Karl Popper's book, within the *logic of scientific discovery*.

In order both to accept that fact, as he ought, and to be consistent with his own moral and psychological views, as he is entitled and no doubt also ought to be, Mr Roszak should confine his strictures and grant, where possible, his approval, only within the field of practice and social implication: if aeroplanes in themselves (i.e. actual flying) are all right, then what remains to be decided so that we may remain true to our real needs, potentialities and instincts, is purely environmental – the optimum number, size, capacity, speed of aeroplanes, and of course the uses they may be put to.

Really to allow us aeroplanes then might be consistent with our real best humanity and it would not be inconsistent with the 'natural history' of flight (using that term in its literal as well as my more metaphoric sense – an essential part of the early technical history of flight arose from the study of birds).

Nevertheless it would be inconsistent with Roszak's moral and psychological aetiology of flying – which he allows only because flight is a *visionary symbol*.*

The flight image is natural to us; it is, we might say, part of our proprioception. Indeed as we know from our early dreams and fantasies, which have long preceded under their own power any Freudian-sexual interpretation, this imaginative urge might appear to be universal. According to Roszak the flight symbol is also prior to any attempt at realization. There is a particular sense in which that is true; just as it is true, although not necessarily informative, of all our processes of invention, discovery and imaginative embodiment or incarnation: we want to do something or find something out, and we have an initial idea or intuition of the way we might proceed. Nevertheless the intuition or idea has to be in a medium or material: the symbol alone, however deeply rooted in the human heart or traditional awareness, won't tell us how to proceed, and will not magically incarnate itself. Nor will it tell us where to stop; because it has no operative power for development or inhibition within the medium: here in the matter of flying (and otherwise, too, no doubt) we have to rely on social sense and moral commonsense. Mr Roszak's understanding of symbolism is merely a refurbished Platonism – and for him the symbol is not only prior to the copy, but being more 'real', better.

There is a case, as things are, for saying that if we had contented ourselves with dream-flight instead of proceeding from turbo-prop via jet to supersonic, most of our lives would be, if really not more comfortable, safer and longer. But there is no real ground for saying that all of us would have been content with stopping short of the realization of flight: or that either denying or deploring the actual history of an inevitable development will in itself help to

* He got this from Castaneda.

solve the terrible problem and dilemma which this, like all scientific and technical and indeed most practical, development, engenders: while by diverting intellectual and emotional energy from the realistic contemplation and analysis of our situation, it may lead to a debilitating moral fatalism.

In conclusion it should be noted that the 'scientific world-view' which Mr Roszak persists in criticizing and in comparing unfavourably with an earlier 'magical' world-view, is not really a 'world-view' in his sense at all. And indeed, again in his sense, we have no evidence that a magical world-view ever subsisted, still less that whatever it was that could thus however loosely be described had any of the effects or connections which he claims for it: certainly those who subscribed to it would not, at the time when they were doing so, think of it as 'magical' in either his sense or Maskelyne and Devant's: it was for them a way of dealing with reality as they perceived it.

In claiming that there is a special and distinct (and superior) kind of universal consciousness, he is really opposing the two ways in which our minds and even our senses have received, related and organized the whole sum of their spontaneous experience: namely, the scientific and the imaginative; and trying to reject the one he does not like. For him, they are not only totally alien to one another but they are totally different ways of experiencing what is claimed to be reality: therefore one is right and the other is wrong — you cannot get out of this contradiction by admitting them as contrary or divergent modes of conception or even of imagination.

But science is not, in this sense, a 'world-view' or even a *mode* of consciousness: it does not begin in a mental receptacle which has been moulded by culture and habit, but in the five individual senses and what they tell us; and in this way it is not primarily distinct from the mental and perceptual receptables of both common sense and artistic consciousness. Hence it cannot be a 'world-view': it does not — idealistically or ideologically — universalize categories which in observation are distinct. That is left to *bad* philosophy. (And no doubt Old Gnosis.)

We are in short obliged to distinguish between a conceptual framework and a mode of consciousness even though it is perfectly true that one may arise from the other. Mr Roszak's 'world-view' merges if not obliterates this distinction. And yet it is difficult to see, unless the distinction is maintained, how a valid and trustworthy 'world-view' can emerge. Of that he himself seems sometimes aware:

> Even before our world-view guides us to discriminate between good and evil, it disposes us to discriminate between real and unreal, true and false, meaningful and meaningless. Before we act in the world we must conceive of a world; it must be there before us, a sensible pattern to which we adopt [*sic*] [adapt?] our conduct.

One of the most important characteristics of conceptual frameworks is that they have an inherent tendency towards demonstration – to becoming public. That is to say, that if a conceptual framework is honest and spontaneous – i.e. if it has arisen naturally from open experience, either experimental or personal, on the one hand, or intellectual, on the other – it seeks, or anyway does not wish or try to avoid, criticism; including, and essentially relating to, its status as 'real', 'true', 'meaningful'. That does not necessarily apply to 'modes of consciousness' which in this respect are secondary or auxiliary to conceptual frameworks. Because they open themselves to criticism, conceptual frameworks move towards and even seek consensus. If they do not achieve consensus (confirming their status as defined above by both Mr Roszak and myself) they tend to dwindle, degenerate and vanish, or become submerged: and the modes of consciousness which are affected by them or in some cases depend upon them directly, also evaporate or turn their attention to objects which have superseded their former interests, and whose reality-status has been more reliably confirmed by the new and altered conceptual framework.

Consensus, of course, cannot alone confirm an 'objective' or public 'reality-status'. That should bother me more than it does Mr Roszak – because consensus inevitably arises within a group (a society is only a large cultural group). We can see, if we want to, how, for instance Lévi-Strauss (in, for example, *L'Anthropologie structurelle*) completely identifies the reality-status both of perceptions and moral laws with the conceptual consensus of particular tribal groups: and much more like Mr Roszak than one would suspect at first, especially from someone who in his professional anthropological work adopts scientific methods and standards of 'objective' investigation. For Lévi-Strauss as for Roszak it is the

I

cultural practices of distinct tribal groups which decide both their 'mode of consciousness' and their conceptual consensus and hence their standard acceptance of the 'reality' of their percepts and of their classification of experience. To put it crudely – my 'world-view' or (in this case) my conceptual framework has as good a claim (or better) to independent 'reality' as yours if it is un-exceptionally confirmed by the beliefs and customary behaviour of my group: and the size, composition and history of groups seem to have no relevance provided the group maintains its integrity or solidarity. 'Unexceptionally', it was said; if there are exceptions, as there always must have been, in all communities, they must keep silent or be regarded as morbid freaks (and suitably dealt with, as the history of intellectual eccentricity has adequately shown).

Mr Roszak should ponder the size of groups as validating con-ceptualization and, through that, influencing perception and sense of reality. He would then realize that the scientific consensus-group is now much the largest: and that would at first no doubt re-inspire his support of the relevant 'drop-out' or 'rhapsodic' eccentric. But he might then reflect that if the scientific consensus-group dwindled to its older minority proportions – say at the time of Galileo – the scientists would again be the drop-outs or eccentrics. I am not myself depending merely on consensus-size in preferring the scientific framework, with all its faults of humane application: for the simple reason that it would not have achieved its size if it did not appeal, by rational conviction, to the great majority of acquainted people. Here again 'rational' means 'realistic': over time, they see that the conceptual framework *works* – as magic does not.

Mr Roszak's consensus-groups are small minorities. To hope for their efficacy he must believe that they will grow and spread (not only by emotional contagion but by superior conversion) towards a 'world-view' – in this case comprising both a mode of conscious-ness *and* a new conceptual framework – which an increasing num-ber will see not only as acceptable, but 'real', 'true', and therefore 'meaningful' for the adaptation of conduct.

The bearers of a potential new consciousness and the makers of Mr Roszak's counter-culture are, loosely, the young or the rising generation. Admittedly the young, as young, can hardly be treated as what I have called 'a privileged moral minority' and in this classification Mr Roszak himself is more specific and selective. Nevertheless, he appears to think, not uncommonly, that there is something special if not unique about the young of our particular established generations, both the middle-aged and the elderly. Granted the most elementary knowledge of social history, this is hard to swallow. Every new generation has always been in revolt and a large proportion of them has always reverted to type. Mr Roszak is a great believer in Original Virtue – we begin all right but have been corrupted by technocracy. 'It is the young, in their desperate need to grow up securely amid an insane environment who hunger for lively alternatives.'

What is arguable here is the interpretation of the word 'securely'. There have always been a few of the young who were interested primarily in 'lively alternatives' to whatever their social opportunities or oppressions happened to be. But what, it is more likely, is new, if anything, in our time, is that the niches for the characteristic reversion to type or to joining the establishment are more than ever being destroyed or restricted.

It would be unfair to suggest that Mr Roszak is not critical of youth's Utopian efforts and maieutic struggle for a new consciousness and a new kind of community. Nevertheless his hopes, however tenuous, are in the young; largely, I think, because their education and their experience have not yet lasted long enough, for most of them, to allow them to acquire the 'objective consciousness' which their elders have absorbed (and been corrupted by). Against that one must repeat that objectivistic obsession – excessive interest in things or objects (and also the reification of ideas) – is indeed a major defect of our Western ways of thinking; but that the ability to distinguish between the objective and the subjective, among the classes of objects that are really given to consciousness, is an essential not only of thinking but also of living. And it may just be said that an essential distinction between the young – any young – and their (no doubt few) mature elders, is that the young have not yet been fully tried on our problems and may be unable to envisage these in their practical reality or hence to decide whether or not they are amenable to change or by what developing methods of change. Here, I suspect, Mr Roszak has fallen into another Either-Or: if the old can't solve our problems, then the not-old, as a logical alternative, *must* be able to do so: of which there is no observable evidence.

Mr Roszak's hopefulness, then, faint though it may be, is wishful. He seems to locate it in the various communities dotted here and there across the U.S.A. and elsewhere—beatniks, hippies, flower people, the psychedelics—as well as students in revolt. These are his *'privileged moral minorities'*. Nevertheless he is aware that none of them, or no selection of them, in isolation, is going to make for him his new culture or way of life. He can ask, 'How *is* one to make certain that the exploration of the non-intellective powers will not degenerate into a maniacal nihilism?' Well how *is* one? Indeed Mr Roszak's sketch of a possible counter-culture may cause us to reflect painfully on the eternal and dangerous recurrence of anti-intellectualism: and his cult of youth, to wonder about 'joy through strength'; for young people are usually at least strong.

It is not much good citing the Quakers as illustrations of non-intellective well-doing. The Quakers, as well as being guided by 'moral passion—the Inner Light' were reasonable, prosperous, and *sober*—or soon became predominantly so. The non-intellective culture of the young alienated in their resistant communities might, moreover, strike us, even in Mr Roszak's description, as fairly intellective:

> One can discern ... a continuum of thought and experience among the young which links together the New Left, the sociology of [C. Wright] Mills, the Freudian Marxism of Herbert Marcuse, the gestalt-therapy of Paul Goodman, the apocalyptic body-mysticism of Norman Brown, the Zen-based psycho-therapy of Alan Watts, and finally Timothy Leary's impenetrably occult narcissism, wherein the world and its woes may shrink at last to the size of a mole on one's private psychedelic void.

A continuum of thought and experience is just what one cannot discern: rather a syncretic hotch-potch on which mere membership of a younger generation bestows no kind of unity of consciousness or anything else, in spite of Mr Roszak's wishes. Elsewhere he himself admits that 'The young', in their ignorance, give us a collage of culture—'as if they had simply ransacked *The Encyclopedia of Religion and Ethics*.' That is so; and it is difficult to have it both ways. In remaining—not too sharply—critical of youth's total rejection of existing culture, Mr Roszak also rejects and derides, with them, any need for discrimination; the natural and civilized if awkward fact that one needs to develop, for all purposes, an honest and disinterested critical faculty. Thus he assists in throwing out the baby – or rather the adult – with the bath-water. With the usual reversal: indiscriminately to reject or try to reject existing modes of consciousness will not give you a new consciousness, but only a disintegrated one. Let us note too that 'psychedelic', or drugged, consciousness does not equal 'expanded consciousness': in its blown – or 'blown-up' – registration of objects of perception or of brain-states, it may well be only another (and worse and more distorted) kind of 'microscope': an artificial technique of the sort Mr Roszak must for consistency deplore.

It has been seen that those who want to change the world and mankind for the better, fall, in the first place, into different intellectual and moral categories; and in the second, they differ as to means. Mr Roszak is chiefly concerned with 'truth' and his own definition of it – which is anti-scientific, and which may reasonably therefore impress us as largely negative and heterogeneous: if 'truth' is that of which we are inwardly persuaded we can have as many truths as there are persuaded individuals.

Mr Roszak says very little about 'freedom' and 'justice' – which together provide the liberal with his most important intellectual categories; and which certainly must, or ought to, bring him up against the problem of means of change.

But Mr Roszak appears not to think about 'means' at all seriously, any more than do his 'communities' – or privileged moral minorities. Since the change of consciousness which is his goal depends on an emotional preconception of 'truth' it at least does not have to wait upon or hope for the reasonable methods which bother, disappoint and frustrate the liberal; indeed it must abjure them. Still, if we believe that for the making over of mankind or of culture we must make over consciousness, we must try and think how it is to be done.

To a Marcuse (or for that matter, a Sartre) this change can be only revolutionary or forcible: a conclusion which Mr Roszak does not face. The Marxists, neo-Marxists, Freudian-Marxists, existentialist-Marxists (even some apparently more orthodox Marxists) also expect a change of consciousness, a new sensibility and aesthetic which will open up to all mankind the 'Kingdom' or 'City' of 'Freedom'. It is difficult to see how that will arise except as some unheralded revelation. Thus although they are in a distinct category both theoretically and practically, the Marxist, the Freudian-Marxist and the Existentialist-Marxist, when it comes to changing men, are miracle-wishers, no less than the more liberal-minded democrats.

Scapesheep and Miracle-Wishers

As miracle-wishers there is not much to choose between those who would change either our minds or our behaviour, and those who believe in a change of heart: and if they have nothing else in common both are inclined to assume that their preferred potentiality exists in some sense: either that it has existed and must be resuscitated or that it waits to be released. Thus they all, however unintentionally or unwillingly, select a privileged moral minority and are forced, logically, into futurism. Looking round existing mankind and its present moral poverty, they are almost obliged to select some minority of co-resistants or moral eccentrics—now with lesser potency—as the bearers of power to come. They all tend, that is, to go in for some form of Scapesheepism.

The belief in something akin to Original Virtue can be assumed in prophets of counter-culture. If it is present only in a more negative sense among the varieties of Marxist, it is not very far below the surface in the more democratic kind of socialist. And it can be discerned as a common feature in the two otherwise very dissimilar examples I have chosen; while the supporting evidence is not much more easy to descry.

C. B. MacPherson, author of *Democratic Theory: Essays in Retrieval*, is a democratic socialist rather left of centre. He is obviously interested in what many people believe to have been, and still to be, the liberal ethos, and appears in this book and in other writings to be trying to 'retrieve' its essentials in the political and economic traditions both of Marxism and 'liberalism'; or rather to see them both as rooted in a pre-industrial, pre-capitalistic tradition of political and social morality from which both have deviated, but especially liberalism: at least, he appears to find that liberal-democratic theory as it has developed is the more in need of justification. It has been often enough suggested, and that has also been the direction followed here, that liberal theory is ideological and unworldly, and hence has never taken sufficiently into account the opposition that exists either in established power or in automatic human competitive drive, with the result that it has been too vague both in its understanding of individualism as a natural and laudable human demand and in its realization of the necessary and just restraints that individuals and classes of individuals must impose upon one another. Thus in practice it has been obliged to compromise with power and its existing structures, and to cheat or dilute the notion of universal human justice; and during the laissez-faire period, its political and social heyday, to find an interested and partisan redefinition of the individualism which, conceived as essential justice, had given it all its moral force.

I believe that MacPherson might not necessarily quarrel with any of that. Nevertheless, for a socialist who is certainly not out of sympathy with Marxist economic determinism he takes a surprisingly 'psychologistic', even moralistic, view of the real problems and temptations of a Western liberal-democrat. I have agreed in advance that liberal-democrats suffer a two-fold temptation to the wrong kinds of individualism: our economic and social conditions encourage the extravert to seek and manipulate power; and thus to forget, if in some degree he ever remembered, that individualism is good; not only for him, but for everybody else.

The way MacPherson puts it is that we have the wrong kind because ours is 'possessive individualism'. If by this he meant only or chiefly that those with the will and the ability to compete strongly in a competitive world are likely to get to the top and there to establish and defend their exceptional and enviable position by collaring far more than their natural fair share of goods, services and status, we should regard that as trite but true.

But MacPherson does not locate the possessiveness of possessive individualism primarily in its property-sense and acquisitiveness —in its will to possess what might otherwise be the just possessions of other people. Instead, oddly, he locates it in every Western individual's sense of having a property in his own person.

It is necessary and fair to give the whole quotation where this view early appears, in a perfectly acceptable and realistic context:

The present widely felt inadequacy of liberal-democratic justificatory theory is, I think, due to the possessive quality of its basic individualism ... the philosophy of liberalism has been, since its origins in the 17th century permeated by possessive individualism which assumes that the individual is human qua proprietor of his own person, that the human essence is freedom from any but self-interested contractual relations with others and that society is essentially a series of market relations.

There is some truth in this if we apply it to the most passive members of our societies: to those in fact who are most directly challenged by the unsatisfactoriness of the market relations and who may, when conscious of the challenge, grab at the only property they certainly have, their individual being. But in the case of those individuals – extraverts and 'alpha-types' – who, in our 'market' conditions, are most likely to get to the top, it is doubtful that they are, at any high degree of consciousness, much concerned with their own individualities, possessive or not. The type is generally inclined to take itself for granted, so that the sense of its own value is comparatively effortless. Its natural lack of self-criticism and its faith in its own merit are reinforced by success. True, success will lessen any chance that it might reflect at all on possessiveness: moralizing on one's shortcomings is more often a side-benefit of failure. Thus unreflectingly possessing its own individuality, it can move into the territory of other individualities with a good heart and an unburdened conscience, if not with enhanced self-righteousness.

Which makes it all the harder for those other individualities, potential or developed, to possess themselves.

Surely it is an essential and an established tenet of democratic liberalism that we *must* possess ourselves? If we are to begin to be humanly free and responsible we must have an identity and a location; and that also entails a minimal property in our own livelihood and labour-contributions. Moreover we can add the rider that if we are not thus morally and legally entitled to this 'property' in ourselves and our own natures, someone else, by private domination or by public invasion, will take us over. *Some* vigilance, some 'looking-out' for ourselves, *is* part of the price of liberty – the alternative is some degree of enslavement, and of diminution from full humanity. Thus self-possessing individuality is one of the elements of the human definition.

The desirable contrary to the possessive-individualist, according to MacPherson, is the *developmental* individual, someone who is concerned with developing his own powers and gifts and who abjures the 'extractive' kind of individualism, both as behaviour and as definition – the true liberal-democrat rejects exploitation, both of his neighbour and of the world's necessities and goods. Both right and laudable: but MacPherson is no clearer than any of the other miracle-wishers as to where this correctly liberal morality is to be found nor, if it is discovered, how it can be implemented with power: least of all how it can be created in conditions that make it unlikely or unnatural. MacPherson, in short, also believes in or at least hopes for 'change of heart' – or of consciousness: by miracle or magic? That he has done no more than arrive at and become jammed in this common impasse is practically illustrated by his doctrine of 'equal access': 'equal access' to the means of labour and development must be guaranteed if democracy is to have any meaning. Again true and laudable. But surely this is no more than old 'equality of opportunity' writ in small print that obscures the implications? Certain suggestions have already been made about what is likely to be the real value of that slogan under competitive social and educational conditions. It is significant that while discussing 'equal access' MacPherson gets involved in an abstract intellectual discussion which is of no particular relevance:

> The difficulty ... [is] that the beneficiaries of extractive (exploitative) ... power in an unequal society *may be assumed* [my italics] to have developed their human capacities further than the non-beneficiaries could have done, so that any reduction of their extractive power [their exploitative power] and hence of their command of resources and leisure would reduce their developmental power, their ability to use and develop their already expanded capacities fully. The question is whether such a loss would be as great as the others' gain.

The question is on the contrary nothing of the sort: and it hardly seems a question at all whether or not those who have established themselves for long enough to provide a test in the advantages of unfair extractive power have made anything like the contribution to moral development, either their own or that of the community whose resources they use, that might fairly be expected.

It is the quality of the capacities that the individual might develop if we were able to turn from our 'extractive' goal that matters: but as usual any concrete picture of this moral individual is lacking.

Rather plaintively MacPherson says that some men obviously are 'developmental' and others are potentially so – 'man is for the most part seen as a striving being'. And what he implies – an ancient sub-assumption of Original Virtue – is that if all men had equality and the leisure they had earned they would move towards creative doing and enjoying. Here again we have the partial definition of 'human nature'. And the inevitable shunt to scape-sheepism. The scapesheep is sometimes located in the past, some-times in the future, sometimes, as here one suspects, in both. MacPherson seems strongly to suggest that there is or was a pre-capitalistic, pre-industrial and pre-democratic tradition (meaning perhaps Marx's 'primitive communism' and also the various com-munity movements of, e.g., the fourteenth and seventeenth cen-turies) that, resuscitated, would give us the right relation between leadership and individuals in a society: and he points to this possibility in many of the emergent nations; in, for instance, some of the new African states that appear to him to have an inbuilt sense of egalitarian humanism, somewhat in the tradition of Rousseau, which by-passes both Marxian communism and our Western version of liberal democracy. He finds too that many of the international movements – for instance, 'Black power' and 'student' power – reflect a similar moral tradition and are also more concerned with and more able to seek 'developmental' individuality, or individual moral power, than our 'liberal' democracies have ever found possible.

MacPherson's book was published as recently as 1973: up-to-date enough to give us all time, including MacPherson, to wonder whether in his conception of African leaders and revolutionaries there are not signs of inventing a 'privileged moral minority'. We might look at Fenner Brockway's *The Colonial Revolution*, a study by no means unfavourably disposed towards African nationalism which, in spite of its careful documentation of bloodshed, cruelty and tyrannical extraversion, still seems to entertain some demo-cratic hope. It is true that Lord Brockway puts most of the blame for the present horrors on the insidious establishment of a financial and economic neo-colonialism – our 'extractive' experts having found new friends and new ways of work. Nevertheless he seems hardly trying to convince us that the new African 'developmental' individuals, if they exist, have the ability or even the will to resist it, even though under the new African leaderships Charters of Human Rights and Liberties have proliferated.

Brockway's documentation may make us wonder whether MacPherson's African scapesheep do not sometimes follow a goatish track.

Karl Popper's *The Open Society* was first published in 1945. The date is significant: he was then an anti-Nazi intellectual in exile seeking in intellectual history the roots of totalitarianism. To say that, however, is not to charge him with any want of objectivity, but rather to attribute the merit of a concrete relevance.

Obviously the book was written at one of the highest peaks of illiberalism: and perhaps through the very stimulus of so great a danger to European civilization it exhibits a surprising degree of hope – the belief that a rational warning based on intellectual history could still help us in later times to avert the worst. Thirty years may or may not be long enough to decide whether the hope looks even faintly warranted. But it can be said that Popper's liberalism is not free from some of the conceptual weaknesses I have discussed. And when we have finished reading this honest, clear-headed and most sympathetic book our questions will remain: how open would the Open Society be; and how can that be brought to pass?

In its basic theme, *The Open Society* is about the damaging historical trail of Platonic Idealism and its connection with totalitarianism and with anti-individualistic trends in social studies and practice. Popper's main target is the political Plato. Not only popularly and in hearsay, but in the higher reaches of professional intellectualism and particularly among theologians, Plato has been regarded as somehow 'above' the phenomenal world of human conflict, not only pursuing, but mystically revealing, a higher kind of noumenal unity. Popper's portrait emerges very differently. It is rather that of a shrewd practical politician sharply aware of the opposing party and the ideas and behaviour which it represents and which he proposes to fight with all the intellectual arms at his disposal.

That does not mean that Popper neglects or minimizes the metaphysical and ontological issues: quite the contrary. He brings into sharp focus the fact — admittedly it has often been pointed out, and more than once in this book — that the way one thinks or has been taught to think and conceive is inextricably involved with one's feelings and general attitudes and even one's perceptions.

He has, for instance, some interesting passages on the association of authoritarianism with a preference for irrationalism. That, as we constantly see, is one common version of a view or an assumption about the Real — that to by-pass the processes of evidential reference and inference that can be reasonably or logically maintained, may often, if not always, put you in touch with a deeper, more instinctive, and therefore *superior* human consciousness — a natural Authority, one might say (for obviously the oracular is authoritarian) — against which one ought not to try to rebel. That can lead to doctrines of divine right, to genetic alphaism, to Laurentian blood-and-soil hierarchy, and to other versions of a mystical pecking-order which are all based on the assumption not only that in our humanity we are fixed entities, but that the natural relations of those entities with others are also fixed.

If it is only one example of the integration of metaphysical and ontological assumptions and doctrines with human, social and political views — and also with psychological and emotional prejudices — the Platonic conception of justice is one of the most important, both for our interpretation and our evaluation of his whole philosophy: and Popper gives it due prominence; and successfully shows how Plato's metaphysical picture is a kind of magic mirror which reflects the real social world of his time — but chiefly as Plato would have chosen to distort it.

'Justice' as defined and described in *The Republic* amounts to 'everyone minding his own business' — his proper business having already been defined and prescribed by his status: 'the carpenter should confine himself to carpentering, the shoemaker to making shoes'. Plato allows, it is true that two workers might swop their skills, but *not their working-class status*:

> Should anyone who is *by nature* [my italics] a worker (or else a member of the money-earning class) ... manage to get into the class of the guardians without being worthy of it ... then this kind of change and of underhand plotting would mean

the downfall of the city [or the state, which Plato regards as having absolute priority over its individual members].

When each class in the city minds its own business, the money-earning class as well as the auxiliaries and guardians, then this will be justice.

Popper comments, warrantably, that 'this means that Plato identifies justice with the principle of class rule and of class privilege ... the *state is just* if the ruler rules, if the worker works, and if the slaves slave'.

The moral warrant for this hierarchical description or prescription comes from Plato's Idealist metaphysics, which claims that Reality resides in the Ideas or Forms, the divine archetypes, of which what we earth-dwellers loosely and as it were colloquially call the 'real' world and its objects and occupants are only copies: naturally, inferior ones.

That the metaphysics is a class-doctrine is illustrated by the famous image of the Cave in Book VII of *The Republic*. Outside and beyond in the upper world of light dwell the Gods and the Ideal (but *Real*) Ideas and Forms — the Patterns — to be imitated comparatively feebly by the works and days of us below, the dwellers in the shadows of the Cave (and of an inferior Reality) — the troglodytes, the predestined mine-workers as we might call them. Popper is no doubt justified in suggesting that this Idealistic metaphysics, whatever its other significance and uses, offers a more palatable disguise for what he describes as Plato's hatred of the democratic and anti-slavery movements of the time which might have led out of the tribal world of caste and authoritarian domination, a world that Plato instinctively preferred.

Most of the rest of Popper's obloquy is directed against Aristotle and Hegel. Either in its Aristotelian or in its Platonic-mystical forms, Idealism has conflated comfortably with Christian theology and dogma, medieval and more recent; and Popper leaves us in no doubt that the practical result of these associations was to delay and divert understanding and remedy of our real human problems and miseries. Popper thinks that Aristotle did not add anything original to Platonic teaching. The main philosophic difference between Plato's Idealism and Aristotle's Essentialism, which both assert the prior 'reality' of Ideas or Forms as compared with material events, is that for Plato the Idea or Form is an archetype or original pattern, while for Aristotle it is an entelechy, a Final Cause or goal of an organism. Aristotle's understanding and account of nature or reality is biological; but it none the less belongs to the Idealist philosophical camp. It is true that the Form or Essence is, as it were, immanent in the organism, whatever it may be, and is only detected and revealed in the behaviour and procedures of that organism—the Tree-yness of the tree, let us say, or the Femaleness of the woman—in which examples, with many others, it has some biological validity. But the Form or Essence is supposed also to be found in other non-biological concepts and structures which many of us—and the whole non-Idealist side in philosophy—would not accept as organic; and we should be inclined to say that in those cases, anyway, the Form or Essence is merely superimposed as a pure verbalism or logical abstraction on the phenomenon or phenomena, thus artificially imputing a natural or biological organization where none exists: and claiming a Real existence for what is only a concept or a generalization, with the further unwarranted implication of growth or development that can be foreseen, or is even foreordained.

It is at this point that Popper detects the Aristotelian fallacies of Hegel and of the Hegelian ideology which among other things poisoned the social philosophy of Marx. Popper in many ways approves of the social and economic philosophy of Marxism: but disapproves of it as social prophecy.

This refers to the doctrine of historicism which Popper attacked at length in *The Poverty of Historicism* and showed, anyway to my conviction, to be both false and dangerous. He treats Hegel as the founder of modern historicism, in its explicit form.

It has been suggested more than once that ideas in their direct and undistorted form have little influence on events. Nevertheless when they engender attitudes their itinerary is worth tracing, if only to see how they go wrong and mislead us: for they may reappear in other departments and studies which superficially at least look unrelated. Popper, for instance, has discovered 'historicism' not only in Marxist philosophy, but also in psychoanalysis and in some forms of sociology. In practice this refers to the self-fulfilling prophecy (which Popper calls 'oedipal').*

* Not wholly satisfactory nomenclature, for it does not distinguish Oedipus's destiny from other forms of fatalism: i.e. the prophecy did not *cause* him to kill his father and marry his mother; whereas in Marxism the foreknowledge of the

Historicism is the belief or claim that there are ascertainable laws of historical development. Thus it is a fatalistic doctrine which implies that the course of human destiny is predetermined. It also entails futurology or the possibility of prophecy, at least, of large-scale developments. It is worth noting that a totalitarian movement — Nazism — was also millenarian: and it is comforting that we did not have to wait longer than we did to see that it could also be wrong.

It is easy to see how Hegel could extract a philosophical basis for his historicism from Aristotelian Essentialism. The Ideas, or Ideal Forms or Universals, contain in potentiality all reality — everything that is capable of coming into existence. They not only shape and as it were foreordain its course and its category of existence — the kind of thing or class of living individual or event that it is, or in which it will be actualized as a phenomenon — but because they are in the nature of goals or Final Causes they also represent an actual evolutionary urge to realization. Aristotle did not pay much attention to the theory of history as such and so, as Popper makes clear, his Essentialist teaching had to wait some centuries to be put to historicist usage. But accepting his premisses, there is no difficulty at all, logical or otherwise, in also accepting that human history is simply a realization of human destiny: what was to be, became, is and will be.

Whatever his formal philosophical connection with Platonic Idealism or with its Aristotelian version, Hegel obviously assumed these premisses, and thought, as Aristotle did, in terms of an evolutionary emergence; carrying it a good deal further than Aristotle. History, according to Hegel, is the realization of the immanent Idea (which must exist in the mind of God, since there is nowhere else for it to be). But, also according to Hegel, this Idea (or World-Spirit) moves towards an ultimate perfection. Moreover the World-Spirit (or immanent Idea), realizing itself in the actuality of human history, does so by the method of the (Hegelian) dialectic: initiating the order of events and thereby stimulating

---

victory of the working-class theoretically helps to bring it about — knowledge of historical origins and past development in history can be used to divert its course; similarly with the individual history laid bare by psychoanalysis. Popper can hardly object to anybody, individuals or theoreticians, learning lessons from history, but only to *inventing* a selective conditioning historical force.

(nay, positively inviting) the next stage of contradiction, both practical and logical, and overcoming them in a higher synthesis of logic and situation. The World-Spirit or Idea thus *reasons* its way towards world-perfection: it thinks it all out for us.*

As Popper points out, the Aristotelian addition to Platonism which, for Hegel, was important and indeed necessary, is Aristotle's teleology. For Plato, the Idea of the Ideal Form was prior to and detached from the phenomenal world – from that sum of all human events and experiences which was a feeble and inferior copy of its pattern and prototype. As a result the universe, including the human world, must be regarded as in decline and human history henceforward as a continual degeneration. But, on the contrary, if the Idea (or World-Spirit) is immanent in phenomena which realize and develop it towards an ultimate perfection, we have, as with Hegel, an optimistic or progressive doctrine. However we must not forget that this realization or actualization of perfection will obviously remain on the ideal plane (which is, let us also not forget, a higher, ultimately the highest, Reality). That might seem to have little or nothing to offer to the mass of human beings as they deem, or imagine, they experience reality from day to day and from moment to moment, in what they assume to be their real lives – so often perceived as really miserable or problematic; those human beings who must be at least part of the actualization of the Idea or World-Spirit. Their Hegelian consolation is that what they believe they suffer, as limited but striving and hence frustrated individualities, realizes or fulfils its Real Reality (as we may surely name it) only in the collective perfection of the state, the ultimate realization of the idea. (There is an obvious structural parallel here with Rousseau's General Will.)

Hegelian historicism, as and when it was promulgated, was associated with real grounds for optimism; for the realization of the Idea in the perfect state was only just round the corner.** We might even say that it had only to wait till Hegel had had time to unveil the absolute Prussian state of Frederick William III and thus fulfil the function for which he had in effect been called to Berlin by

---

* For Hegel the 'Rational' is the Real – and vice versa: this depends partly on whether or not you accept the medieval definition of 'Rational' – with a capital R – or whether you mean that what is rational results from our ability to use reason to become reasonable.

** According to Schopenhauer as well as Popper.

the monarch in 1818 as first official philosopher and Great Dictator of philosophy.

Popper makes a strong case for connecting Hegel via the rise of German nationalism with the development of totalitarianism. It is an interesting and obviously important question, for necessary psychological and social analysis, if not of immediate relevance, how far there is an actual and natural affinity between a peculiarly German nationalism and ideology on the one hand and totalitarianism on the other: and hence how far Hegel is to be held both representative of Nazi ideology and in part responsible for it. It may just be mentioned that not only Popper but also Ralf Dahrendorf (op. cit), a German in origin, who experienced his formative years under Nazism, believes that Idealism, particularly in its Hegelian form, not only distorted formal German thinking — not least in its capacity for grasping the methods and concepts of science — but also corrupted the German sense of reality, including its political and social judgment. There is no racial or genetic implication in this: I do not believe that there is a peculiarly 'German' nature or character. I do however believe in a real conditioning by historical events and cultural situations: in other words that history and culture are real or actual and not Ideal; not even an actualization of the Ideal.

It may also be noted in passing that John Halliwell in *The Failure of German Liberalism* puts much, if not most of the blame for the advent of German Nazism on the German liberals and accounts for this to his own satisfaction by their positivism and their desertion or rejection of Idealist philosophy, with its 'Eternal Values' — something which is as near as possible to being the exact contrary of the truth.* The failure of German democracy rather resulted from the historic German weakness in developing social and legal institutions and from a hierarchical structure of education. The liberals, with other classes, may have been partly reponsible for a failure to guard and realize what rights and freedoms they possessed. But the fault can be traced rather to under-concreteness in political and social awareness than to want of Idealism — in short to over-abstraction. We have seen since, if not before, that this is one of the chief dangers to immature democracy — and most democracies have had too little time to mature.

* The liberal is the whipping-boy for both sides, the materialistic and the Idealistic. To (e.g.) Marx and Sartre he is the typical *bourgeois*-Idealist.

It may indeed be said that the failure to develop free institutions directly depends on an abstract or Idealist suprastructure, although this is not the only cause. Popper, who believes that the development and maintenance of free institutions is essential though not sufficient for liberal democracy, seems to suggest that the freedom in free institutions is somehow self-validating and will continue to be understood as such by those who have the habit of the institutions. Thus in his proper objection to Idealist historicism he appears to disregard the causality of real historical events and habits and hence to assume that free institutions will be maintained or can be reformed in the direction of further freedom by those (his social engineers for example) who, however well-intentioned, may not have a clear or overriding concern with the freedom of individuals nor a concrete understanding of what people really mean and want by freedom: and moreover may lack a synoptic view of its real relations often because of over-specialization on one of its aspects.

Popper criticizes historic doctrine not only in philosophy, but in sociological theories. Marx, for instance, as every student, if not yet every schoolboy, knows nowadays, 'stood the Hegelian-Idealist dialectic on its head' but accepted and preached historical determinism in a materialistic form; that is to say, he (with Engels, Lenin, etc., and many others, our contemporaries) accepted the Hegelian belief that there were laws of historical development which could not only be ascertained from the analysis of past human history, but which thus enabled prediction of the human future. The dialectic proceeds by thesis, antithesis and synthesis — a historic 'stage' or period when one set of attitudes, beliefs, religious and political ideas and forms, structures, and habits of behaviour, predominates, followed by another 'stage', opposing or contrasting; followed, and as it were concluded, by a third 'stage' synthesizing these contradictions into a higher unity. The difference was that the movement in the case of Hegel took place in the realm of Ideas (or the suprastructure); while with Marxism it takes place in the realm of economic life, especially of material production, and in the conflict between the labouring and the capitalistic classes, and the working out of the internal contradictions of their relations to productive existence.

Popper accepts what he calls Marx's 'economism' — the theory that the material and productive forces and the opposition of classes that necessarily results are the main determinants of the behaviour of human masses. But he rejects the Hegelian hangover which persists in all the developments and consequences of Marxism: which means that what he chiefly rejects in Marxism and the Marxist reading of human history is precisely its historicism.

Historicism is two-ended. In Marxism and Hegelianism it is mainly a prophetic doctrine: it tells us our inevitable future; which in the Hegelian variety will come about through the emergence and establishment of the Ideal form of state organization and rule. In the case of Marx, our still inevitable but quite different future will be brought into being by the victory of the proletarian working class. This version is saved from mysticism — if it is — by the claim that this last resolution of the dialectic conflict of classes can conceivably be shortened by going along with it instead of trying to resist it: throwing in one's lot with the militant workers. For Marx, Engels and their followers, this futuristic historicism amounts to a scientific prediction. Popper makes it amply clear, both here and in *The Poverty of Historicism* and *The Logic of Scientific Discovery*, that this is a misunderstanding of scientific prediction and of the methods by which it is attained. Science does not go in for large-scale prophecy; according to Popper, it cannot even predict what new kinds of knowledge will arise (with their retrospective adjustments of what we now regard as knowledge): science is a challenge to refutation, not a claim on omniscience.

To put it another way: in the scientific sense of *knowing*, we cannot know in advance that we or any other class of persons will logically and inevitably turn out to have been right. The prophetic historicism of Marx and his followers contains such an implication; thus we can see in it a disguised and self-deceiving version of the old Hegelian Platonism, which in this context amounts to the claim that there is a class of persons — particular or special individuals or the class as a whole — with an abstract and entailed right to rule. (Or a privileged moral minority.) This description applies whether we are thinking of workers, bourgeoisie or aristocrats, because it is the leaders of either, often largely self-appointed, who achieve and maintain their 'right' to rule, partly by believing that they have a natural claim to do so. In analysing the sociological variety of 'historicism' Popper finds that its chief preoccupation is with origins — a conjectural history of how things began, either in prehistory or in individual psychology – and how they thus implied or dictated the subsequent course of development of human societies. That appears mainly like a difference of stress; both types of historicism are both aetiological and eschatological – they refer to origins and to a future more or less predetermined. But the Marxian picture of human history and development is 'economic' (or materialistic); that is, it effectually denies that there was ever a pre-social stage when human life was not organized, or seeking to be organized, into some form of productive relations which not only maintained human livelihood, but largely dictated the ways in which human beings thought, felt and behaved.

The other form, to which Popper gives the name 'psychologistic', looks for the origins of human society and the roots of all developing forms of human behaviour in something called 'human nature'. Popper finds the classic example of this in Mill, the father of our English liberalism, who also believed in the possibility of a scientific sociology. Popper points out, rightly I believe, that this is only a psychological version of the Social Contract.

Both in the context of *The Open Society* and in the present context what is being discussed is the possibility of a working and truly democratic liberalism; the important objection to all forms of historicism, psychologistic or materialistic, is that they lead like the Platonism, from which they derive, to collectivism and the predominance of the state over the individual; in other words, in a totalitarian direction, or anyway to varieties of hierarchism, as we saw in discussing contemporary ethology.

In Mill's case that might seem strange and even uncalled-for. Mill surely held the classic liberal view that the individual's individualism had the right to go as far as it could until it was checked by that of others; the role of the state was merely to keep the ring and, one might say, maintain the rules of combat and of course the handicaps, so that the weak were given a fair chance against the strong: in short the jostling market view of society, with the state keeping out as far as possible and with no more than an instrumental status, certainly with no trappings of authority or pre-eminence of wisdom.

Nevertheless I think that Popper's historicist criticism with its charge of psychologism casts a new light on Mill and on classical liberalism. The 'human nature' in which Mill grounds his description, his analysis (and his hopes) of the development of human society has, as we saw, not only an essential propensity for freedom, but is essentially progressive; and by progressive, Mill means 'morally progressive'; and by moral progress he means that we shall come to be predominantly social beings: in other words that we shall *prefer* to surrender or at least to pool our individualism for the greater good of the whole. *Preference* must be emphasized: it is unlikely that Mill would have endorsed state intervention and the collective control of individuals even to the extent that we have developed it in the liberalistically well-intentioned Welfare State.

One may reasonably guess that he foresensed, if not foresaw, the inevitable dilemma of trying to work his (or anybody's) liberal principles – that there has to be *some* compromise with government and organization. Human beings *have*, for survival, to learn to behave like social beings. The simplest way – least painful, too, to the self-assertive and doctrinaire pride of a *principled* individualism – is to diagnose the social propensities as instinctive or innate.

I give here the whole of the relevant quotation from *Utilitarianism*:

> Not only does all strengthening of social ties and all healthy growth of society give to each individual a stronger personal interest in practically consulting the welfare of others: it also leads him to identify his feeling more and more with their good.
>
> He comes as though instinctively to be conscious of himself as a being who of course pays regard to others. The good of others becomes to him a thing naturally and necessarily to be attended to, like any of the physical conditions of our existence.
>
> This mode of conceiving ourselves and human life, as civilisation goes on, is felt to be more and more natural. Every step in political improvement renders it more so, by removing the sources of opposition of interest.
>
> If we now suppose this feeling of unity to be taught as a religion to the whole force of education, of institutions and of opinion, directed, as it once was in the case of religion, to make every person grow up from infancy surrounded on all sides both by the profession and the practice of it I think that no one who can realize this conception will feel any misgiving about the sufficiency of the ultimate sanction.

On the contrary, I think that, with experienced hindsight, we must view our present educational capacity in this direction, as we have revealed that we understand education, with the utmost misgiving: as we must also view what Mill understood by the human individual.

We may agree that Mill did not escape 'psychologism' in the particular sense that he tried to root beneficent social change in the possibilities of 'human nature' — our Original Virtue. And also, in a rather more specific sense, Popper's detection of a 'historicist psychologism' is convincing. Mill assumed that there were 'laws of human nature and mind' which were originative and continually causative in social development: and this may well represent at least a vestigial Idealism; one may add that it would be surprising if his education, both in being dominated by a parental Guardian, and in its mid-Victorian upper-class range and scope, had left him wholly purged of Platonic abstraction.

But we must now ask whether, at any of its degrees, or in any of its forms, a liberal approach to human possibilities and human social and moral problems can avoid being 'psychologistic' in Popper's sense; and whether Popper is indeed free of it himself.

Indeed, in Mill and in others, Popper gives a limited approval to what he still continues to call 'psychologism': that is, so long as it means only that

the 'behaviour' and the 'actions' of collectives, such as states and social groups, must be reduced to the behaviour and to the actions of human individuals.

Nevertheless, this is only true ... if we mean individuals in situations and reacting to situations, not merely functioning because of the peculiar psychological structure of 'human nature'.

To that latter or 'methodological collectivism' (or 'Methodological Essentialism') he opposes his own concept and classification — 'Methodological Individualism'.
This allows that

institutions and traditions are ... the results of human actions and decisions.

But, Popper continues,

> that does not mean that they are all consciously designed, and explicable in terms of needs, hopes and motives.

The important distinction between the two concepts of the individual with his social relations and effects is contained in the next part of the paragraph:

> On the contrary even those which arise as the result of conscious and intentional human actions are, as a rule, *the indirect, the unintended and often the unwanted byproducts of such actions*.

One might regard that as nearly truistic if one reflected that the actions of individuals, or any of them, intentional or not, are inevitably opposed by the actions of other individuals. But that is not quite sufficient ground for dismissing 'psychologism' from sociological relevance, as Popper would like to do – seeking what he calls an 'autonomous' sociology which would not have to assume any 'laws of human nature', but would only study and attempt to assess how human beings actually behave in their social conditions and relations and their real situations.

That sounds eminently desirable: but it is still possible and relevant to ask whether such a behavioural sociology – if its uses were also to be desirable and if its explanations were to be humanly satisfying or even illuminating – could disconnect itself from what real individuals think and feel, their 'needs, hopes and motives'; or even from what they *believe or assume* they feel, need, hope and are motivated by.

Individuals do all these things: and these things have their effects. It is also true, as Popper says, that many, indeed most of the effects, *are* inconsequential – unintended. But it might be simpler and more accurate to say that individuals are liable to be conflicting: they disagree about how to fulfil wishes, needs, hopes, motives and very often do this by means of contrasting even if untenable and emotive arguments – which for liberal honesty, both justice and reform have to try to meet, however irrelevant or even fantastic they may appear to be.

Popper grounds what faith and hope he has for the continuance and flourishing of liberal democracy in institutions for the control and balance of power, and not, or hardly at all, in any instinctual or universal urge towards a social morality which only oppressive conditions manage to frustrate — as the classic liberals, as well as doctrinaire socialists, have been disposed to do.

To the Platonic question, *Who* shall rule the state? Popper opposes a liberal-democratic one: How can we develop and maintain the political and legal institutions by which we can control those who come to power? Most important is the legal and political framework which enables us to get rid of the government without violence. That would subsume such institutions as a free press and equality before the law.

It will be seen that Popper has — or anyway had — continuing faith in the possibilities of liberalization by democratic political change. Even in the better democracies, it is obvious, liberalization still needs advancing — it is never complete and it often retrogresses. In particular our institutions — the more hallowed, not the least — need inspecting, overhauling and changing, if their human value and often their original intention is to be maintained or indeed if it is to be stopped degenerating. There must be change and it must be reasonable and intelligible; it must be both just and logical — or rather its logic must be based on revealing and clarifying and we might say cleaning up the inherent justice of the institution.

What then should be the role of a valid and acceptable sociology in relation to our institutions — either to those we still more or less willingly accept and employ; or to those which we criticize or would even reject?

What Popper offers us as a process and means both for selective maintenance and reasonable and ordered change (as also, we may assume, for a prophylactic treatment, political and social) is '*piecemeal* social engineering'. We should not promise large-scale changes or solutions, nor even attempt large-scale problems: we should begin by tackling what is obviously wrong and, as Popper puts it, by doing what we can to prevent or cure unhappiness, not claiming or even expecting either the duty or the privilege (or having the arrogance) to try and create positive happiness. (This is a general attitude with which I am in complete agreement.)

That ought however to imply that 'social engineering' — with its techniques and apparatus for effecting change — must work from local and communal bases upwards and outwards (grass-roots, for want of a better cliché), and without any necessary concern with an overall and co-ordinated plan for social amelioration. But we can see here, surely, that an 'autonomous' sociology, one which was based on a behavioural, materialistic, or even situational conception and explanation of human existence, is unlikely to function in this way: and we may perhaps wonder if the stress is not, after all, more on 'engineering' than on 'piecemeal'. I cannot thing of any kind of engineer, however metaphoric, who can work without knowing what he is doing in some overall sense. From the aeronautical or nuclear scientist or inventor to the radio or gas technician, however much they work by rule of thumb, they all operate within a general technological and scientific structure, and, more immediately, to a plan: they *know* at least that it is there for checking or appeal. In other words, they know that some people know some accepted – and perhaps tested – rules for the longer-term objectives of the common operation, and have the final theoretical responsibility.

The 'piecemeal' social engineer can be in no different situation, socially speaking: however deeply involved with the immediate urgencies of his task, professional or voluntary, at the back of his mind (however unconsciously – and therefore uncritically) he adheres to some sort of social theory *in which someone is expert* or *more expert*. Is it unjust to ask if Popper's autonomous sociology does not really mean the same as a sociological science: and that that implies some sort of final authority? If he admitted this Popper would say that he does not regard any science as an authority in the 'authoritarian' sense – he was quoted earlier as saying that all sciences are fallible and that indeed their method is a challenge to refutation. But in this case we are not clear where the refutation is to come from, nor how soon.*

In the case under consideration there seems to be some confusion between natural and social science – which Popper is generally careful to distinguish.

What is being said, among other things, is that no social engineering – piecemeal or otherwise – is without a social philosophy: and that unless this is a humane and moral one which can

---

* On the practical side of social science — e.g. 'counselling' in its various versions — a flattened or horizontal hierarchism is already clearly visible: it is not a very exaggerated reduction to absurdity if we surmise that in the foreseeable future, half the population could be ranged as counsellors and the other half as the counselled. And who shall counsel the counsellors?

be clearly recognized by the social engineers, as well as willingly accepted by those they engineer; and unless it is actually derived from the needs, wishes, hopes and idiosyncrasies of individuals who can at least learn to see it for themselves as psychological realism – their engineering will indeed be 'autonomous': detached from its human ends and, at its most disinterested, able only to strike a utilitarian average.

Popper has rejected, it is true, even beneficence, of a large-scale or positive kind, as the deliberate intention or goal of either social theory or social practice. But a great many of the needs, hopes, wishes, etc., of individuals, and these not among the least important, are negative or passive. Not only do people often passionately wish to be left alone and not interfered with, but what they in general don't want or wish or are even unable to think (at least not yet) has an effect on society which is not only real but, even if at a low degree, intentional: and may be relevant to the changes that our most necessary democratic institutions still demand. With all of these – they cover a vast range of culture and all the tastes you cannot really argue about, including the arguments we insist on having about 'permissiveness' and anti-permissiveness alike – an autonomous sociology can have no real truck. A 'piecemeal' social engineering, if it were conceivable, would have to be based on a 'psychologistic' philosophy. And it would have to be a good – realistic – and acceptable psychology, which we have not yet achieved.

Popper not only does not make out a complete case against 'psychologism' – he suffers from it himself in the unacceptable form we have already detected in other liberal thinkers: with the assumption, that is, that there must be and will be a change of heart or consciousness and also with that partial or exclusive representation of humanity one can call Scapesheepism: or the implied selection of a 'privileged moral minority'. As Popper says:

> there are only two possibilities, that a terrible world should continue forever, or that a better world should eventually emerge ... the more clearly men realize that they can achieve the second alternative, the more surely will they make a decisive leap from capitalism to socialism.

He adds that 'a more definite prophecy cannot be made':

> The chances of founding such a society [a liberal- or social-democratic society, he means] will depend very largely upon the devotion of the workers to the idea of socialism *and* [my italics] freedom, as opposed to the immediate interests of their class.

He seems to have settled for this hope: yet still with an inconsistency which actually appears on the previous page and which he does not resolve. Disagreeing with Marx that 'the workers' victory must lead to a classless society', he quotes Marx's own analysis 'that the unity or solidarity of a class is part of their class-consciousness' and comments:

> There is no earthly reason why the individuals who form the proletariat should retain their class unity once the pressure of the struggle against the common class enemy has ceased.

And indeed we have had time to see that they do not. There is no earthly reason why we should turn them into Scapesheep.

Popper's lingering hope for his workers' victory – over themselves as well as over capitalistic reaction – is itself perilously near to 'historicism'. His book in many ways is so admirable, even invaluable. It embodies more than any I have read a passionate awareness of our need for a genuine human liberation, and also of a genuine liberal philosophy. Yet it leaves us still with the moral and philosophical dilemmas unsolved. Perhaps it must be seen in the context of Nazism, which he and many of us must still inconfidently wish to classify as a monstrous mutation – and thus exculpate entirely not only all the victims but all those who did not suffer the temptation to participate. Or divide the human world with another Either-Or.

13

To Change or to Understand?

I have been trying to look at some of the psychological possibilities of liberalism as a problem that enters into all our lives and the atmosphere surrounding us; that is, as it affects ordinary people whether they are aware of it or not; and also from the point of view of a writer who, although she had thought and read about the subject and its contraries and contradictions for many years, does not claim to be wholly objective or without partiality; whose liberalism is as much a matter of temperament and upbringing as anyone else's, and therefore as undefined.

This has implied that for realistic understanding, both of our social and psychological worlds, a genuine liberalism requires a properly sceptical kind of conceptual and semantic criticism.

I cannot guess what hope there is for this. I do not on the other hand foresee much of a practical future for liberalism. I realize that there must be democratic mechanisms; or rather, political institutions and measures which are more nearly democratic or less undemocratic than others. If you have mechanisms you can tinker with them; moreover, mechanisms like Proportional Representation and (arguably) Referenda can (arguably) make a 'fairer distribution' of power. But then I do not see that this 'fair distribution' — any more than the economic kind — will necessarily incarnate justice. And no one can be certain in advance that infinite sub-divisions of power will not change its natural chemical composition, even make it soluble enough to be washed down the social sink.

That everyone should be able to take some real share in influencing the events that concern him seems to be a *sine qua non* of genuine, that is liberal, democracy. But he must also be given the opportunity — the *power* — to understand first what can be influenced and what he himself wishes to influence: in short, of 'understanding the world' before trying, or trying to help, to change it.

I am not a practical politician, nor a professional political thinker, but as a concerned observer I do not see how party politics will ever incarnate the humane and disinterested aspiration which the authentic liberal impulse — with whatever muddle-headed unrealism and with whatever Romantic excess of *Geistigkeit* — has always intended.

But then I see that party politics of any kind seldom or never really embody the lofty principles party politicians almost always profess. Even if we can accept that their principles, whatever they may be, and whether or not they are our own, are genuinely valid for some: even if they actually are those we subscribe to ourselves — between them and their realization 'falls the shadow'.

There is a gulf between desire and fulfilment; between conception and realization; between theory and practice: and this is not only because compromise is part of the art of living. There is indeed a more fundamental, even what we might call an analytic or truistic, truth: that principles in themselves cannot be compromised and still retain their essence or indeed their significance. That may be partly because of the dissolution of Ideas as influences, referred to more than once, and their capacity for turning themselves into their contraries. But here that would imply that it is humanly very difficult to keep a hold on understanding even one's own firmest principles: one can so very easily deceive oneself into accepting the interpretations which social compromise about having to live with others imposes.

And compromising and trying to look as though we hadn't is one of the commonplaces of human behaviour.

That is not because we are all, or even very many of us, either hopelessly unworldly or highminded, or hopelessly self-deceiving or conspiratorial, but rather because even if our beliefs and principles provide us with vision, our eyes cannot, in the nature of our humanity, see very far into the surrounding jumble of existence — they are flat against an opaque medium of circumstances; the X-rays are necessary and they are lacking. We are forced to live backwards: *How can I know what I think till I see what I say — or do?*

Thus acting on a principle or on a theory, with whatever willingness or humanity (or, more often, partisan indignation), often amounts to little more than joining one's signature to a letter of protest whose sentiments sound familiar and proper: sentiments nevertheless which, while one will defend them with one's next breath, one will belie with the one that follows, in all the near and immediate relations and circumstances of one's ordinary life, domestic and public. The conservative is certainly not all conservationist nor generally much beyond his own acres, back garden, market, moor or fishing rights. The socialist has not always, even at the back of his mind, the real people who compose and build cities. The liberal takes liberties with the liberty of other men and women — especially of those with whom he is nearly acquainted.

That sounds pessimistic; and indeed I do not know, any more than anyone else, any concrete and demonstrable grounds for even a limited optimism: though chiefly because I doubt that either optimism or pessimism belong to the actuality of our human métier, any more than they do to the birds, the beasts and the plants. Rather, both are forms of the characteristic self-deceiving faith with which we regard our intellectual and perceptual capacities — as giving us both the qualifications and the promise of our human superiority. Even our pessimism can show itself partly optimistic, as an implicit claim upon a know-all future: while both pessimism and optimism, however much they may back themselves up with statistics and facts (sometimes conflicting and even contradictory), can turn out to belong to one form or another of inflated and unanchored ideology.

I have quoted the two commonest criticisms of liberalism: (1) that it is too Idealistic; (2) that it is not Idealistic enough. And from the general standpoint I have taken these two criticisms are much the same. Both kinds accuse liberalism of being a mere ideology detached from what the critic regards as Reality — a reality generally preselected by his own ideological preferences and claims. Of course there is truth in the criticism, from whichever side it comes: but innumerable pots calling the kettle black do not thereby acquit either themselves or the kettle of being black.

Liberals arouse antagonism from both philosophic sides: perhaps more than they arouse in each other: and less absolutely from the Idealist than from the Materialistic parties. The Idealists, even if they are not orthodoxly religious, believe in the Kingdom — although they may also believe that it is not of this world and that we shall never come into it without aid: from something beyond our present capacities and nature.

The materialistic parties of the Left maintain a token or conventional stake in the Kingdom—or what Sartre, deriving from Marx, calls the City of Ends—but both believe that it is not of *this* world, but will be reached only after our economic and social problems have been solved (or rather liquidated) by revolution. Sartre has even analysed [*What is Literature?*] a complex necessity of moral adjournments: our contemporary moral problems not only cannot, they ought not to be solved in present terms, since as *problems*—and so demanding various and experimental answers —they arise only in private relations which distract us from our social (and revolutionary) obligations, through whose fulfilment alone we may arrive at the still distant City of Ends (and, as we must assume, its totally discontinuous morality).

That tallies with orthodox Marxism or at least does not contradict it; but it is totally alien to a liberalism that might make sense —which can never regard the immediate and personal as irrelevant, but which, on the other hand, must strive to keep the City of Ends in sight—indeed as a kind of teleological or Final Cause which gives a universal human meaning to all those private diurnal exchanges.

To the parties of the Left, all those who believe that a necessary material changing of the world can and must be brought about by direct action, this belief in an intellectual and moral continuity is more hateful than the Idealist or religious millennial expectancy. It seems to them to hold out a hypocritical promise, more like a mirage even than a Pisgah-view: it is not a mere Moses who is to be disappointed, the people themselves are deceived and misled.

It is a reasonable belief that a genuine liberalism does not, indeed cannot, belong to either Idealism or Materialism and there is a sense in which it shows up the weaknesses of either, particularly, on occasion, in the matter of the unity of theory and practice, so essential to Marxist interpretation and action. For the materialistic Marxist, something has to be *done*, to the end of changing the world: it is a reasonably particular something—the establishment of a final human equality through the victory of the working classes. Of course he does not mean that this would be better done without understanding or preliminary interpretation of the existing situation: he means only that the situation must be understood in *his* way. But this does not necessarily exonerate him from the common error, which we have already noted, of most doers and changers: that on the whole it is better to do something than nothing (perhaps specially inconsistent in his case; because it is part of his historic determinism that Something *will* inevitably be done, the theory will work itself out and prove itself correct: our actions can only help it along just because it is correct, although one might say that the prophecy merely renders our action superfluous).

The Idealist, on the other hand, knows that there is nothing to be done except possibly in the different order of the Hereafter — this too is a determinism, but extramundane.

A realistic liberalism, different from either, may well become aware that on a large-scale there is nothing certainly or advisedly to be done; that 'to understand the world' has still to be completed, or even perhaps begun: but the passivity that may lead to will be of different quality from the Idealist's or the religious believer's.

There is possible a passivity which is not other-worldly; and not idle or hopeless, but expectant and strategic; and which depends on not living beyond any of our means, physical, psychological or intellectual: thus understanding what we are doing in the near company of our consenting and likeminded fellows, as far as we can see.

The problem is still *first* to understand the world: it depends what you mean by 'understanding' and by 'world'.

If we look round us today and even if we look at past history, with the doubtful benefit of hindsight into that record of repeated failures, we see that some people and some small bands of people whom we are proud to reckon as liberals, did know what to do, and do know, when the circumstances are repetitions, or follow the patterns, of the old and recognizable ones. But they are very limited circumstances of immediate challenge; and if we compare the effort with the abomination and desolation of the ordinary concerted process and action it attacks, both its effect and its scope are slight and vanishing. It is only for brief periods of time; and in general retrospect it is followed by prolonged losses of the art of being a liberal.

When it is not a question of critical immediate survival — and perhaps of some values, some moral tastes rather, which we have

K

only lately managed to turn for some people into needs, without which the appetite for living loses its edge – there can be long lapses of even the memory of freedom. We grow morally senile, fathearted, as well as fatheaded, and forget what freedom could really be about.

But even now, when the committed enemies of freedom are vigilant, the resisters wake up: we saw it in the Nazi war; we see it with a Solzhenitsin, a Sakharov – I mention only these few examples because they are enough to show how the organic molecule of genuine and necessary liberalism is composed: how an instinctive sense or feeling, a kind of instantaneous perception even, which is natural and biological freedom close to the mere impulse to live at all, must and sometimes can be joined to an intuitional understanding or comprehension: one element in the compound is the sense of the self, or of identity; the other the universalized or rational intuition of the common or human situation in which the first is involved.

But it is situational: those freedom fighters, some of the resisters in the Occupied territories, perhaps many of the Russian dissidents, are by natural disposition and in their ordinary diurnal interests and occupations of livelihood and living behaviour people who are indifferent to or bored with the distributive machinery of society, whether lotteries or systems: and not much impressed with its end-product of power and wealth, except in so far as they can be and are being used oppressively. They may well be those, in short, who are the nearest we can know to Shelley's 'Good'.* Freedom then to those people, now and in history, is a sporadic event of brief illumination: although that may persist for the term of their lives or at least for the full time of the emergency.

The illumination nevertheless while it lasts is real, but because it is struck from the resistant body of mere contingencies it constructs nothing – not, certainly, a heritable and growing tradition: as one fire at a time is lit from another, it may be again and again, the old dies down.

* It ought, perhaps, to have been stated earlier that this means not much more than all those who are not recognizably 'bad' in Acton's sense— (it is all perilously like an Either-Or). True, to be moral, they should not only 'want' power in Shelley's slightly archaic usage of lacking it: they should positively *not* want it and, paradoxically, perhaps, should not be too unwisely neglectful of it.

The situation of the guerrilla of our day or of the revolutionary fighter, terrorist or not, is quite different. Even if they could persuade us or themselves that their long-term aims are similar to the liberal wish, even if they are professedly committed to a City of Ends, a free and open society — one day — for all men and women, they can seldom act upon their own insight and understanding of large-scale effect, even with the momentary illumination of the freelance freeman. There is an inevitable split between their theory and their practice, because the theory is in general that of others: there is a moral division of labour; it belongs to and helps create an intellectual tradition, but this may be more of a professional mystique, more like an alchemy than a handbook or guide to practice and action. They *know* not what they do. There is not, either for themselves or the world, that momentary but real illumination of structure, the best we can expect when we try to look for, and into, the laws of our human relations.

That applies to all ideologies (including the pseudo-sciences — some, too, of the 'human' and social sciences — and whether they are authoritarian or libertarian) — indeed it is their hallmark.

This is specially marked where the ideological or propagandistic stress on the unity of theory and practice is strongest: there the real unity is weakest and the split is widest: and theory is furthest from being a real induction or valid and referential categorization of what men can do. Those who are the doers have most to do and least time and capacity to see what they are doing, or light to see it by. The doers know least what they are doing, just because it is so expertly known *for* them. Thus theory is in a way unified with practice but by a *Gleichschaltung* of living criticism: ideology becomes self-fulfilling prophecy — with its tail in its mouth.

We have to stand Marx on *his* feet. The problem is not after all to change the world, at least not primarily: not even on the other hand just to interpret it, because we shall merely interpret it into particular languages, which will not be universally or even commonly understood, and in which instruction will be given which will certainly be misinterpreted and misapplied, and which in many cases will be simply wrong.

On the contrary, the problem is to do for the first time what has not been done, not even by the philosophers: to understand the world and ourselves.

There might seem to be an inconsistency here with the reiterated claim that ideas have little political influence. It is true that ideas in themselves, as Marx put it, do not 'change the world' – he excepted of course the ideas of Marxism. But ideas are not the same as understanding, which they often obfuscate. And it may even be a fortunate disposition of our nature that people mostly get them wrong: for at least that may give a balance or mutual cancellation of contrary bad effects.

In practice, people make use of them only when they conform to or seem to substantiate preconceptions; and only here in conditions of unbuttoned rumination; or following slogans whose intellectual content has already been manipulated out of recognition: but seldom in direct application to their own concerns where they can only use what immediate judgment they have. If the ideas either begin as, or soon become, false or inadequate abstractions – and thus are wrong – at least people are often prevented from trying to apply them because they generally arrive without a book of instructions for use.

The great notional generalizations: Love, Truth, Beauty, Goodness, God, Sin – and plenty more, we multiply them all the time – are always based on incomplete induction or none at all. It is not that these notions do not, or did not at some point, refer to the actual behaviour of men and things, but rather that they rapidly take off into the blue and, like maverick pigeons, cease to home to the experience of facts which ought to have given them their origins and which ought also to check or test them.

Nor is it because of a subjective origin that these great notions are always wrong, or a misfit: that is not the necessary source of their tangential deviations and their errors in application. Original and formative thinking always begins, and cannot help beginning, with one's own senses, one's own history of habit and awareness and one's powers of immediate intuition (in the strict and non-mystical sense of instantaneous coherence or ordered unification of perception). There is no real defect, I believe, in the human potential and apparatus for natural thinking, which prevents us from genuinely universalizing those real experiences *which we have made our own*: from comparing our visions – provided that, though narrow, they are direct and honest – with those of others; because the vision, where it exists, is subjective, it is, as it were by definition, common, that is, characteristically human. The error arises in *confusing* the subjective and the objective: in failing to stick to the meanings one can substantiate—the meanings for oneself—and in accepting the diluted meanings with which, so far it seems inevitably, we construct our media of exchange at the necessarily average level, the highest common *denomination*.

Of that which we cannot speak of that we must remain silent. Wittgenstein might have meant by this (although I don't think he did) that we can only say or speak sensibly about objects of reference which we certainly know to exist; when we are all speaking about the same subject-matter; thus that the rest must be silence because the difficulties of authentic communication appear to be insuperable.

We might interpret this more popularly or metaphorically, and advocate a prolonged Trappist spell, a moratorium on spoken or written utterance. But social humanity, having words, is obliged to exchange them (clearly if we have a tool, we are compelled to make use of it), if only to pass the time of day: and the words have if no other a 'value-in-exchange'—they support the social circulation. (For instance, it is perhaps only in this abstract verbal sense that 'love' can be said to make the world go round.)

But all these necessary media of social exchange, including the established or traditional conventions of behaviour, soon become both worn and inflationary: they provide both a bad coinage and a bad paper money.

Philosophers, even linguistic and conceptual practitioners, don't help and bad philosophers do more to water the circulation. And modern philosophers, including those concerned with 'ordinary usage', do very little to purify the actual language and other real exchanges of the tribe. One reason for this is that they *neglect* the (often contemptible) 'Ideas' instead of deflating and correcting them: the big loose generalizations which everyone uses and assumes to have referential meaning, and to stand for a common reality (although often for no better reason than that they are used in the same way by everybody else). Yet these stand most of all in need of the conceptual analysis which is the best, if not the only, instrumental contribution of typical contemporary philosophers.

It is true that those of the 'Ideas' whose corresponding colloquial iusage has been, or must be, subjected to some rough standardizaton (for instance for political purposes or legal definition) are also treated philosophically: examples are Freedom, Equality and Justice: and Truth (which is a borderline case with Goodness and

Beauty: like the last two it has a bad history of free-floating abstraction, yet it *can* be referred to by way of demonstrating its objects: and there are new philosophic techniques for treating in the same way the other pillars of Platonism). But hardly anyone pays attention to the ordinary or haphazard usage of these inflationary terms, or to the circulation of meaninglessness and failure of communication, both intellectual and human, it is bringing us towards.

What conceptual analysis has been applied to 'Love'?—or 'Fraternity' or the 'Brotherhood of Man'? Yet they are paid out from every pulpit, every studio, every platform, every school assembly, every hippie-camp and are continually bandied by all sorts of average people. We urgently need to know: What do people themselves think they mean when they operate these exchanges? And what, if anything, do they expect the exchange-relationship to be, with its subsidiary effects, which is set off by this operational usage?

Liberalism is an attitude which as much, and perhaps more than most, is operated by these great and gaseous commonplaces, some of which, I suggested, are not only abstract concepts but structures or instruments conditioning and organizing the very fabric of what one thinks or talks about.

As we have seen, the great nebulosities, or some of them, can be made use of by either of the two main families of philosophic thinking; Idealism and Materialism, structurally, are mirror-mages of one another, Popper, for one, clearly tracing the shape of Platonic Idealism in Marxist materialism—which might be thought to be most inimical to it. For both sides the Liberal slogan (and Trinity) has provided historically and still provides two invaluable nebulosities—Liberty and Equality—(whatever they may think of Fraternity).

The usage in either party's case remains an abstraction or, at its humanly most meaningful, a generalization of experiences—or more likely emotions—many people believe they have had, although this may be largely imaginary or even a matter of hearsay.

The usage, still nebulous, may be either too Idealistic or too Materialistic. When John Halliwell (*The Failure of German Liberalism*) refers to Liberty—as what should be preserved or defended by liberalism—he grounds it on the *Eternal Values*: he leaves us with the feeling that Liberty belongs up in the sky with all those other absolutes and universals, and has been there *ab initio* and has no connection that we can trace with the freedoms or liberties from which many of us think that it is actually abstracted or generalized: indeed it may be difficult to see, if we start from that end, how any implementation could be found. Halliwell's main reason, we saw, for blaming the German liberals in large part for the success of Nazism is not primarily that they allowed their traditional rights to be filched and their legal and constitutional establishment to be overthrown but rather that they were disloyal to the universal and extramundane morality of Idealism.

The nebulosities, on the other hand, not least these two, can be conceived and used with an exaggerated materialism, often in a statistical and utilitarian form or even as an over-particularity.

'Equality', when it is not being used as a 'Hurrah-word', an Idealist's slogan, is often treated only as qualifying proper distribution. According to Rawls (op. cit.), a real equality would depend on a perfectly fair distribution of goods and benefits: that leaves us, whatever we may achieve in actual distribution in particular groups or associations (even to the perfect satisfaction of all contributing or receiving parties) still in want of a definition of fairness: or if not a definition, some way in which we can recognize it, any of us, in operation.

Of Fraternity, the Brotherhood of Man, something must after all, no doubt, be said, but perhaps the less the better (as I, in effect, suggested of the social feeling progressively developed by the practice of social living which Mill, for one, thought that he discerned). With liberals, it is obviously a Romantic abstraction of Idealist type though it has been appropriated by socialists and Communists as a rationalization of their own social and material prescriptions and allotments.

Human social existence, it still at present seems, cannot function without general ideas which, however nebulous, act and will continue to act as regulative and normative: in spite of the fact that they and their verbal expression may habitually and exponentially deviate from real and commonly acceptable reference.

At the semantic level, where we suffer from the complementary temptations of over-abstraction and over-particularity, we stand in need of a common language of concrete universals.

The morality of language – and obviously and increasingly a great part of our language-usage is immoral – depends upon real description or reference, and a real intention of communication as precise as we can make it. (That does not rule out ambiguity: ambiguities and contradictions are existents of authentic experience; they are also part of the structural economy of poetic realism.) Knowing what one means, saying what one means, meaning what one says – and abjuring rhetoric – these constitute the morality of language.

The philosophers reacted from the rigidly scientific standard of referentiality proposed by the logical positivists and the earlier Wittgenstein, which if strictly interpreted and put into practice would have meant that, without risking the charge of gibberish, no one could have opened his mouth except to utter the baldest propositions about what was immediately under his nose. The philosophers advocated instead the study of 'ordinary usage' to provide the standard of sense.

This is a great advance on some earlier epistemological behaviour; for instance, in the theory of perception, where they favoured such propositions as 'That pink patch is a pig not an elephant', which may be undeniably true and which may even bear on the difference between reality and hallucination, but is certainly something that no actual person ever *volunteers*. In turning to the study of 'ordinary usage' philosophers were admitting that, in the first place, human beings do try to say what *they* mean: we have, the most illiterate of us, a natural capacity for finding words and expressions which we adapt quite subtly to anything we really want to say: even if we find the wrong words they come to let our meaning show through, they are at least as good as gesture: and if we are very illiterate indeed, our thoughts may merely be uncomplicated, but they may still be urgent. In the second place, philosophers were admitting that language spontaneously used did reveal rules which could be classified and generalized. Thus it is legitimate for them to deal in generally very short propositions or 'sentences' or statements with the minimum content of connotation so that the logical or grammatical structure will not be obscured by wealth of imagination and imagery. As a corollary the illustrations, paradigm-sentences, or propositions, could hardly suggest that philosophers were talking about ordinary *people*.

Naturally, too, there has been still less indication that knowing and saying what one means (quite apart from meaning what one says) has any moral connotation.

Yet surely what has just been referred to as our semantic temptations really are just that — and not only for rhetoricians and crooks, but even for ordinary people and their ordinary usage.

Discourse, even at the lowest level of ostensiveness, of actually nodding or pointing at what we are talking about, is impossible without some degree of generalization: in fact we speak in essential part for the purpose of generalizing our experience, for finding out and fitting it into the common classes of experiences of others. But it is immoral to generalize beyond what we can actually see for ourselves as existent and valid: whether we do so by inventing our own unrelated or inflated abstractions or whether we simply absorb and recirculate those derived from general hearsay.

Admittedly this is one of the commonest kinds of language-behaviour which uses Ideas — at least in our megalo-civilization.* It is often deliberate, but even when it is not it forms part of the circulation of untruth and meaninglessness, auxiliary to the primal offence, like the receiving and uttering of stolen goods.

That is not to blame the ordinary users, the semantic tribe. It is to say that from infancy they should be taught a better, more moral usage: although it would be here — if anything of the kind were possible — of no advantage to begin from a purely formal linguistic or grammatical angle: that is, objectively, or even regulatively: just because the prime intention *would* be morally therapeutic: not less than that of laying the foundation and first elements of a living community; starting us off straight with one another.

I am aware that such a revolutionary change in educational theory and practice is highly unlikely; even that one may partly suspect such a speculation of being in the same category as 'change of heart' or of consciousness — of which I have earlier complained. But here as well as in other ways we may find that the unlikely is after all the necessary — for survival; that some such change or changes are none the less necessary because we have progressively made them more difficult and more unlikely.

---

* If we are to believe Lévi-Strauss, still primitive tribes can be more meticulous — obviously seeking to avoid abstraction as far as possible and also to substitute non-verbal structures of communication whose reference to values are fairly clearly standardized.

There is nothing in itself remarkable about semantic intervention in education: all over the world, throughout history, sects and groups, religious and secular, have thought that it was natural and proper to exercise control over the speech-habits of their communities and to include this form of education in the rules for initiation, and one may guess that the realization that this would reflexively govern their habits of thought has not been very far below the surface of consciousness. To develop this instrument and to teach it as a necessary and honest skill is by no means beyond human ingenuity: all that is lacking is the needed will and integrity.

But there has never yet been a sect or a group or a department which was content with merely instrumental intervention and without restriction of subject-matter: the *how* and the *when* those *in statu pupillari* should talk, or be silent, leaving the *what* to take care of itself.

In this century, the philosophic explorers of linguistics and semantics have often thought to secure their theories by the standard of scientific discourse. But the languages, at least of the 'human' sciences, are as liable to over-generalization as others: spreading their concepts from the phenomenal field under investigation into wider social implications. It is not always the fault of the scientific users, but sometimes because they are tempted in their role of invited 'expert'. Not, on the other hand, so much because they are also sometimes tempted to speculate: but much more because a technical language, which may be useful shorthand for intra-scientific communication, easily corrupts into jargon outside that inner circle, so that the scientists themselves forget that their generalizing concepts do not always represent repeatable experiences. (I am not referring to the 'natural' sciences.)

It may be a long way of saying that a lot of 'scientific' language, in psychology and social studies, isn't strictly 'scientific'. On the other hand the language of science can be over-particular, in the sense that it excludes, or tries to exclude, the imaginative use of its concepts and observation. (Imagination is different here from speculation – or even from science-fiction.)

It may be said that the sciences and the scientist do not and cannot act with this exclusiveness. Certain poets, for example Shelley, have made good imaginative (and accurate) use of scientific perceptions and concepts. The defect lies in the determination to be 'value- and interest-free', which often amounts to a highly esoteric refusal to be part of a human world and whose invitations to a human scientific mind, if its curiosity is open and vivid enough, might seem to have some natural priority.

No doubt this kind of 'negative capability', with its assumption of scientific – and other – 'mind', is becoming and will become increasingly rare. The mass- and world-organization of research, with its imposition of subjects and directions for commercial ends and technological proliferation, can only discourage it: and what might have been a creative scientific intelligence (at any rank) becomes tied to a routine not less exhausting than a factory-hand's, and just as exclusive of genuinely imaginative generalization: although perhaps better paid.

Imaginative insight into the structure of phenomena is what teaches one to write well: and the ability to write well should not be thought of as a weakness in a scientist: even if it entails mastering the art of communicating simply – though of course without falsification. Here, as Polanyi says in *The Tacit Dimension*, some subjects are of greater intrinsic interest. That also implies that they are of greater interest than average to some *person*: generally because he has grown up with them and their constitutive phenomena – which have in essential part made him the person he is. In learning, as in art, there is a natural and individualized circulation of the phenomena of a living and lived world: in this way the language even of the inanimate may be tacit but it is not dumb: it is one we can learn to decipher; and to interpret our own humanity and its status and situation in the world, we need to try.

It may be true that by nature we cannot help being animists, given even to the pathetic fallacy. If we need it, television programmes about the natural, particularly the animal, world give us some confirmation that we are more interested in life even than inflation or political in-fighting. Among scientists, the zoologist and the animal ethologist have a pull. That still leaves us trying to define what we mean by writing well while remaining a scientist.

These apparently privileged animal studies give us the clue that the fascination lies, among other things, in direct and on-the-spot description. Here the scientist's eye and word provide a natural ciné-camera: we can be in the real presence of the object while it lives and changes, free of interference, even that of preconception.

Educationalists who look at the problem (or cliché) of the 'Two Cultures' with a preference for the 'Humanities' (as if education had the option of educating for anything else but humanity) generally look on 'good' literature as their best aid: but do not necessarily give enough attention to the elementary essential of writing well—an 'innocent' eye in unimpeded relation with its object, whatever that may be. A great deal more is needed: that is only the *sine qua non*.

Dr Leavis, for instance, who has distinct if limited ideas about what makes literature 'good', does not give enough, if any, attention to this simple subject-object relation as possibly a primary qualifier for 'writing well' and therefore being at some level 'good'. The highly exclusive membership of his 'Great Tradition',* he tells us, qualifies by being deeply and essentially concerned both with morality and 'art'—but in what way is far from clear. All of them write well, perhaps most of the time. But when they write badly— say, George Eliot in *Daniel Deronda*, or too much of the later Henry James, or much of D. H. Lawrence in his prophetic times—it is partly because in some way the eye's innocence has become clouded and its natural patient receptivity obscured. The writer is looking at his own ideas and preconceptions and not straight at the object as it is given. This makes in one way or another for bad language: and good literature, whatever else it requires to be good, cannot build itself on language that is intrinsically bad.

Obviously the language of some scientific writers is good in this meagre sense that I have suggested: and though Dr Leavis does not allow, or at least he does not mention it as a possibility, there have been some scientific works which qualify as literature—providing us even with this essential part of the definition.

Otherwise it is difficult to know what common minimum makes for 'goodness' in the special sense, too, that makes for literary morality: what it is about any literature that might make it a fundamental and necessary tool in changing people (including ourselves) in a direction which they could come to recognize as fulfilling both to themselves and to their species, eliciting the best of their natural selves. It is worth noting that the 'morality' in literature of which Dr Leavis approves consists of the 'objects' of which he approves—in the case of the later D. H. Lawrence, often

---

* F. R. Leavis, *The Great Tradition.*

ideological and unnatural; and exclusive therefore of other ideologies of which they both disapprove.

It may be impossible to define in any comprehensive sense what makes literature either good in itself or good for mankind. Less difficult perhaps to point to what is bad and why. Taking the whole body of verbal production most of 'literature' has been bad — that at least we can recognize — including the liberal 'literature' which Dr Skinner (op. cit.) objects to, though not, I should say, for the reasons that he gives.

An essential if not sufficient cause of badness lies in the kind of conceptualization the writer has inherited or acquired, by which his selection of language is, as a rule unconsciously, directed.

Here again we can find the usual complementary defects: over-generalization and unwarranted or unrepresentative particularization.

Sticking for the moment to 'imaginative' or anyway non-factual 'literature', we might employ as two roughly delimiting extremes, Romanticism and pornography (taking into account that some pornography is highly Romantic, for instance Lawrence's).

Romantic literature, when weak or bad, over-generalizes and inflates some human capacities: pornography over-particularizes others and rubs our noses in material details.

I am not saying that all pornographic writing — all vivid and intimate description of sexual behaviour — is bad: but when it is certainly bad that may be, as in Lawrence's case, because it is referring to inflated and sometimes phoney general concepts as if they were natural description.

These are reasons for saying that an essential if not sufficient intention of literature that will turn out to be good, is finding and manifesting the concrete-universal. This, good poets do naturally and spontaneously while they are being good. Unfortunately there is not enough certainly good poetry available to provide good natural semantic therapy: and what there is is often badly prescribed by educationalists (that is, *prescribed*) and not so willingly swallowed. The best we might conceivably do, in the way we have at present to conceive, is to try to find and encourage parallel (but more palatable and digestible) attitudes to thinking and verbalizing.*

* Nevertheless nothing in English schools is done about teaching children to think at all let alone think correctly, while I am not alone in thinking that the time is overripe. Cf. Edward De Bono, for example.

I do not imagine that I have discovered some kind of educational panacea: or for that matter an applicable if partial cure: either would be presumptuous to the point of insanity.

Even if the diagnosis is correct and if the treatment were sufficiently and generally accepted, there is the eternal and always dual problem: Who shall begin and who will be able to follow on?

The school does not (and ought not to) exist in a vacuum: but the home is the seat of an older generation whose general ideas and whose capacity to conceptualize at all is in large part anchylosed in error and unrealism.

All I am saying is that if we intend or even hope that our education should become the instrument of a humane development, we must find out how to teach and encourage children to think realistically and to express their thoughts accurately, fully and without superfluity. Primary—and fundamental—scholastic education then would consist in learning to use one's own language with the intention of honesty and accuracy to the best of one's natural ability, under the guidance of older people who have learned how to do it themselves, and in ever fuller communication with them. Most of them would have to be people who had seen for themselves the necessity of training themselves out of their own age-old and traditional bad habits. I do not foresee colleges of education that will give them their courses and diplomas. I do not see that it will happen anyway.

Yet there must be some people who even if they do not know how to purify the language of the tribe, still less how to clarify their conceptual minds, feel and believe that they have a duty—also to themselves—to pull the beam out of their own eyes.

I have in one way and another been proposing that the function of realistic understanding both of the social and the psychological worlds, a properly sceptical conceptual and semantic criticism, is one, perhaps the only certain one, that belongs to a genuine liberalism.

It might be a remedial exercise to look again at some of the liberal's stock-in-trade of conceptions and see if we can substitute others which we can reasonably claim will be more nearly what ought to be occupying his mind. The improvement, if we could make it, would depend on two qualifications: that our substitute conception should be drawn from and always remain attached by some kind of guy-rope, to some minimal need or characteristic which ordinary human beings, tacitly or perhaps unconsciously, with whatever imperfections and aberrations, in their ordinary daily doings, recognize as their common belonging. The second qualification is that when we have built on this basis the general conception which we shall obviously need for communication and instructions, it should always remain capable of intellectual or analytic correction: there would always be the tug of the guy-ropes; we should always be able and in readiness to show to ordinary users that our conception does fairly, honestly and recognizably represent their minimal need or characteristic, and is not just another balloon floating off into the Empyrean.

The liberal Trinity will do as well as anything else. None of its three parts comes up to the specifications. It is true that, in the negative sense of the captive animal, people need freedom: but in the positive, creative or 'developmental' sense of the leading and most high-minded liberal propagandists there is little evidence that most of them do: that is to say, it is not a defining characteristic of all human beings on which we can build our general conception of liberty and to which therefore we can refer our conception for correction.

Similarly in the case of equality. 'Equality', as we have got into the habit of using it or even of defining it, does not represent a recognizable minimal need or a qualifying characteristic of human beings. Most people, when their attention is drawn to the matter, as it commonly is, want not merely to catch up with, be as good as, their neighbours and colleagues, they want to be better: a natural insurance or safety factor against falling too short. Some people do not mind being in an inferior position, generally because they have not thought about the matter: this category can cover those people who are genuinely content with cultivating their gardens (one of the other illustrations which are probably as near as we can get to Shelley's 'good'). But even here if circumstances after all oblige them to think about it, they may well enter the race, handicapped too by their previous neglect of competitive practice.

It is just possible that one reason why nobody naturally wants equality is that people do not know how to define it in a way that responds to their inner sense of worth. We conceive it, and liberals have so far mostly conceived it, as something prescribed and imposed from outside by merely distributive and statistical methods and therefore based on a partial psychology.

'Fraternity' even more obviously than the others is inflated to the point of imminent departure for outer space: and hence the 'minimal requirement', or need, is among the hardest to define or isolate. We are talking of the 'minimal requirement' as a natural need: in this sense, and if we define it as protective association in immaturity, most likely maternal, people do need 'love'. But this also has slipped its guy-rope. In its sexual manifestation, Sartre's description in *Being and Nothingness* as 'reciprocal alienation of the other's freedom' is unfortunately close to the mark. On the other hand, the 'brotherly love' of fraternal delegates to a Labour Party Conference looks (in the end-of-conference photographs) as if it would balloon off as soon as they stop singing *The Red Flag*, while, on the ground, normal competitiveness would be moving in.

All of these terms which imply an instinctive or spontaneous feeling for others, with the possible (and temporary) exception of a mother's identification and involvement with her infant, seem to be due for a prolonged semantic fumigation. But apart from that I leave the third of the Trinity aside, because I believe that if we can find satisfactory substitutes for the other two, fulfilling the 'minimal requirement' of the concrete universal, the third will be covered too.

For 'Liberty' and 'Equality' then I propose to substitute 'Identity' and 'Justice'. I shall try to show that those need not be merely another kind of abstract concept but that they refer to minimal needs of human psychology: also that at ground level they are inseparably connected.

The appearance of 'Justice' is against it: we need not go further than Popper's analysis (op. cit.) to see that it can be a Platonic barrage balloon. On the other hand, those who identify the concept with fair distribution, either of goods or opportunities, afflict it with over-particularity: from which we have to regress to a further definition of the abstractions 'fairness' or 'equality'.

I am proposing, it will be seen, that for an authentic liberal 'justice' – or 'justice in society between men' – has conceptual priority over freedom and openness and that the foregoing difficulties are in his way.

The liberal nowadays can hardly appeal to any theological sanction or to any extramundane metaphysical absolute. He cannot demonstrate his principle analytically – it is not self-evident that *All men must strive for justice*. There is, too, no evidence that any impressive majority of mankind can intuitively recognize what is just or unjust in any particular solution of a real and immediate problem or situation or that they will accept or even understand a reasonable and impartial demonstration in the given case. Moreover it is difficult at times of discouragement – that is, most times – to believe in an overriding principle of justice even in the pragmatic sense that a liberal may well accept (namely, that our species will not survive and cannot even define itself as specifically human without committing itself to this qualifying pursuit).

There is one consolation that can be offered to the liberal inclined to suspect himself of idealism or ideological abstractions: that all those who use without defining, or who avoid defining, or dismiss the possibility of defining justice (either what would be thought 'the just society' or what, in a situation would be just) are in the same ideological boat as himself. All, as well as the liberal, have to show that they are successfully avoiding over-generalization on the one hand and under-induction on the other. The latter, the fallacy of over-concreteness, is common with the 'human scientists', often manifesting itself as a partial definition of human being ('partial', too, in the sense of preselective). In this case, justice or fairness is treated or even defined as a method or technique. This specially applies to those who feel obliged to talk in terms of a 'just society' with 'equality of opportunity', when they are really advocating some form of hierarchy.

In practice they are all obliged to seek a principle even if only for the purpose of circumventing it. Or, rather, they all have to assume that they have found some standard of what is just and that we all know what they mean by it and *ought to accept it*. The liberal here may not be all that much better or more successful in his search: he may not find any definition of universal justice that is less vague than the one average mankind uses to grope its way, or one which is generally acceptable for any reason better than just being vague. But at least he has nothing to hide from the rest of his fellow-beings; the pursuit is not enemy action and many of them would like him to succeed.

There is a strong human feeling in favour of justice: though there is a widespread sense of resignation to its inevitable imperfection in realization upon this planet. But it might be suggested without cynicism that in this case the remains of hope is better than certainty one way or the other: it is better to rely on these human feelings, vague no doubt, but world-wide and age-old, than on 'answers' from statistical tables and computers. And for this there is one good reason—in my opinion an overriding one: justice is not now and may never be quite calculable or even exactly definable. But what is *unjust*, however particular, can, when the circumstances are not manipulated or distorted, be universally recognizable. We all know what we mean by injustices and, given the facts, everybody else can tell us whether we are right or wrong.

There are then two alternatives for those who intend to speak or write about 'justice in society'—meaning here the avoidance of injustices: either justice is a fundamental moral rule, no matter how it originates, which we take as our principle when we try either to describe or to help initiate a just society: or it is a method or technique which is supposed to represent and implement what 'we' (various interests, specialities and groups) have selected and will maintain as a preferred form of distribution of 'necessities' and 'goods'.

To adopt a moral principle and to treat it as an absolute does not necessarily make one an Idealist, either in the philosophic or the popular sense. Moral principles have to be treated as absolutes in the sense that one is *committed* to them: they do not have to represent any noumenal or supernatural authority; they are normative and methodological rules in the first place *for ourselves*; adopted, if honestly, because they satisfy, as far as possible, sense, reason and experience. That allows that, though not ephemeral, they are alterable: they are also never a perfect practical fit, and their goals are never perfectly attained; and moreover a great many people, doubtless a majority on the earth at any given time, so it appears to external judgment, get on quite well without them. But they are such that without them we arrive, as human beings, at a condition of moral paralysis: we have to do, and to choose, and we do not know what. Sooner or later, whatever judgments we may make and whatever actions we may take, are revealed as meaningless. Meaningless, that is to say, for human beings: because, in one permissible and essential definition, *humanity* includes developing as a system of communicable meanings.

I am aware that that may look like begging one of the essential questions; because it is a question and, as already indicated, one very often asked with increasing frequency, whether one can recognize our species as all that distinct from our animal forebears and by what characteristics we qualify the claim. Obviously all animal life at whatever stage of complexity operates by some system of signs, and that implies some degree of communication or something commonly recognized.

But to the best of our knowledge animal systems where they exist are in no recognizable sense reflexive, nor therefore critical or self-judging: they do not refer back to nor therefore criticize, re-adjust or adapt the signs and guides that continue to come to them and which constitute an environment sufficiently stable to preserve them in their average, if short, span of survival. Thus their lives are always starting from scratch.

It is true that in many, perhaps all, of the connotations of our communications, by speech or gesture, we hark back to what we share with all other biological species and confirm our unelected membership of this planet — in our passions, our alimentary and sexual needs, our rhythms of sleep and waking, even in our social, and social-moral awarenesses of our kind. But we are the only species that also, in language and the gestures and performances with which we communicate, constantly refers back not only to our given earthly environment and its reactions and interventions, but also to the ways in which we have made over that environment, to our cultural achievements and conflicts; in short, to a part of our history that is predominantly *human*: and of course artificial. One may say, if one likes, that we have invented ourselves. But in that case we must also say that every being that has appeared during our evolution from the most primitive specimen of mankind has contributed to the invention, and has helped to make us what we are — and uniquely — a self-reflexive species. That our image of ourselves is not consistent but conflicting does not alter the case.

That is not to say that the vastly greater part of our species has ever consciously or actively participated in the effort to become and to define humanity. It is to say that, on the other hand, the moral and intellectual teachers and would-be teachers, the philosophers, the artists and the scientists, have never existed in a moral and intellectual vacuum: they would never have arisen without what seemed to them a potentially human material to interpret — more often, to misinterpret.

For the leaders and teachers of mankind have never been much better than anyone else in identifying the truly human potential nor therefore the best direction it might be encouraged or assisted to take: and often they have been worse; because they have had skills, more highly developed than the average, in instituting and defending partisan, often polemic, attitudes and beliefs which they often mistakenly claim to represent the whole of human potentiality. That often implies that they have fallen in love with their own definition of human being and universalized something highly exclusive: and the most liberalistic ideologies and the most committed fideists of a general Original Virtue (that includes some contemporary 'free' educators) are covertly just as partial.

The intent and effort to become human (even where it recognizably exists) is not essentially, perhaps not even at all, benevolent or altruistic: primarily it does not even take other people or beings into account, except in so far as they are inextricably involved with the original intent and effort of self-definition.

The only essential postulate here is that we are all members of a species that characteristically moves towards individuation: if we are normal we do not want not to be ourselves. It has to be put at this rudimentary level and in this negative way because obviously a great many, maybe the great majority, give no thought at all to the matter of a self and having or being one.

Yet it is visible and physical fact that all beings that are even legally or statistically classified as human assert their living existence and even their right to it — a physical and mental *Lebensraum* that cannot be infinitely compressed by pressures from outside it. The biological evidence, admittedly, appears to be that this is true, even truistic, of all living beings, including animals and plants. But those beings, to all appearances, do not suffer the temptations which again are characteristically human. These include the illusions of fantasy — that we can imagine ourselves living other lives and even find them really enviable, and in our contemporary technological and medial dream-world, often do so: the projective behaviour of pop-fans is only one among many examples.

They include, too, the older, if not more adult, preoccupation with the private lives of stars or royalty, an example of which has the advantage of making it more easily discernible that this identification or even envy is generally nothing more than a spree. Ordinary normal people do not really want to change places with those other people; they prefer their back gardens, their domestic life, even often their work, however routine and boring, if for no other reason than that it provides them with the necessary material power to purchase their off-periods when they cannot be pushed into being *not* themselves; or can even—in the face no doubt of internal and intraspecific resistance and interference—try to be themselves, however rudimentary the achievement turns out to be.

The significance of this negative conception of individuality or personality is mostly neglected or ignored, no doubt just because it is negative; and not least by liberals. Yet it is for them probably at its greatest; because in a species, a world and a society where the prizes have gone, and go, as much as ever to the illiberal and the anti-liberal, their only realistic position appears to be defensive; and looks as if it will continue to be so.

I am referring to that other world of the weak, the 'meek', the ordinary men, still more the ordinary women and children: those who 'want' power—ambition, self-assertion of a kind we could honestly see to be potentially justifiable, and also any skill or gift even to discern how they could organize themselves to achieve it. (That other world of course includes the many people of totally different or even opposing cultures whom our forms of organization have drawn in, in large part against their natural will and aptitude.)

It would be nice to call these ordinary people the 'Good' (as opposed to the Powerful—the alpha-types). But Shelley provided us here with a classic Either-Or, in its way as fallacious as all the others. The omega-types number among them plenty of would-be but failed aggressors. Their significance here is that they are the actual or potential material of those who feel called upon to organize, to rule or to lead: without them the alpha-types would be ineffectual devils stamping their hooves in a void.

Looking at this vast and fairly silent majority under the moral microscope, we can discern that whatever their attitude towards subjecting their actions, and in some cases their thoughts, to the will of others (whose claim to be more capable and enlightened, even whose substantiality of power they may not be able to estimate), none of them wants or can even very well bear their distinct being to be invaded. That applies even to slaves and to the members of long-subjected peoples; more clearly, to primitive tribes which have up to the present remained as autonomous cultures.

All that is meant to sound perhaps even more crude and obvious than it is. It looks as if it might only be saying that all distinct beings will fight for or defend, as best they can, their lives, their bare existences. It is also obviously true of the animal kingdom: while the struggle for bare survival extends to plants as well.

But that extension of the obvious is also a way of pointing up a minimal distinction. The bare existence which will at some point turn and fight for its survival factually entails, under the moral and analytic microscope, at least one other characteristic. What is potentially but characteristically human here is that this exist-ence is also an identity. That is what minimally but absolutely differentiates the mass.

Identity doesn't have to have much or perhaps even any discern-ible content. To make its human and moral demand it doesn't even have to be conscious or reflexive. People naturally behave as if, at some level, however rudimentary, they were, each, an identity; as if they had, for their own purposes, an awareness and partial comprehension of their immediate 'world'; as if by nature they had an address, a local habitation and a name.

Initially that is put forward not as a moral rule — something which among other things could be conceded or rejected during the process of necessary socialization and which could also there-fore be turned into precise descriptive or polemic language — but as a simple fact of observation. That means too that you either see it or you don't — the capacity here may have a great deal to do with willingness.

It makes no difference to the psychological reality of this 'mini-mal identity' that it is probably learned rather than innate: that the fact of one's identity is first established as reflected in the behaviour of others: at the same time recognized as one's *kind*.

It would be agreeable to think that this awareness, this bare perception or registration of the self-in-the-other, were the germ of 'love' or anyway social feeling, as not only Mill but Christianity and some kinds of idealistic socialism would have us believe. But the existentialist belief that its emotional accompaniment, if any, is more often anxiety and guilt, looks more plausible. Our next step in social consciousness is difficulty in admitting, as we often feel we ought, the equivalence of all those reflected identities with our own. And if we feel no guilt, we commonly feel a need of heavy rationalization. That need, realized or not, is most obvious in the behaviour, theoretical and practical, of the alpha-types in politics, sociology and the 'Human' sciences, who have succeeded the priests and also the cruder tyrants, and who, with their enlarged I.Q.s, are not likely to be without skills in the use and abuse of the moral microscope: if signs of rationalization and of class- or caste-categorization are signs that they do not really like what they see, those are also signs that they see what they do not like.

I have now two postulates: (1) that 'identity' is a discernible fact; (2) that becoming aware of it and accepting it as a fact either for oneself or for others entails a principle of reciprocal recognition.

I am obliged to treat these two postulates as axioms because to try to do without them would entail the rejection not only of an absolutely minimal meaning for liberalism, but also of any rational communication about what we mean by both mankind and a human being: it would be a denial that we are 'free' and 'individual' even in the minimal sense that we are discernibles, that for certain purposes we can be distinguished from the mass; that we have at least the identity (or discernibility) of a blade of grass. That would amount both to total thingification and to a totally abstract conception of 'humanity'.

Metaphysically these two errors are not easy to distinguish: in principle the authoritarian does not distinguish them; the totalitarian neither in principle nor practice.

It may be held that to cover my two axioms I am using the word 'identity' in two different meanings; moreover that neither of these two senses entails the other. It is true that 'identity' has both an objective and a subjective meaning. The first is generally, at least in theory, now admitted, anyway as a mere statistical usage, by all parties, points of view and convictions.

To establish the subjective meaning lands us in all the metaphysical and ontological difficulties of solipsism. But then, Western philosophy has never been able to solve the problem which Hume so clearly (and so cheerfully) put before it: the existence of other minds or even the continuity and predictability of one's own experiences including the experience of having a self. (The Behaviourists of our day have solved the problem to their own satisfaction and without any philosophic attention by implying or actually asserting the practical meaninglessness of such concepts as 'minds' and 'selves', as also therefore of philosophy, at least as it bears on such concepts.)

To substitute for 'mind', 'self' or 'consciousness' some such term as 'identity' may look like a mere verbalism. If 'I' become aware that 'I' have an identity, 'I' should also become aware – logically and in course of time – that 'I' cannot claim more content than is implied by the capacity for saying (and feeling) 'I'. That provides no logical ground for attributing even the same capacity and content to you, let alone a particular identifiable existence: nevertheless your observable behaviour obliges me to award you both. Keeping the content to the logical minimum is what makes it reasonable for me to do so – to deny your 'I'-saying would be to annihilate my own most exiguous world and reduce my own minimal identity thus defined to a dream without a dreamer.

This 'I'-saying is in content considerably more reduced even than the Cartesian 'I think therefore I am' which Descartes asserted as both an irreducible and a warrantable minimum of real existence.

Nevertheless, if it implies less about what kind of being 'I' am, it also implies, as Descartes's version does not, that 'I' have – and assume – a need for communication: and that hence in my 'animal faith', as Hume called it, I assume the existence of other 'identities' similar to 'me', because I have also to assume that my sayings can be heard somehow somewhence (and perhaps even understood and misunderstood). It is perfectly true that 'I' can talk to myself and may do so in conditions of apparent isolation, as a suburban housewife or on a desert island. But there are always *some* occasions when doing so implies that 'I' assume other 'identities' are somewhere to respond, or have been at some time.

It may be said that 'I think therefore I am' equally assumes an objective reality, a world external to one's own awareness and perception, and this is true in the sense that it is impossible to think without thinking of something. Nevertheless that something is not necessarily something human: nothing is logically implied about other comparable identities, as in the example of 'I'-saying. What is being said is that the sense of identity is a subjective *reality*: most psychologists will support the observation that the minimal self-discovery is a real event, even a moment in the development of children: and that if not thwarted or distorted it develops through a stage and into a principle of recognition – of one's own distinct being representing at the same time a human category: in short that identity is a concrete universal (or, to adapt Kant, *a synthetic a priori judgment*).

To say that we have a principle of recognition of other identities which entails recognizing our own, and also that it is because we have the germs of an identity that we are able to make the recognition, certainly looks circular.

In practice we have not the essential logical ground (in the analytical sense) for a universal attribution of 'identity' (nor therefore of a full humanity). Nevertheless the attribution is justified if we can reasonably judge that the sense of identity (as I have tried to define it) is within universal human capacity, given favourable circumstances — although we may have to admit that those may not be realized or realizable within any particular lifetime.

Moreover it is obvious from the consistency of their behaviour (given a sufficient spell of observation), in its preference for certain directions and its avoidance or rejection of others, that some people do have this sense of identity and act as if they were thus centres both of 'freedom and responsibility' and *loci* of reciprocal human recognition. That they may be in a minimal minority and that on any macroscopic scale they are largely helpless to propagate or even to communicate this human sense does not annul either its moral status or its significance as fact. Nor does it minimize the corollary that, if not among the omegas, they are usually for the most part non-alphas. Certainly they do not resemble the 'New Men'* of C. P. Snow or Teilhard de Chardin: they are not a freemasonry and their 'principle of recognition' is not conventional or left-handed or ritual or even conscious. Perhaps, as the less competitive, the Beatitudes might have blessed them as 'Meek': but they show no evident sign of inheriting the earth.

To save even a barely observational minimum for my principle of recognition, I have to keep my human definition as negative as possible. Can we find any common habit of behaviour or conversation which might appear to confirm that even that minimal observation is acceptable?

When do we say '*It's only human*'? Curiously, often when someone has felt their identity and its perquisites infringed and has repelled — by whatever means are socially allowed — an invader. (And of course we do invade one another, or try to, and not only

---

* See C. P. Snow, *Science and Government* and *The New Men*.

by force or even by real superiority, let alone by showing off.)

We *don't* say 'It's only human' of a deliberate, still less a cruel aggressor, but instead of someone who *resents* an unsatisfactory situation—which may all the same be part of a social structure which we have to accept or live with: even if the individual moral situation is one of wounded pride, wounded even by envy born of a feeling of inferiority. I am talking about spontaneous human reactions or feeling—natural or unreflected 'recognition'. Unless we are anchylosed by collective, particularly hierarchic, ideology, we respect and sympathize with the spontaneous assertion of a minimal existence which in its circumstances respects its own claim to a common if minimal recognition: even if that has to be evinced in attitudes or behaviour which we find, in general terms, un-amiable. Human individuality is a moral fact: and those who fail to recognize it suffer from guilt or, quite commonly, schizophrenia, which they cannot cure but only hide by retreating into fortifying some *inhuman* abstraction.

I should note here that 'identity' is not verbal smuggling for 'personality' or 'person', either in the fairly clear if abstract Christian definition, or in the contemporary journalistic sense which seems merely to refer to a moral ragbag: that, too, may be said of the vulgar usage of 'individuality' or 'individualism', although these more often represent the purely abstract ego with its statistical lack of content.

In discussing a range of theories and ideologies about Man in the social and human world which I have made as varied and representative as I can, my essential aim has been to show that they are real and applicable to ourselves, our perennial problems and our planetary future only in so far as they are founded on a justifiable assumption of the nature of human being. I avoid 'definition' because I do not mean verbal formulation, or not necessarily: although it is true that many of the ideologies, the theologies and the theories, especially the political and social ones, actually go in for definitions of 'Man'. All the definitions turn out to be partial, distorted or tendentious; and since all of them at some times have found their contradictions and their opposing parties and arguments, it appears that all of them are in some important aspects, wrong.

Whether or not they use definitions they all base themselves on assumptions, at least partly concealed, about human being, and exist in a framework of expectations thence derived about 'humanity'.

In the case of the contemporary 'human sciences', the assumptions are often much more nearly tacit; possibly because they also often derive from earlier theorization or ideology which has not been examined or even not thought worthy of examination, for instance, Skinner's contemptuous and sweeping dismissal of any purely philosophical analysis of the concepts with which behaviouristic psychology operates.

One may reasonably expect that being tacit the assumptions are all the more in need of exhumation. When exhumed and examined we find that these assumptions, too, even if they are not notably distorted or tendentious, are partial — often with the added disadvantage (or is it an advantage?) of vagueness or obscurity. Or they still function within a framework of ideas which have sunk below the ground-level of realistic criticism: e.g. both Skinnerism and Freudianism, as also what Polyani* and others call Scientific Rationalism, *assume* nineteenth-century physical determinism: while Christianity *assumes* the reality of Sin. It is all rather as if the overwhelmed Pompeians had maintained a robot functioning.

Obviously the authoritarian, theological or secular, has favoured one set or colour of assumptions, and the libertarians and reformers another and contrary one. But as we grow nearer to the contemporary world, the assumptions sometimes lie deeper and are more confused: and can also produce some surprising cross-associations, once they are unearthed. One can trace the Augustinian-Pelagian controversy of the early Christian centuries in the psycho-archaeology of the opposition between authoritarian and libertarian. For instance, 'aggression' — bandied between psycho-ethologists and, say, Spockian-type psychologists — assumes a genetically fixed constitution that puts one in mind of Original Sin. The more fundamental, because structural, assumption that present human behaviour is genetically derived from animal behaviour is only half-emergent. If it was fully expressed it might well reveal itself as the *logical* fallacy of *post hoc propter hoc*: as if by merely preceding us the animals have conditioned our nature.

There are other classes of theory and ideology about men in

* Op. cit.

society whose adherents do not willingly recognize themselves as authoritarian or hierarchic and who, on the contrary, preach equality and the other liberal slogans without admitting their liberal and Christian-humanistic provenance. In time they reveal themselves as after all authoritarian: in so far as they admit this, they may at least in part claim the inadequacy of liberal analysis and method. At first anyway, before the smoke of revolution has ceased to obscure the situation, their authoritarianism or even totalitarianism may be proclaimed as temporary, or a transient but necessary evil. Nevertheless it remains settled, with the implicit excuse that in the process of revolution or in the maintained situation many of the desired and desirable changes of society have actually accomplished themselves, so that the new kind of Man is at least well on the way to existing and functioning: or that after all the new men and women have got the kind of society they like: thus ignoring that their average man or woman, new or old, has not been presented with an adequate range of social situations to choose from.

All authoritarian societies must move towards totalitarianism, among other reasons because the best, perhaps the only, way to deal with mavericks and dissidents is to iron them out or remove them.

The first step towards this economical and efficient ordering of a society is in some form to categorize the opponents and resisters as subhuman or inferior in humanity (according to your definition, which, even if honest, is partial, distorted and/or tendentious: also, to illustrate Popper's word — 'oedipal' — it tends to make people what it says they are).

The philosophies of neo-Marxism, in all its forms, inside and outside the Soviet Union, with Nazism and the various forms of neo-Fascism, all obviously come within this framework of ideological assumptiveness.

In this context what they have in common is a totally objectivist treatment of the human phenomenon, a total disregard of the subjectivity of human existence. For them all — if we may dip for a moment into Sartrean language — the human animal exists in-itself, not 'for-itself'.

Introspection, as a method or technique of self-preservation or analysis, is nowadays, by the dominant professionals, much derided. Nevertheless, we do it; at the most shallow level it assures us that we do, however insensitive, extravert or for that matter altruistic, indeed live 'for-ourselves': as intentional beings, with wishes, needs and purposes which are sometimes, if only sporadically, conscious; and even adventurous and heuristic – seeking the means to fulfil themselves.

I have tried to give reasons for including behavioural science, with its infiltrations into the statistical sciences, on the objectivist or anti-human side: and there are good grounds for believing that even the 'natural' sciences, those which are exactly quantifiable but claim to tell us nothing direct about social and humane matters, are based on unexamined human assumptions.

It is understandable that their methods of quantification have enabled these sciences to achieve their equally undeniable triumphs. But the very method and its success involve a certain exclusiveness of interest. The 'human' sciences have learned to approximate their methods (with its implied narrowing of interest, moreover) to those of natural science as an ideal: or conversely the methods of natural science have acted upon them as an infection.

Where do liberalism and the liberal fit into all this? Certainly, no less than other (and often opposing) ideologies, liberalism bases itself on concealed or unexamined assumptions about what constitutes the human being, which are no less partial and are often as distorted and tendentious: typically the assumption (sometimes a professed belief) that human nature is originally 'good', has been damaged or slanted by vicious social and familial pressures, and will spring back into shape when these pressures are released (or sometimes, less optimistically, when we know how to do it); that this will simultaneously release to the average individual his so far dampened creative and developmental powers; with the wishful corollary that this will equate both with individual 'freedom' and with continuing moral progress or social evolution.

One might think that this 'humanistic' assumptiveness (with the usual selective drawbacks) is the chief or the only certainly common characteristic of the various kinds of liberalism. In the course of time it has surely become clear and in the last two centuries, very clear, that 'liberalism' refers to a bunch of attitudes: what they have in common, the nearest they can offer to an acceptable unity, is negative: in origin they are distinct: they resemble one another in dislike and resistance to imposition, particularly if its authority appears to be usurped: and the dislike and resistance can be sporadic, even quite momentary and evanescent. Hence not only the lack of an all-embracing definition, but the poor effectiveness of 'liberal' action – although it has not been denied that there have been plenty of local and temporary causes which induced unified action: and even provided a transient recognition of freedom as a defining human potential.

It appears that the most practical business of liberalism is not with Freedom, but with freedoms; with trying to defend those that have been won by whatever local and temporary victories, in thought and speech, in writing, in social relations and manners, in civil and economic rights or concessions: and with resisting the renewed and inevitable encroachment which will always be made upon them, in some quarters with increasing intensity and perhaps with a ferocity worse than we have so far witnessed.

Even its theoretical business, perhaps, is not primarily with 'Freedom', for the reason that has been suggested: that we do not know how to define it or even recognize it except in concrete or 'minute' particulars. It may be that both the persistence and the progress of liberalism depend instead upon recognizing its real self-portrait in justice – developing like a photographic image from vagueness to clarity.

Justice – not as the ideological or Platonic symbol on the one hand, nor, on the other, as a mere distributive and utilitarian egalitarianism, but rather as the 'solution' (using a mathematical metaphor) to a perennial and immensely complicated problem with a dialectic structure: the problem of being or becoming human.

Liberalism would then be seen more and more clearly as a special critical philosophy; critical not only of the concepts and precepts (and also of the vices) of social and ideological moralities, but of the metaphysical and even epistemological assumptions on which we build both our theories and our societies; striving to clear not only our understandings but even our perceptions: because Justice is a form of perception and a minimal principle of recognition – that one is one and that another is another and comparable one.

I said that, residing in perception and awareness, recognition might be inculcated. 'If there were world enough and time' is a warranted expression of doubt, but that is true of any attempt at a genuine personal education. And there might be some intensive moral education which might improve the general level of moral *accuracy* — something similar is certainly being done in mathematical education.

To train one's perceptions has nothing to do with either duty or emotion: perception is what happens to us if our eyes are open and our vision is not wilfully distorted. Squints, too, can sometimes be corrected (although because I know no grounds I have no confidence that they will be, this side of the Millennium — or Armageddon).

Thus it is not true that 'We must *love* one another or die' — if by 'Love' we mean what has been and is commonly meant: either as an individual emotion of Christian altruism bouncing off the telstar God, or even Mill's 'social feeling'. Its only realistic and usable meaning is as a form of perception and acceptance of the identity of at least *some* others. And it is still learnt best, if at all, in the natural family within the generation of the children. Many other things are learnt there as well, as undesirable as all the other predictable manifestations of Old Adam and Old Eve. But there in early relations an uncritical equality *can* be absorbed, the only one there is — of brothers and sisters in all three possible combinations. That is more significant than any generation-gap or any attempt to close it; and though it may well imply some sympathetic preference, for siblings over parents, it is not merely a variety of the 'hating-together' which so many of us mistake for friendship and loyalty.

The liberal may come to be the one who interprets — at least more realistically than Eliot would have wished — the moral meaning of the religions, including Christianity, which have undoubtedly been woven into the tangled branches of his descent. He may come to acknowledge that moral salvation is after all the business of our lives; and that while salvation is of individuals it can only come about in some community which feels natural to most of us; but which we have yet to discover and develop.

Bibliography

Sydney Anglo, *Machiavelli: a Dissection* (O.U.P., London, 1969).

Robert Ardrey, *The Territorial Imperative* (Collins, London, 1967).

Robert Ardrey, *The Social Contract* (Collins, London, 1970).

Hannah Arendt, *Crises of the Republic* (Harcourt Brace Jovanovich, New York, 1969).

A. J. Ayer, *Language, Truth and Logic* (Gollancz, London, 1936).

Isaiah Berlin, *Four Essays on Liberty* (O.U.P., London, 1969).

Fenner Brockway, *The Colonial Revolution* (Rupert Hart-Davis, London, 1973).

Herbert Butterfield, *The Whig Interpretation of History* (Penguin, Harmondsworth, 1973).

Maurice Cowling, *Mill and Liberalism* (C.U.P., Cambridge, 1963).

Maurice Cranston, *What are Human Rights?* (Bodley Head, London, 1973).

Ralf Dahrendorf, *Society and Democracy in Germany* (Routledge, London, 1973).

T. S. Eliot, *For Lancelot Andrewes* (Faber, London, 1928).

T. S. Eliot, *Poems 1909–1925* (Faber, London, 1930).

T. S. Eliot, *Dante* (Faber, London, 1965).

H. J. Eysenck, *Sense and Nonsense in Psychology* (Penguin, Harmondsworth, 1957).

H. J. Eysenck, *Fact and Fiction in Psychology* (Penguin, Harmondsworth, 1965).

H. J. Eysenck, *The Inequality of Man* (Maurice Temple Smith, London, 1969).

Frances Fitzgerald, *Fire in the Lake* (London, 1972).

Sigmund Freud, *Moses and Monotheism*, trans. Ernest Jones (Hogarth, London, 1951).

Christopher Hill, *The World Turned Upside Down* (Penguin, Harmondsworth, 1972).

Rodney Hilton, *Bond Men Made Free* (Maurice Temple Smith, London, 1973).

Thomas Hobbes, *Leviathan*, edited and introduced by M. Oakeshott (Blackwell, Oxford, 1946).

Liam Hudson, *Contrary Imaginations* (Penguin, Harmondsworth, 1966).

Liam Hudson, *Frames of Mind* (Penguin, Harmondsworth, 1968).

Arthur Jensen, *Educability and Group Differences* (Methuen, London, 1973).

F. R. Leavis, *The Great Tradition* (Chatto & Windus, London, 1955).

Claude Lévi-Strauss, *L'Anthropologie Structurelle* (1960). *Structural Anthropology*, translated by C. Jacobson and B. G. Schoeph (Penguin, Harmondsworth, 1972).

Konrad Lorenz, *On Aggression* (Methuen, London, 1966).

James Mackinnon, *Origins of the Reformation* (Longmans, London, 1939).

C. B. Macpherson, *Democratic Theory; Essays in Retrieval* (O.U.P., London, 1973).

Herbert Marcuse, *One-Dimensional Man* (Routledge, London, 1964).

Herbert Marcuse, *Essay on Liberation* (Penguin, Harmondsworth, 1969).

Herbert Marcuse, *Five Lectures* (Allen Lane, London, 1970).

J. S. Mill, *A System of Logic* (Longmans, London, 1843).

J. S. Mill, *The Subjection of Women* (Longmans, London, 1869).

J. S. Mill, *On Liberty* (Dent, Everyman, London 1924).

J. S. Mill, *Autobiography* (Columbia University Press, 1960).

J. S. Mill, *Utilitarianism* (Routledge, London, 1974).

Kathleen Nott, *The Emperor's Clothes* (Heinemann, London, 1954).

Kathleen Nott, *A Clean Well-lighted Place* (Heinemann, London, 1969).

Kathleen Nott, *A Soul in the Quad* (Routledge, London, 1969).

Kathleen Nott, *Philosophy and Human Nature* (Hodder and Stoughton, London, 1970).

Plato, *The Republic*; trans. J. L. Davies and D. J. Vaughan (Macmillan, London, 1872).

Michael Polanyi, *The Tacit Dimension* (Routledge, London, 1967).

Karl Popper, *The Open Society* (Routledge, London, 1945).

Karl Popper, *The Logic of Scientific Discovery* (Routledge, London, 1973).

Karl Popper, *The Poverty of Historicism* (Routledge, London, 1973).

Giovanni Prezzolini, *Machiavelli* (Robert Hale, London, 1968).

John Rawls, *A Theory of Justice* (O.U.P., London, 1972).

Theodore Roszak, *The Making of a Counter-Culture* (Faber, 1970).

Theodore Roszak, *Where the Wasteland Ends* (Faber, 1974).

Jean-Jacques Rousseau, *A Discourse on the Origin of Inequality*; trans. G. D. H. Cole (London, 1952).

Jean-Jacques Rousseau, *The Social Contract*; trans. and edited G. D. H. Cole (Dent, Everyman, London, 1955).

Guido De Ruggiero, *The History of European Liberalism*; trans. R. G. Collingwood (Humphrey Milford, London, 1927).

Bertrand Russell, *The History of Western Philosophy* (Allen & Unwin, London, 1946).

Jean-Paul Sartre, *What is Literature?* (Methuen, London, 1950).

Jean-Paul Sartre, *Being and Nothingness*; trans. H. Barnes (Methuen, London, 1951).

B. F. Skinner, *Walden II* (Macmillan, New York, 1948).

B. F. Skinner, *Beyond Freedom and Dignity* (Cape, London, 1972).

C. P. Snow, *The New Men* (Macmillan, London, 1954).

C. P. Snow, *Appendix to 'Science and Government'* (Harvard University Press, 1962).

Anthony Storr, *The Natural History of Aggression*, Symposium (Institute of Biology, London, 1963).

Anthony Storr, *Human Aggression* (Penguin, Harmondsworth, 1968).

A. De Tocqueville, *Democracy in America* (O.U.P., 1972).

Lionel Trilling, *Sincerity and Authenticity* (O.U.P., 1972).

James Watson, *The Double Helix* (Weidenfeld, London, 1968).

Evelyn Waugh, *When the Going Was Good* (Duckworth, London, 1946).

A. G. Woodhead, *Thucydides on the Nature of Power* (Harvard University Press, 1970).

Index